Inflections
of the
Pen

Inflections of the Pen

Dash and Voice
in Emily Dickinson

PAUL CRUMBLEY

THE UNIVERSITY PRESS OF KENTUCKY

Copyright © 1997 by The University Press of Kentucky

Scholarly publisher for the Commonwealth,
serving Bellarmine College, Berea College, Centre College of Kentucky,
Eastern Kentucky University, The Filson Club, Georgetown College,
Kentucky Historical Society, Kentucky State University, Morehead State University,
Murray State University, Northern Kentucky University, Transylvania University,
University of Kentucky, University of Louisville, and Western Kentucky University.

Editorial and Sales Offices: The University Press of Kentucky
663 South Limestone Street, Lexington, Kentucky 40508-4008

01 00 99 98 97   5 4 3 2 1

Library of Congress Cataloging-in-Publication Data

Crumbley, Paul, 1952-
    Inflections of the pen : dash and voice in Emily Dickinson / Paul Crumbley.
        p.   cm.
    Includes bibliographical references (p.   ) and indexes.
    ISBN 0-8131-1988-X (alk. paper)
    1. Dickinson, Emily, 1830-1886—Technique.   2. Women and literature—United States—History—19th century.   3. Dickinson, Emily, 1830-1886—Criticism, Textual.   4. English language—19th century—Punctuation.   5. Point of View (Literature)   6. Dash (Punctuation)   7. Literary form.   8. Poetics.
    I. Title.
    PS1541.Z5C75   1996
    811'.4—dc20   96-25520

This book is printed on acid-free recycled paper meeting the requirements of the American National Standard for Permanence of Paper for Printed Library Materials.

♾ ♻

Manufactured in the United States of America

For Phebe

Contents

Illustrations

Acknowledgments

I AM GRATEFUL TO the many people who have helped make this book possible. Chief among them is Everett Emerson, friend and mentor, for making me prove to him that Dickinson's dashes are connected to voice. I also owe special thanks to Martha Nell Smith for her advice about final revisions and her invaluable assistance in thinking through the intricacies of translating Dickinson's holographs into print; to Linda Wagner-Martin for her careful critiques of early drafts; and to Robert Bain for helping me understand the literary environment Dickinson inhabited. I am grateful to all those who read the manuscript at various stages, especially Cristanne Miller, Nicole Mitchell, Beverly Taylor, and Joy Kasson.

I could not have completed the crucial work with Dickinson's manuscripts had it not been for the generous cooperation of John Lancaster and his staff at the Robert Frost Library of Amherst College, Leslie Morris and her staff at the Houghton Library of Harvard University, and the Department of Rare Books and Manuscripts at the Boston Public Library. I want also to thank Jeffrey Smitten and the English Department at Utah State University for the financial and moral support that enabled me to see this book through the final stages of publication.

This book would not have been possible without the continuous support of Phebe Jensen, whose insistence on clarity of expression never interfered with her love for me. She is my Tribunal.

Print Representations of the Dickinson Holographs

Most of the poems and many of the letters printed in this study attempt to capture primary visual features of Dickinson's handwritten productions. Special attention has been given to holograph lineation, placement of variants and their flags (represented here by plus signs in varying positions), word spacing, and punctuation—particularly that category of marks widely referred to as the "dash." Our solution to the difficulty of matching print to Dickinson's variable "dashes" has been the creation of sixteen dash types, each of which stands for a range of similar handwritten marks. The end result is visual semblance rather than exact replication. We have, for instance, angled all the upward- and downward-slanting marks at 20 degrees, not because Dickinson's angles were uniform but because this angle fairly reflects the visual character of her multiple angles. To represent the different lengths of Dickinson marks, we developed six types that either extend or reduce the en-dash, the most frequent length: · | - | – | — | — | —— ; and have positioned the marks at five heights relative to the line of type: _ | ⌣ | – | — | ⌐ . Several other types are represented by combinations of these lengths and heights: ⌐ | ~ | ⌣ | . | - | .. . These dash types represent categories of holograph marks that appear with great frequency throughout the poems and letters, as well as marks that may be unique to the materials discussed in this study. Future studies may require additional dash types. Our intent throughout has been to communicate in print the visual complexity so important to a full appreciation of Dickinson's artistry.

Introduction

"You know I have a vice for voices"[1]
—Emily Dickinson

A FEW TANTALIZING QUESTIONS lurk at the center of the mystery that is Emily Dickinson. What drove her to copy out more than a thousand poems between 1858 and 1865, largely in the privacy of her room, destroy all but four of the rough drafts, and meticulously preserve fair copies on special paper bound into forty fascicles and fifteen manuscript books?[2] How could she be so prolific, so thematically diverse, and still carefully write, perfect, and save almost two thousand poems while fulfilling her obligations as elder daughter in a prominent Amherst household? In the following I approach such conundrums through an analysis of what is perhaps Dickinson's most intriguing stylistic characteristic, her signature "dashes."

I propose that the marks all but a few recent editors have reductively designated as either em or en "dashes" are central to a graphocentric poetics within which they perform as highly nuanced visual signals intimately linked to Dickinson's experiments with poetic voice. The broad category of marks that come under the heading "dash" suggest subtle gradations of inflection and syntactic disjunction that multiply the voices in poems and letters. Precisely because these dashes can expand rather than restrict voicing options, they play an important role in defining a poetic project designed to present readers a wide range of simultaneous meanings. The succeeding close examination of the way dashes perform within the larger context of manuscript chirography aims to increase appreciation for the visual and vocal richness of

Dickinson's writing, while also clarifying a key aesthetic project: her strategy for investing readers with the authority to challenge the social determination of linguistic content.

The process through which I began to understand the aesthetic importance of the dash may sound familiar to others who have also been simultaneously enthralled and mystified by Dickinson's poetry. When first examining Dickinson's work, I quickly discovered that my efforts to pin down Dickinson both psychologically and aesthetically were consistently derailed by the poems themselves. Instead of finding one single poetic voice, even within individual poems, stylistic countercurrents—provoked primarily by punctuation, capitalization, and diction—invariably suggested a divided self. Dickinson's dashes in particular seemed to belie the orderliness of her poetry's common measure and ballad and hymn meters, transforming a poem such as "This is my letter to the World" (*P* 441, *MBED* 548)[3] from a paean to universal harmony to an angry assertion of the poet's outsider status in the cosmos. In my search to find a single explanation for such apparently irresolvable oppositions, I read John Cody's *After Great Pain*, Albert J. Gelpi's *The Mind of the Poet*, Rebecca Patterson's *The Riddle of Emily Dickinson*, and many other studies that exhaustively trace the emergence of Dickinson's creativity to a single biographical origin in unrequited love, psychological trauma, or a combination of the two—a catastrophic event that, it was assumed, must have shattered a previously whole psyche. But helpful as these works were, none provided the combination of biographical information and textual acuity that would explain both the range of the poems and their appearance.[4]

Unsatisfied with such scholarly efforts to place Dickinson's poems in the context of a single event, I began to read them again, this time looking more closely at the points where Dickinson's language most obviously defied codification. As my focus shifted from a concern with unifying patterns to an awareness of the ways in which the poems resist easy coherence, I began to see that the dashes perform a key function by disrupting conventional thought patterns. As Dickinson's primary punctuation, they tell us that the poems introduce polyvocality as a direct challenge to the primacy of a single unified voice. Familiar child, bride, and Queen or poet speakers, for example, which recur throughout the poems, speak from a spectrum of positions that stretch from the conventional to the wild.

In the following chapters I divide Dickinson's speakers according to the voices of the child, the bride, and the Queen in order to represent paradigmatic relationships speakers have with conventional discourse, rather than as labels for unified identities. In general terms, the child communicates shock at the discovery that discourse limits personal power; the bride seeks to acquire personal power by conforming to discourse; the Queen proclaims personal power that exceeds containment in discourse. My discussion of "This is my letter to the World" in chapter 1 demonstrates the way that early, normalized print versions of her poems encouraged the view that her speakers ultimately embody conventional voices, albeit with slightly eccentric twists.[5] As long as I continued separating the mundane speakers (those concerned with robins on walks and certain slants of light) from Dickinson's more oracular or demonic observers (those who see life as a pit or a still volcano), I was reaffirming the theory that something horrendous had happened to splinter a unified psyche. Had I believed this, my task would have been to locate the source of the disturbance and from there build a comprehensive story accounting for all speakers and voices as fragments of a larger coherence, now lost.

But rather than reenter the search for a reductive master narrative, I considered the possibility that varying speakers and voices were not meant to function exclusively, according to a hierarchic logic validating one over all others. Instead, I came to see that the poems provoke a continuum of readings that endorse social conformity at one extreme, rebellion and even anarchy at the other. The poems show us that conventional behavior is the product of choices that readers, speakers, and subjects make at every turn; they tell us we are participants in a reality that infinitely exceeds the familiar habitations charted by orthodox social practice.

This is not to say that Dickinson's poems advocate a rejection of all monologizing impulses; rather, they point to the process by which culture urges conformity. Some sense of identity is normal and healthy. One needs to achieve coherence and unity—the momentary housing of the self—to take action in a material world.[6] But the poems iterate the belief that identity is the temporary product of specific discourses within a given historical context and that the self is limited neither by such discourse nor by the unity upon which discourse depends. Dickinson's poems do not tell us that as readers we must resist the impulse to locate specific, unified meanings; rather, the poems celebrate the positive pull toward unity by positioning it in the context of opposing impulses. In this important respect, Dickinson's writing is unusual because it so consistently foregrounds the reader's choices, making it clear that any delight her poems afford is in some sense the product of negotiating tensions that would not exist if contrary tendencies were not operative.

This project, it soon became clear, could not be accomplished simply by rereading standard published versions of the poems. For the editorial and print practices through which Dickinson's poems have been reproduced are themselves, at least in part, an inevitably conventionalizing process. Certainly, these practices historically have been predicated on a belief in the centrality of a unified poetic voice, a belief, I had become convinced, Dickinson was determined to refute.

The conformity forced on Dickinson's poetry by conventional print practices can be illustrated by the two versions, manuscript and print, of "Dare you see a Soul" (*P* 365).[7] In manuscript, the speaker in this poem issues what may be considered a general warning to all potential readers of Dickinson's poetry:

> Dare you see a Soul at the
> "White Heat"?
> Then crouch within the door –
> Red – is the Fire's common tint ‿
> +vivid
> But when the +quickened Ore   5
>   +vanquished
> Has +sated Flame's conditions ‿
>   +it
> +She quivers from the Forge
> Without a color, but the Light
> Of unannointed Blaze –
>
> Least Village, boasts its Black-   10
> smith ‿
> Whose Anvil's even ring
> Stands symbol for the finer Forge
> That soundless tugs – within ‿
>
> Refining these impatient Ores   15
> With Hammer, and with Blaze
> Until the designated Light
> Repudiate the Forge –
>   [*MBED* 440-41]⁸

As the poem follows the progression of a soul metaphorically described as raw metal ("Ore") through the forging process that yields a socially determined object ("designated Light"), it raises questions about what is lost in the process. The soul, having absorbed "the Fire's common tint," emerges "Without a color," stripped of its prior majesty by an "unannointed Blaze."

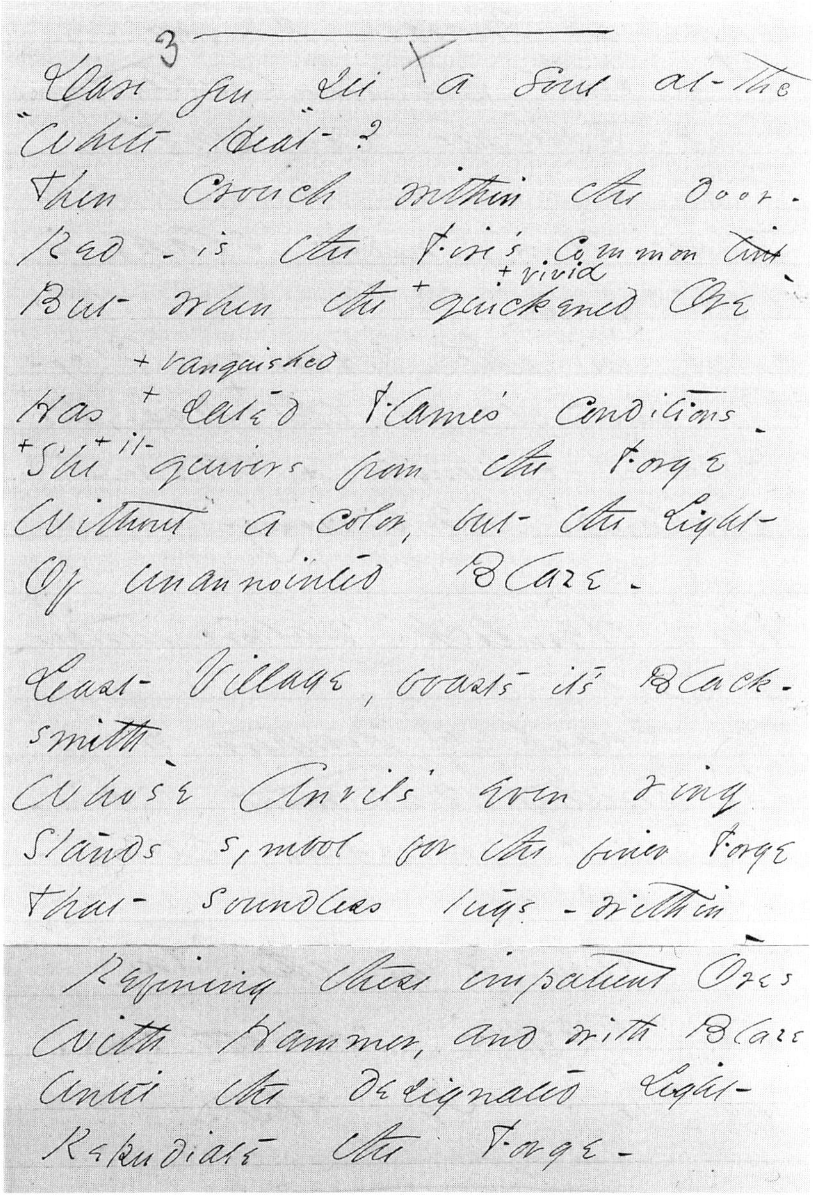

Figure 1. Poem 365, Fascicle 20. *The Manuscript Books of Emily Dickinson*, 440-41. © The President and Fellows of Harvard College. Reproduced by permission of Harvard University Press and the Houghton Library, Harvard University.

Mention of the "Least Village" draws attention to the exemplary nature of this activity; we are told that the "Refining" concludes only when a predetermined "designated Light" is powerful enough to "Repudiate the Forge." Is the final product all the more admirable because it outshines the forge? Is it a vastly diminished substitute for the fearsome "White Heat" of the soul? Or is the refining that goes on in the last stanza a superior kind that repudiates the public accomplishment of the blacksmith and recovers the awesomeness of the soul?

The normalization of the poem performed by Dickinson's first editors, Mabel Loomis Todd and Thomas Wentworth Higginson, significantly reduces the interpretive options reflected in these questions. By conscientiously altering manuscript eccentricities, they produce a much different poem, one that provides sharp contrast with the manuscript version. Where the manuscript disrupts conventional discourse, their poem makes discourse seamless; where manuscript dashes combine with other visual signals to multiply voice possibilities, this poem urges perception of a monologic and unified self. Here is the severely edited version that appeared in the 1891 *Poems, Second Series:*

> Dare you see a soul at the white heat?
>   Then crouch within the door.
> Red is the fire's common tint;
>   But when the vivid ore
>
> Has sated flame's conditions,   5
>   Its quivering substance plays
> Without a color but the light
>   Of unanointed blaze.
>
> Least village boasts its blacksmith,
>   Whose anvil's even din   10
> Stands symbol for the finer forge
>   That soundless tugs within,
>
> Refining these impatient ores
>   With hammer and with blaze,
> Until the designated light   15
>   Repudiate the forge.
>   [*Collected* 100]

The most obvious physical differences between this poem and the fascicle version include removal of capitals in all but first words of lines, elimination of all nine "dashes," deletion of all three word variants, exclusion of quotation marks around "White Heat," and regularization of punctuation and lineation.

These changes introduce a narrative map that guides reading and significantly diminishes opportunities for independent reader participation. Placing "White Heat" on the first line, without preserving capitalization or quotation marks, immediately reduces the unique status of these words as special subjects of inquiry. Readers are not encouraged to question the meaning of these terms but rather to accept their application to the soul as part of the conventional mind-body opposition that characterizes the rest of the poem. The second line establishes the reader's perspective and the following six-and eight-line sentences clarify the way that the soul is refined by mortal experience. The first six-line unit (lines 3-8) focuses on the physical forging of the soul through the exhausting ("sating") of "flame's conditions"; flame here symbolizes the red blood of the physical body and the change to which the body is subject. The concluding eight lines point to the purely spiritual dimension of this process whereby "impatient ores" at last "Repudiate" the physical "forge" that is the body.

Such a reading confirms traditional religious belief and asks little of the reader. As such, it may be considered the codification of discourse Dickinson introduced into her fascicle poem for the purpose of interrogation. In a sense, the editors have lifted Dickinson's speaker out of heteroglossia and ironed out so many of the syntactic disruptions that she appears passive. In comparison with the manuscript speaker, this speaker is notably stripped of her ability to see through conventional thought patterns; instead of a polyvocal Queen who entertains multiple voices while enthroned in heteroglossia, we are given a priestess of patriarchy. It is important to stress here that print practices do not obliterate Dickinson's unruliness entirely, but that such practices muffle and hence silence important contrary voices. Regularized versions like this one represent the poetry that Dickinson knew current editorial practices would yield if she allowed publication of her poems. As a result, early published versions of the poems that insistently regularize the language can be extremely useful both in clarifying her reasons for not publishing and in isolating the dominant discourse she sought to dismantle.

One of the most significant features of the manuscript poem is its demand that readers acknowledge the surrender of personal authority implicit in the affirmation of mind-body dualism. Consequently, the blacksmith, whose role was insignificant in the monologic reading, assumes much greater stature in the manuscript. As shaper of raw material, he demonstrates the translation of desire into language common to all speakers, but as the person to whom society assigns special responsibility for refining language, he acts as a poet. As poet, however, his determination to create a poem that effaces the stages of its creation is at odds with the manuscript Dickinson left. Where he would remove evidence of production, Dickinson's version infuses the poem with unusual punctuation, word variants, irregular line breaks, and odd capitalization—all features that foreground the constructed nature of "poetic" discourse while suggesting by contrast the irregularities of speech or "natural" discourse.

This pronounced violation of conventional practice impedes syntactic closure, introducing the possibility that the forge is not repudiated after all. Breaking "blacksmith" into two words on separate lines, for instance, contrasts "Black" with the brilliance of forge and heated ore, while the "smith" portion connotes the anonymity of a common profession and surname; the result exposes the blacksmith's aim to repudiate, while significantly diminishing his power to do so. The reader is forced to consider whether as poet the blacksmith is an artist or a wordsmith. In addition, the variants "vanquished" and "sated" at the beginning of stanza two introduce opposing views of the ore: does it triumphantly vanquish "Flame's conditions," or is it consumed? Similarly, the variants "She" and "it" at the beginning of line 6 raise questions about whether or not the feminine survives the forging process. Is the blacksmith a successful neutralizing, neutering agent of convention, or does the "soul"/ore free herself from containment? As long as this degree of verbal instability persists, resolution is impossible.

Read according to the manuscript evidence, the poem proclaims the accomplishments of poets who fabricate seamless works of art, while simultaneously revealing the sacrifices required for such achievements.[9] The information on the page does not recommend one reading over the other; rather, weighing all the evidence encourages the view that at least two equally compelling possibilities coexist. Dickinson's poem, then, offers a third possibility made available when such a dialogue is sustained: a reading that comments on the act of reading and illuminates the performance features of poems that acknowledge their own dialogic potential.[10] In such a view, poetry captures in microcosm the predicament of the individual who must use language to enter the social world but does so without surrendering independent selfhood. The poem's nine dashes barrage readers with visual reminders that speakers use provisional vocabularies incommensurate with the self, thus drawing attention to the multitudinous potentiality of that self and its innate resistance to reification in social discourse.

From the standpoint of this third reading possibility, the poem provides an interesting description of the process by which the soul achieves "White Heat." The speaker's first word, "Dare," cautions the reader preparatory to a potentially unsettling encounter. The rest of the poem then moves through the blacksmith's handling of the ore to a final concentration on "the finer Forge / That soundless tugs – within ⌣." This silent forge also works ore but does so in a manner conspicuously devoid of sound. As a contemporaneous but silent forging, it points to unexploited possibilities inherent in prevocal language, thus opening the poem to a simultaneous proliferation of meaning that ultimately repudiates the blacksmith's forge with the "Light" of "a soul at the 'White Heat.'" Here it is important to bear in mind that awareness of the effect language has on the reader becomes possible only if the semantic content of the poem is sufficiently complex to make meaning *generation,* and not specific meaning, the subject of reading. A dialogue of meaning-bearing discourses must occur before heteroglossia can enter the text and illuminate the infinite self (soul) that language would otherwise transmute into self-effacing monologic discourse. To see "a soul at the 'White Heat,'" then, readers must gaze backward through speech into the limitless abyss of heteroglossia.

Through her innovative use of the dash in combination with other unconventional writing practices, Dickinson strains coherence in order to make reading occur simultaneously on the multiple levels sketched out here. All of Dickinson's poems potentially activate at least three kinds of movement: the centripetal, linear movement of conventional discourse; the centrifugal, spatial expansion of heteroglossia and polyvocality; and the cessation of movement that occurs when heteroglossia overcomes centripetal unity and arrests consciousness with raw physicality. These mechanisms force readers to recognize that discourse is created rather than predetermined, that readers themselves control linguistic meaning, personal identity, and the voices heard by the mind's ear.

This study concentrates specifically on the dash, a focus that proceeds from the belief, as Sharon Cameron has put it, that "the relation between words in Dickinson's poems . . . like the relation between poems . . . [is] emblematized by the dash" (*Choosing* 56). Even when I do not mention them specifically, my readings reflect sensitivity to the disjunctions dashes indicate; throughout the following chapters, I touch on other features of her chirography as they inform and extend the dislocations signified by dashes.

The necessity of providing multiple readings for poems has meant giving considerable space in each chapter to the discussion of single poems. For this reason, I have not attempted to cover the canon, as I might otherwise have done. I have also tried to focus my comments as much as possible on complete poems rather than fragments. Both of these decisions reflect my belief that it is all too easy to impose unity on Dickinson's texts and, by doing so, fall into the habit of overlooking important elements of her chirography and her social critique. Once parts of poems are lifted out of context, the textual interrelationships that make those parts crucial to the entire poem's performance are lost. And because Dickinson is so interested in exposing the inadequacies of social discourse, it is especially important to avoid confusing the limited perceptions of speakers with the larger aims of the entire poem.

In the first chapter, I provide readings of key poems that demonstrate the usefulness of a dialogic approach. My aim here is to explore the difficulties associated with discussing the polyvocal character of the poems and to provide a method for reading that respects Dickinson's employment of dashes. I also establish the usefulness of both Mikhail M. Bakhtin's work in dialogics and Julia Kristeva's work on the constitution of the self in my analysis of Dickinson's poetic voice. Tracing the activity of voices in the poems, even with the assistance of these theorists, is complicated, because any poem may have a primary speaker with multiple voices or multiple speakers with single or multiple voices.[11] In this first chapter I focus narrowly on primary speakers in specific poems, treating syntactic disjunctions as potential ruptures that reveal the assumptions underlying each speaker's utterances.

The second chapter explores Dickinson's treatment of discourse prominent in the literary culture of her day. I argue here that Dickinson deliberately draws on elements of high and low culture in an effort to create a new poetics. I look especially at poems that Dickinson scholars have placed within Gothic and Romantic traditions, repositioning them in the context of sentimental and anti-Romantic readings that demonstrate serious play with prevailing literary conventions. Central to this chapter is the argument that Dickinson unhinges language from primary assumptions about the nature of truth as part of a strategy to free discourse for artistic play.

Chapter 3 examines the emergence of dashes as a central stylistic feature in Dickinson's letters. I argue that Dickinson uses dashes in the letters as she does in the poems: to disrupt discourse and suggest voice shifts. Consequently, I identify multiple voices in the letters; I also show that in the process of creating these voices Dickinson becomes increasingly aware of homelessness as an important expression of poetic illocality. Dickinson's repeated descriptions of herself as being "at sea" in her letters, I argue, bear directly on her freedom to create multiple voices.

These voices become the basis for the fourth and fifth chapters, where I explore the voices of the child, the bride, and the Queen. Though I designate characteristic speakers, I also show the ways these speakers illuminate one another by provoking voice shifts or competing for dominance in poems. My purpose in proceeding this way is to establish connections among speakers widely recognized by Dickinson scholars and to expand my analysis of dialogics and the speaking self.

The final chapter concentrates on the relationship between Dickinson's manipulation of literary form and her presentation of the self. I argue that Dickinson uses form to clarify the link between discomfort and the constructive self-knowledge that accompanies her serious interrogation of external truth. The truth about the self that Dickinson insists must be told "slant" arises from an uneasy balance between the stability of unified identity and the limitlessness of the semiotic out of which all language emerges. Knowledge, then, directs consciousness to the limits of any discourse and, by that means, to the limitless potential the semiotic offers any speaker. This movement is diametrically opposed to Romantic definitions of the egotistical sublime, where the individual achieves transcendence and thus affirms the hierarchic logic implicit in discourse.

Given the centrality of the Dickinson fascicles to this book's argument, the difficult mechanics of *how* to represent this manuscript material within the parameters of late-twentieth-century printing technology remains to be discussed. Fortunately, I am aided in this endeavor by several critics whose work has pioneered Dickinson manuscript studies and, not coincidentally, deeply informed and enabled the present study.

Despite the divergent aims and arguments of their work, Sharon Cameron, Susan Howe, and Martha Nell Smith agree that the manuscripts, rather than Johnson's variorum, should become the basis of scholarly analysis; all provide useful recent examples of innovative ways that manuscript materials can be translated into print, as well as insightful critical interpretation of that material.[12] Along with these critics, I approach Dickinson with the assumption that the fascicles and most other manuscript versions are finished works, a conclusion partially founded on the belief that coherence and unity are not goals of Dickinson's poetics. Further, Dickinson's decision to publish her poems personally is an act that both assumes the importance of audience to her work and suggests that she rejected the conventionalizing impetus of print—or, in Cameron's stronger language, "refused to collaborate with the institutions of publishing" (147). Rejecting standard print conventions signaled aesthetic independence, as Howe suggests when she claims that "[c]onventional punctuation was abolished to subtract arbitrary authority" (*Emily* 23).

Short of simply reproducing Dickinson's poems in manuscript, a solution that creates its own problems of legibility, some translation into print of Dickinson's poems is necessary for the present study. The compromise adopted here is indebted especially to the Dickinson Editing Collective and their ongoing efforts to provide a responsible readers' text.[13] Graphically, to emphasize the openness of Dickinson's dash, I use the en-dash length to preserve space at either end of the mark, while attempting to match in print the slant and position so important to Dickinson, thereby visually distinguishing Dickinson's dash from the standard em dashes in my own text. I will also respect Dickinson's lineation, capitalization, and placement of variants as closely as possible.

In the broadest sense, the interpretive conclusions reached in this study about the disjunctive potential of the dash, the importance of audience to Dickinson's poetics, and Dickinson's experiments with voice are generally shared by Howe, Smith, and Cameron. Howe sees the dash contributing to the "polyphonic visual complexity" of manuscripts as "visual productions" (*Birth-mark* 141): "spaces between letters, dashes, apostrophes, commas, crosses, form networks of signs and discontinuities" (143). As I will also suggest at length in subsequent chapters, Smith links Dickinson's punctuation with the importance of reader participation to her aesthetics: "Certainly Dickinson's punctuation marks, 'dashes' . . . suggest an author who expects readers, who must decide whether to regard the marks as substantial or accidental, to engage in textual production and in effect become co-authors" (*Rowing* 52-53). Smith also interprets Dickinson's "angled marks" as reminders of "tone's importance" (144) in the reader's creation of voice: "Since the reader invents the voice of the written text and can return to the work time and again to generate new texts, thus 'hear' new voices, the tone of any reading seems infinitely variable" (145). Cameron similarly understands the dash as related to voice, observing that "according to the indeterminacy conveyed by the dashes" readers encounter "overlapping, disparate meanings" (*Choosing* 26) that evoke a sense of multiple voices speaking simultaneously: "So voice is at odds with itself in these poems, so much so that the proper term for the disagreement is in fact heteroglossia in another form" (27).

The consensus on the disjunctive potential of the dash is joined even by recent critics who do not share a belief in the importance of Dickinson's manuscripts. Cristanne Miller describes the dash as a signal of disjunction; Gary Lee Stonum observes, similarly, that the dash performs an important role by "isolating words or phrases," thereby "slowing or interrupting the cumulative effect of the poem" and inviting readers "to linger over their full potential as single words" (50-51). Along the same lines, Robert Weisbuch argues that dashes highlight the poetic process; they are a "means by which Dickinson takes us backstage to view the struggle of poetic process, a struggle to find the right word, and they serve to represent a hesitancy . . . to reveal the word which in turn reveals the poet's mind" (73).

A broad consensus, then, currently exists that the Dickinson dashes signal disjunction. But what significance do we attach to this disjunction? And how, in any individual poem, do we assess the *degree* of disjunction and corresponding voice tonalities indicated by dashes ranging in length, position, and slant? When should readers internally regularize the verse—occluding syntax Dickinson scrupulously preserved in fair copies and letters—if the disjunction seems negligible; when should the dashes be trusted as serious markers that potentially introduce voice changes wherever they appear? These questions, I will argue, can never be definitively answered; they must be confronted and wrestled with anew with each reading of a Dickinson poem. How to conduct that confrontation, and how a dialogic theory of language can help in understanding, if not resolving, its implications, is the subject of my first chapter.

1

Dashes and the Limits of Discourse

 UNTIL THE LATE 1980s, surprisingly little critical attention was paid to Dickinson's punctuation, an oversight partially resulting from a century of editors who consistently downplayed the importance of the poet's unusual manuscript style. In editions of Dickinson's poetry published before Thomas H. Johnson's 1955 variorum edition, the dashes were reduced and/or replaced by more common punctuation. Johnson included Dickinson's dashes, but failed to distinguish between the range of marks as they appear in manuscripts: their different lengths, angles, and positions relative to line of inscription. Not only did Johnson reduce what in the manuscripts are a variety of different dashes to a single, conventional printer's mark, he made painfully clear how insignificant he believed these particular Dickinson eccentricities were: "such 'punctuation,'" he wrote in his introduction, "can be omitted in later editions" (Dickinson, *Poems* lxiii).

The work that *was* done on Dickinson's punctuation, and particularly the dash, though some of it quite strong, suffered from this generally dismissive attitude. Brita Lindberg-Seyersted insisted in 1976 that punctuation is "an inherent feature" of Dickinson's "style" (*Emily* 2); eight years earlier she had argued similarly that in the drafting process Dickinson "did not discard the dashes . . . but retained them as essential to the poem" (*Voice* 196). Similarly, in both his 1967 book *The Editing of Emily Dickinson* and his 1981 introduction to *The Manuscript Books of Emily Dickinson*, R.W. Franklin acknowledged the difficulty editors face in transcribing Dickinson's writing. But both Lindberg-Seyersted and Franklin concluded that the dashes represented by Johnson's variorum were about as accurate as could be expected. Until quite recently, the only book-length study to focus on the dashes was Edith Wylder's notable, though vexed, 1971 study, *The Last Face: Emily Dickinson's Manuscripts.* Arguing that Dickinson's "punctuation system is an integral part of her attempt to create in written form the precision of meaning inherent in the tone of the human voice" (4), Wylder acknowledged the dash's importance in guiding intonation and inflection. But partially because her objective was to specify unitary meaning in each poem, uncertainty about interpretive procedure troubles Wylder's readings.[1]

Why, aside from these few exceptions, has an otherwise adoring public and attentive scholarly readership been reluctant to embrace Dickinson's stylistic innovations until so recently? A clue can be found in the words Sandra M. Gilbert and Susan Gubar use to describe the Dickinson dashes: as "rending pauses, silences like wounds in the midst of speech" (626). As this language suggests, the disjunction produced by the dash can appear to threaten to dismember both the speech conventionally associated with poetic voice and, as the metaphor of the wound suggests, the self that language presumably communicates.

My aim in this chapter is to argue that, instead of seeing the Dickinson dash as the sign of both linguistic and personal violence, it can be read as an indication that Dickinson has rejected the myth of wholeness implied by the possibility of rending. Rather than being a painful symbol of loss and division, the dash suggests that disjunction, to Dickinson, is one of the defining characteristics of the self in language.

The connection I suggest between Dickinson's punctuation, aesthetics, and metaphysics is partially supplied by the "dash" entry in the 1828 edition of Webster's *An American Dictionary of the English Language*. There the dash is described in a manner that would strike the eye of a young poet as highly suggestive: "A mark or line in writing or printing, noting a break or stop in the sentence; as in Virgil, quos ego—: or a pause; or the division of the sentence" (55a verso). The words of Virgil, "quos ego—," which mean "what I am" or "that which I am," are an assertion of identity, but a markedly inconclusive one: Virgil asserts that he is something, but does not further define what this something is. The appearance of Virgil's assertion within a definition describing the disjunctive function of the dash associates identity with syntactic rupture. The dash, then, becomes a form of punctuation that both challenges the linear progression of sentences and emphasizes the uncertainty of identity. Given Dickinson's friendship with the Webster family, the presence of a family dictionary inscribed by Noah Webster in the Dickinson household, and numerous references to the importance of her "lexicon" in her writing, we can readily accept Cristanne Miller's conclusion that Dickinson "spent a lot of time reading her dictionary" and that doing so liberated her "to speak as she might not otherwise dare" (153).

A familiar poem like "This is my letter to the World" (*P* 441) can introduce my argument on several fronts: by showing more precisely how the dash is linked to a definition of human identity based on disjunction; by demonstrating how editorial normalization of the punctuation has tamed Dickinson's poetry, suggesting the poet's belief in an ideally unified self; and by indicating how the disjunctions signaled by the dash encourage readers to participate in the poem's meaning. As published in the 1890 first edition, the poem contains only one dash, and that is softened by a preceding comma. In this way the disjunctive power of the dash is diminished, and each of the two stanzas becomes a complete sentence.

> This is my letter to the world,
>   That never wrote to me,—
> The simple news that Nature told,
>   With tender majesty.
>
> Her message is committed   5
>   To hands I cannot see;
> For love of her, sweet countrymen,
>   Judge tenderly of me![2]

According to this representation of the poem, the "simple news that Nature told" is conveyed in the speaker's "letter to the world" with the hope that future readers will, out of love for Nature, "judge" the letter writer "tenderly." The speaker is communicating Nature's words and therefore trading on the authority of Nature to win the approval of unknown readers.

The hierarchic distribution of power from Nature through the poet to the audience is altered significantly, however, when dashes are acknowledged in the text. Suddenly, the speaker seems to be saying not that she is communicating news transmitted to her by Nature but that Nature is part of a "World" that never wrote to her:

> This is my letter to the World
> That never wrote to Me –
> The simple News that Nature told ‿
> With tender Majesty
>
> Her Message is committed   5
> To Hands I cannot see -
> For love of Her – Sweet ‿ country-
>   men ‿
> Judge tenderly – of Me
>   [*MBED* 548]

Read with an eye to the dashes, the poem suggests the possibility that the speaker never received the "simple News that Nature told" and that Nature's "Message" was sent to others, whose "hands I cannot see." The very possibility that there could exist such things as "simple News" and "tender Majesty" is placed in question.[3] By means of dashes, these clichéd depictions of nature and nature's sympathetic bearing on human life are held at arm's length, suggesting the speaker's rejection of the discourses to which they are attached.[4] As Sharon Cameron has noted, this "is not necessarily a poem about a benign telling of nature's secret"; rather, "the secret being told is ominous" (*Choosing* 33). And here, in this recognition of ominous possibilities, lies the key to the text's multiple voices: as the speaker questions the validity of culturally determined voices, she distances herself from these voices, so that through her we hear voices that no longer confine her.

Dickinson's multiplication of discourse possibilities through the dash magnifies the importance of reader assent in attaching meaning to language. As readers who become aware of the speaker's ambivalent relation to prevailing thought, we do not "Judge tenderly," precisely because we detect the speaker's anger at an indifferent Nature that counters the rhetoric of "simple News" and "tender Majesty." The manuscript lineation that separates "country" from "men" increases our sense of the speaker's detachment from communal values, particularly those articulated by the male voices of patriarchal culture. Cameron effectively captures this element of the poem, describing the voice qualities refracted through the speaker's angry delivery: "the letter to the world . . . is inescapably to be read as analogous to those stern communications the speaker has herself received" (*Choosing* 33). The reader's response to this poem now grows from an appreciation of the speaker's outrage, an outrage directed to a "World" that never wrote.

In addition to presenting Nature as uncertain and antagonistic, the speaker also undermines the authority of her audience. The insertion of a dash between "Sweet" and "country- / men" separates the terms of an otherwise positive salutation, suggesting that the speaker is once again distancing herself from conventional discourse and, in this case, twisting the meaning ordinarily attributed to a congenial epistolary form of address. As previously indicated, the maleness of addressees is here singled out as a potentially damning attribute. Yet as we hear the speaker's tone become ironic, instead of sincere, we do not entirely reject her sincerity and replace it with something more akin to sarcasm. Rather, we observe the speaker's moving through the network of discourses that constitutes the socio-symbolic domain of language, interrogating and manipulating culturally determined voices. By this means the speaker admits to complicity with her audience in assenting to the very voices she finds most offensive.

At the same time, we can see that the speaker's participation in this process acknowledges the power of the larger culture without accepting that power as determinant; we hear voices that are not the speaker's and yet contribute to a discussion in which the speaker is a party. In this way, the poem traces the speaker's movement away from conformity without excluding the influence that conventional discourse has on the self—a self that both includes and exceeds the voices that permeate it. Like many Dickinson poems, this one alerts readers to the importance of not becoming settled in any particular linguistic locale. As she indicates in her 1883 letter-poem to Maria Whitney, creative minds are never fully at home in language: "Fashioning" and "Fathoming" "dissolves the days / Through which existence strays / Homeless at home" (*L* 771, #815; *P* 1573, no ms.).

While the dashes, in particular, point to the open and unresolved character of Dickinson's poem, this very open-endedness militates against any exclusionary tactic that would deny the possibility of a poem's achieving closure. The poem emphasizes resistance to closure by respecting but not submitting to its appeal. A truly dialogic reading of "This is my letter to the World," for example, would respect this quality of being "Homeless at home" by not dismissing the interpretation made available through the regularization of punctuation; rather, the dialogic approach builds on interpretations that assert unifying movement in the poems. In fact, the voices in the poem acquire distinction as they depart from unified discourses, making such discourses a necessary part of readings that acknowledge the dialogizing influence of the dashes. Consequently, the regularization practiced by Dickinson's editors usefully clarifies impulses toward univocality and closure while unfortunately muffling forces that urge polyvocality and the multiplication of meanings crucial to dialogic readings.

But if by disrupting speech dashes alter the status of the speaking subject, what should we make of this shifting self and the corollary shifts in voice? What implications might these elements hold for Dickinson's sense of both language and identity? Julia Kristeva gives us a way to approach this question through her discussion of poetry as a signifying process that shatters discourse and "reveals that linguistic changes constitute changes in the *status of the subject*" (*Revolution* 15). Poetry that is "revolutionary" in Kristeva's sense of the term presents the stages by which subjects enter language instead of the end result of that process. To understand this poetry, instead of attempting to discover the formal unity that suggests a single voice, the reader must observe the subject's participation in multiple discourses. Through these many voices, the subject expresses a self that is always in process, never entirely realizable in spoken language. In Kristeva's terms, Dickinson's poems provide the image of a self emerging *through* rather than *in* language. As a result, normal oppositions between self and other, inner and outer that depend upon a clear and present "I," distinguishable from its surrounding environment, are impossible to maintain.[5] Instead, the poems present us with a speaking subject whose utterances reflect an emergent self, a self who is a mix of personal and social languages not containable within a unified voice.

The work of Mikhail M. Bakhtin, the theorist most centrally associated with dialogism, provides a useful means of understanding this mix of languages through which the subject Kristeva describes moves. "Each word contains voices," he writes, "that are sometimes infinitely distant, unnamed, . . . and voices resounding nearby and simultaneously" (*Speech* 124).[6] Within this multiplicity of voices and corresponding ideologies, "consciousness must actively orient itself . . . , it must move in and occupy a position for itself" (*Dialogic* 295). Like Kristeva, Bakhtin helps to illuminate the movement of a subject through language, but unlike Kristeva, he prioritizes not the speaking self but speech and its relation to surrounding discourse. "The author speaks," Bakhtin tells us, "*through* language . . . that has somehow become more or less materialized, become objectivized, that [she] merely ventriloquates" (299).

For a literary and creative mind like Dickinson's, this movement through language requires conscious awareness of the contradictory voices that proliferate in discourse. By suggesting that meaning is created through the tension between centrifugal and centripetal forces, the dashes emphasize that speech is an amalgamation of discourses. For these reasons, reading the poems with attention to the dashes encourages the reader to participate in a selection process parallel to the one the speaker enacts while uttering words that are themselves "chosen" from other discourses. Martha Nell Smith further emphasizes the necessity of reader participation when she argues that Dickinson's "manuscripts . . . will not let us forget that reading is a dialogic drama, always a matter of editing, of choosing what to privilege, what to subordinate" (*Rowing* 53). Such an understanding naturally extends the "dialogic drama" to all elements of the poem, including interpretation of the speaking self.

A crucial strategy in this empowerment of readers is Dickinson's creation of speaking selves that reflect the entire spectrum of linguistic success and failure. Thus through her speakers she incorporates instances of surrender as well as liberation, demonstrating through them the inevitability of periodically succumbing to conformity. David Porter is therefore correct to observe that Dickinson does not provide a road map or a clear destination for her poetic tour of the individual's experience of language.[7] The category of visual markers referred to as the "dashes," together with unconventional line breaks, capitalization, multiple variants, and calligraphic chirography, disrupts the syntactic linearity suggestive of specific linguistic destinations. In such a linguistic context, instead of finding maps readers must reconsider the very notion of specific locality. Poems like "A still– ~~Volcanic~~] Volcano– Life–" (*P* 601, *MBED* 546)[8] direct consciousness to closer scrutiny of a "quiet–Earthquake Style–" like Dickinson's that can explode foundations of thought, forcing reconsideration of preexisting maps.

Bakhtin's identification of "heteroglossia" as the point where the *centripetal* history of words intersects with the *centrifugal* force of unique utterances is particularly useful in explaining the way Dickinson's poetry frequently reveals that destinations, and the roads leading to them, have no existence independent of reader consent. Bakhtin identifies two important relationships each person maintains with ideological discourse: first as closed "authoritative discourse" perceived as external and "organically connected with a past that is felt to be organically higher" (*Dialogic* 342); secondly, as "internally persuasive discourse" emerging through an open dialogue with language and yielding "ever newer *ways to mean*" (346). Accordingly, writers can assist the reader's growth by creating images of speaking subjects who act out the process of freeing internally persuasive discourse from subordination to external authority: "This process—experimenting by turning persuasive discourse into speaking persons—becomes especially important . . . where someone is striving to liberate himself . . . or is striving to expose the limitations of both image and discourse" (348). As Denis Donoghue has observed, "heteroglossia and polyglossia name the conditions in which people no longer assume that the authority of discourse must be recognized in a single voice. The question of voice is always a question of authority" ("Reading" 118).

By requiring inclusion rather than exclusion, Dickinson's poetics indeed challenges definitions of authority born out of hierarchic and monologic visions of truth.[9] Dickinson's poems provide a locus within which conservative, monologic notions of self contest with dialogic notions, challenging culturally founded assumptions about the unity of nature, the logic of language, and the need to define one's identity as a speaker or a writer. Once we are sensitive to the range of voices Dickinson signals by means of dashes, we can understand the poems as her refusal to silence the many rebellious voices that registered clearly in her own mind despite the considerable social pressure of more orthodox opinion seeking to enforce conformity. Speakers' efforts to express voices at variance with conventional beliefs about nature, religion, and the centrality of marriage in the lives of women, for instance, provide illuminating instances of the range of Dickinson's opposition to social confinement.

And here—through her insistence on inclusion and her refusal to silence the voices that inform the self—the feminist implications of Dickinson's poetics register with greatest force. Because the voices conventionally attributed to a patriarchal "other" are shown to exist within and not outside the speaker's mind, any power associated with those voices is in some sense accessible to the speaker. As Mary Loeffelholz points out in *Dickinson and the Boundaries of Feminist Theory,* the boundaries that Dickinson describes "exist to be breached" (111); when this breaching of boundaries takes place, the metaphorical border that distinguishes self from other and male from female is illuminated in order that it "might be seen deconstructively, not as irreducibly 'primary,' but as the effect of its own undoing" (111). Dashes contribute to this "undoing" by revealing the interplay of speakers' voices and the mix of discourses so crucial to the perpetuation and reification of boundaries. The self that surfaces in the poems and is no longer restricted by the border, no longer subject to its power, comes very close to fulfilling the project Kristeva outlines at the end of "Women's Time": "to demystify the identity of the symbolic bond itself, to demystify, therefore, the community of language as a universal and unifying tool, one which totalizes and equalizes" (210). By demonstrating that neither speech nor the speaking self is unified, Dickinson demystifies the discourses that impose social control, forcing readers to recognize their complicity in the creation of the conventions that restrict them.

Two poems, read with attention to both dashes and dialogics, can illustrate the way Dickinson's poetry simultaneously registers and rejects monologic social discourses. Both dramatize the enormous difficulties speakers encounter when they seek to express a multitude of voices in the face of unremitting social pressure to silence all but the voice of convention. The first, "Doom is the House without / the Door–" (*P* 475), traces the path followed by a speaker who painfully recalls how he or she was unconsciously seduced by the desire for certainty:

> Doom is the House without
> the Door –
> 'Tis entered from the Sun -
> And then the Ladder's

thrown away,   5
Because Escape – is done –

'Tis varied by the Dream
Of what they do outside ⌣
Where Squirrels play – and
Berries die –   10
And Hemlocks – bow – to
God –
                    [*MBED* 802]

As the final stanza tells us, doom is equated with a house from within which
the speaker dreams of what an unspecified "they" "do outside." By telling us
that the dream varies the speaker's experience within the house, this line
communicates the monotonous nature of life inside. Because the speaker's
perception is situated within the context of a dream, her removal from the reality of waking life strengthens and develops the discourse of inner and outer,
confinement and exclusion—defining characteristics of "doom." We see how
the world the speaker originally inhabited outside the house has been reduced to a few natural details depicting the cycle of life and death in a world
dominated by God. But what is the speaker's attitude toward this state of
affairs?

The poem can yield dramatically conflicting answers to this question;
as with "This is my letter to the World" (*P* 441), the poem's tone depends
on whether the reader takes seriously the disjunctions signaled by dashes.
What might be called a "linear" reading grows from the assumption that the
speaker has a single voice and that the dashes enforce that voice, if they are
significant at all. In this interpretation, the speaker inhabits a world that con-
forms to a romanticist vision of the self and nature.[10] The house of doom is
entered through a process resembling humanity's fall from innocence; the
dreams that take place within the house suggest the paradise from which the
speaker is alienated. According to this reading, confinement within the house
is constructive because it establishes the speaker's proper position within a hierarchy ordained by God.

A very different vision of the speaker's situation and identity emerges if
we attend to the dashes. In this "spatial" reading we can hear voices that express extreme dissatisfaction both with the speaker's physical entrapment in
the house and, more profoundly, with a system of thought so totalizing that
it employs dream images in the objectification of subjects, so that speakers
become tools in their own imprisonment. This speaker rejects the romanticist

vision within which imprisonment is a way to imagine absolute freedom in a divinely ordered universe, but she remains frustrated by the difficulty of fully imagining an alternative freedom, one separate from the hierarchal paradigm implicit in images of an imprisoned humanity and an omnipotent God. In this reading, the dashes show how the speaker "quotes" from this romanticist system of thought only to damn it. As Margaret Dickie has observed, "By indicating just how stultifying conventional form can be, [Dickinson] subverts the Romantic habit of making dejection a subject that denies its exhaustion of power" (72).

If we examine the lines and words set off by dashes in light of such a "spatial" reading, we can begin to hear degrees of surprise, anger, shock, and, finally, resignation that challenge monologic assumptions about self and voice. The initial mention of "Doom" in the first two lines introduces an ominous atmosphere at the same time that it provides a relatively straightforward declaration that the general topic of doom is metaphorically expressed as a house with no door: "Doom is the House without / the Door — ." Though a certain mystery surrounds this image, the sense at the beginning of the poem is that Doom has been contained and to some extent safely sealed. Setting "the Door" on a separate line enhances perception of the house as sealed. The first two lines, then, sound like a nominally conventional voice authoritatively setting the scene for the poem. The third line reverses the expectations raised by the first when it suddenly shifts the focus from outside the house to inside: "'Tis entered from the Sun - ." And here the dash points to the potential for disjunction that regularization disregards. The speaker, who discovers—only after it is too late to avoid being trapped—that there is no "Escape," may have assumed that the sun would provide protection from precisely the sort of gloomy atmosphere attributed to this house. There is, after all, no evidence in the poem that the speaker either chose to enter the house or even knew of its existence prior to discovering herself in it. This line, then, could easily be spoken with the sort of shock and dismay associated with the recognition of deception or betrayal. The fourth, fifth, and sixth lines suggest bitterly that a malevolent intelligence is at work in the world the speaker inhabits, an intelligence that preys on naive trust in the sun deliberately to manipulate and disempower its victims.

Again, any determination of the way to read the lines depends entirely on how dramatically we as readers interpret the disjunctions represented by dashes. The most radical disjunction would magnify the shock and anger reflected in a speaker so distraught that his or her voice changes as new impressions dispel previously held assumptions linking sunlight with security. Only after the speaker gains sufficient composure would the second stanza (the longest uninterrupted syntactic unit in the poem) begin: "'Tis varied by the Dream / Of what they do outside ⌣." These two lines communicate the view available to the speaker once he or she is resigned to captivity. And here we begin to see a very different concept of dreams from that which privileges conformity within a harmony ordained by God. Rather than treating the dream of unity as a heightened perception of divine order possible only through immersion in a monologic universe, the lines bemoan the speaker's radically diminished access to anything resembling a larger world. Indeed, the forced separation of inside from outside is itself treated as an unacceptable surrendering of personal authority.

As the poem progresses, we see that the dream is characterized by the same coercive and exclusive movement that was so clearly expressed in the speaker's entry into and entrapment within the house. The speaker's freedom or "play" in the sun has become imprisonment within the house of doom, just as the "play" of squirrels and the death of berries are brought into conformity with an order or "house" where all things "bow – to / God –." Because we know both that experience in the house is "varied by the Dream" and that the dream itself conveys images of conformity, we can conclude that the dream is a further refinement of the experience from which it varies; it is revealed as another Chinese box that additionally confines the speaker. We can then imagine the speaker's uttering the final two lines with the realization that what is dreamt about the outside is only a reflection—albeit more varied—of what happens on the inside: "Where Squirrels play – and / Berries die –/ and Hemlocks – bow – to / God –." Such stereotypical images of nature can therefore be articulated with a sort of deafening calm, emphasizing the death of imagination once the trap of conformity is sprung. Manuscript lineation that gives separate lines to the death that comes to berries and the ultimate agency of God brings forward for examination the termination of personal authority conveyed by these declarations. Consequently, as the speaker quotes clichéd images of spring and winter or youth and age epitomizing the binary oppositions that characterize conventional discourse on nature, these images acquire deep irony and bitterness. "Squirrels play" and "Berries die" because that is their function within a discourse on nature that at this stage forms the basis for the speaker's dream life.

The isolation of "bow" in the final line can for this reason be read as a dissection of the stereotypical image of sympathetic nature. Here the speaker's tone expresses amazement at his or her own credulousness; the lines are spoken as a sort of mortified confession that is exceeded only by the force of the last word, where the origin of conformity toward which the Hemlocks bow is identified as "God." With this final withering admission, the speaker acknowledges that God is the logical foundation of a monologic worldview that transforms perceiving subjects into objects whose perceptions confirm a preordained order.

The last stanza of the poem, then, confirms that one object of Dickinson's scorn in this poem is the concept of natural theology—one of the most powerfully conventionalizing social discourses of Dickinson's time. This very popular doctrine, which saw evidence of a divine plan in every detail of nature,[11] was the kind of simplifying theory Dickinson resisted throughout her life. From an early age, she was preoccupied with the fear of losing herself in any ideology that demanded conformity to a single unified belief system. In one of the most famous of her letters, Dickinson associates natural theology with patriarchal domination by conflating sunlight with male power and stating her fear of being trapped within that power. Writing to Susan Gilbert in June 1852, she describes the undeniable attraction this male power holds for women. Like flowers in the morning "satisfied with dew," young women are bowed by the sunlight that "Scorches them, scathes them." "Oh, Susie," she writes, "it is dangerous, and it is all too dear . . . the spirits mightier, which we cannot resist! It does so rend me, Susie, the thought of it when it comes, that I tremble lest at sometime I, too, am yielded up" (*L* 210, #93). Though the situation described in the "Doom" poem does not explicitly involve sexual attraction and the sort of gender conflict overtly described here, the figurative linkage of sunlight with male power and a consequent loss of the speaker's freedom provides an undeniable parallel.

Letter and poem together iterate Dickinson's awareness that the security associated with sunlight and the sun threatens the independent existence of female consciousness. Vivian R. Pollak states the matter succinctly in *Dickinson: The Anxiety of Gender* when she writes that the "comparison of women to flowers who depend on the sun's phallic potency" is a favorite metaphor of Dickinson's and that "the structure of society is based on this metaphor. That is, society is based on a hierarchy of social status, and women's accomplishments . . . are correspondingly devalued" (159-60). Dickinson undermines this hierarchy of male dominance in letters where she identifies Susan with the sun's power, but here she appears to be drawing on the socially determined system of sexual opposition in order to explore its implications for female identity.[12] Systems of thought like this one, that anchor experience in unified identity at one extreme and in deity at the other, leave no room for the surpluses of self that Dickinson's poetry expresses.

Linked, then, to the discourse of natural authority, were the powerful social conventions associated with marriage, the institution that most consistently implicated women in the silencing of their own voices. Of Dickinson's many poems on marriage, none more clearly expresses the speaker's sense that she has been drawn into a house of Doom than "A Wife – At Daybreak –" (*P 461*). From the first line on, the poem uses dashes to set off the thoughts of the speaker from phrases familiar in the contemporary discourse on marriage:

> A Wife – at Daybreak –
> I shall be –
> Sunrise – Hast thou a
> Flag for me?
> At Midnight – I am   5
> yet a Maid –
> How short it takes to
> make it Bride –
> Then – Midnight – I have
> passed from thee –   10
> Unto the East – and Victory -
>
> Midnight – Good Night –
> I hear them Call –
> The Angels bustle in the Hall –
> Softly – my Future climbs the   15
> Stair –
> I fumble at my Childhood's Prayer –
> So soon to be a Child - no more –
> Eternity – I'm coming – Sir –
> Master – I've seen the face – before –   20
>   [*MBED* 781][13]

Unlike the speaker in the "Doom" poem, this speaker does not reflect on past experiences but rather takes the reader through her experience as it unfolds. The chronological sequencing of lines suggests that we are approaching a glorious moment of marital consummation, when the bride will become "woman." Instead, the speaker is shocked and dismayed when the anticipated spiritual ascent by means of a husband who is also "Master" suddenly reverses, and she is struck not with newly altered and elevated perceptions consistent with spiritual enlightenment but with a familiar face that the speaker has encountered "before." Paula Bennett's observation about this poem in *Emily Dickinson: Woman Poet* establishes the basis for the speaker's dismay: "So closely does Dickinson identify the male lover with the male governing principle that . . . it is impossible to tell whom the speaker is addressing: a lover or a God" (158). For this reason, when the speaker discovers that the face is part of her mortal past rather than the herald of a new spiritual dispensation, her astonishment is profound. The dash that concludes the last line suggests that the experience she had expected to consummate her life has instead left it open-ended.

From the first line to the last, readers are presented with the thoughts of a hesitant, naive speaker who consoles herself with language that she has apparently learned from others. The dashes establish a dialogic tension in the speaker's thoughts by indicating that spoken words and phrases are being repeated almost mindlessly from outside sources. Matters that trouble the speaker, for instance, stimulate responses that sound like a litany of unconvincing assurances lifted from a handbook on bridal preparation. The word "Wife" triggers the hesitant response, "at Daybreak −/ I shall be −," just as the word "Sunrise" triggers first the question, "Hast thou a / Flag for me?" and then the catechistic formula: "At Midnight, I am / yet a Maid −/ How short it takes to / make it Bride −." We see how platitudinous the phrases are in proportion to the degree of anxiety evident first in the question about the "Flag" and the "Victory" it would signal, and later in the speaker's fumbling at her "Childhood's Prayer."

In the second stanza, where the speaker moves even more completely into the domain of culturally engendered figuration, we hear women who say "Good Night" at "Midnight" and we are told that they become "Angels" in the hall. The husband on the stair, who becomes first the speaker's "Future" and then her "Master," fits the hierarchic model that leaves no room for a self not unified and solidly contained within a totalizing system. Like the speaker in the "Doom" poem, the bride awakens to the realization that she has contributed to the prison she now inhabits. As Loeffelholz writes, "it is important to remember that the prison is not in any direct way a simply external, masculine force, but an aspect of the speaker's own identity" (107). The irony of the bride's discovery that she has committed herself to repeating the past—and hence to complying with what threatens to become a pattern of containment—acquires considerable dramatic power in this poem, because her expectations are so much more thoroughly defined. As a result, the final word, "before," followed by a dash, releases centrifugal force that gathered pressure through the bride's questions, producing an explosion even greater in intensity than that achieved in the "Doom" poem.

The dashes here contribute to our sense that the speaker may finally be able to escape this onerous sentence. They introduce degrees of disjunction in the speaker's thought process that allow us to distinguish throughout the poem between the bride's thoughts and those imposed from without. For instance, the formulaic litany that moves from "Wife" to "Victory" in the first stanza introduces the sort of rhetoric Pollak describes as "the language of nineteenth-century Christian evangelism, language suffused with the tone of the Book of Revelation and Watts hymnal" (165). When in the last line the astonished bride exclaims, "I've seen the face – before –," we sense that we are hearing *her* voice for the first time, that up to that moment she has been fumbling at childhood prayers handed down through history. The dash that precedes "before" sets that word and the final dash apart as an expression of the speaker's loss of coordinates, or her entry into the abyss of uncertainty that both frightens and offers promise of release from the infantalizing discourse that takes her back to childhood prayers. For this reason, her preceding commentary on maidenhood and her expectation that she will under-go some mysterious translation into wifehood all the more clearly reflect voices from the culture she inhabits.[14]

Joanne Dobson understands this language as part of the "cultural mythos" of Dickinson's day, according to which "a new and transcendent identity awaited the married woman": "It is the seductive lure of this mystical transformation co-existing alongside the nagging awareness of identity loss in conventional marriage that informs the complex and self-contradictory figure of the wife/bride in Dickinson's highly charged marriage poems" ("'Lady'" 50). The bride's concluding uncertainty could reflect her struggle with the social judgment that says there is no life outside marriage.[15] One outcome of this reading, then, is the reader's hope that by discovering other, less conventional voices the bride will refuse to accept containment in the trap she has helped to devise.

A dialogic approach to Dickinson's poems that acknowledges multiple voices requires a model for reading that opposes both linear constructions of meaning and interpretations that conform to the requirements of a binary logic. This way of reading allows readers to treat the poems as independent utterances rather than as expressions of an elusive "fugitive identity" (Porter 5) and encourages readers to take seriously the uniquely Dickinsonian grammar, orthography, and punctuation. Such attentiveness to detail not only respects the syntactic integrity of the poems but is consistent with hints about reading that Dickinson gives in her letters. As she states in an August 1862 letter to Thomas Wentworth Higginson, hierarchic organization was antithetical to her practice: "I had no Monarch in my life, and cannot rule myself, and when I try to organize - my little force explodes ͜ " (*L* 414, #271). In the same letter, she explains why she is unwilling to adopt Higginson's recommendations, linking her refusal to her ability to see "Orthography": "You say I confess the little mistake, and omit the large – Because I can see Orthography ‿ " (*L* 415). Looking at these words closely, we see Dickinson's informing Higginson that his confusion as a reader of her poems is the result of his search for an ordering system that she has not used. Her sensitivity to orthography, in particular, suggests that she attributes meaning to features of the text that conventional approaches to reading treat as only secondary.

When in another letter to Higginson—this of August 1876—Dickinson observes that "a Pen has so many inflections and a Voice but one" (*L* 559, #470), we sense her continued concern with the control a writer can impose on written language. Without the speaker's physical presence to specify the relation of thought to word, words become increasingly susceptible to the assumptions readers bring to texts. Precisely because words are so unruly, orthography takes on additional significance. Rather than seeking to confine the meaning of words in her poems, Dickinson uses each poem to liberate the words of her speakers. As the speaker of "A word is dead" (*P* 1212) tells us, the stating of a word is the beginning, not the end of its life: "I say it just / Begins to live / That day" (no ms.).

Close attention to the expanding life of words within the poems means reading with an eye toward spatial rather than linear progression. The dash liberates meaning from a syntax that would ordinarily narrow the field of reference for specific words; at the same time it alerts readers to the role they play in expanding these fields of reference. In this sense, the poems trigger imaginative responses to conservative, centripetal impulses within language that aim to stabilize meaning, so that readers personally experience the explosion of centrifugal force that Dickinson described in her letter to Higginson and that we remarked in "A Wife – at Daybreak –." As participants in the poems, readers share the experiences of speakers who encounter the limiting syntax of culture.

By confronting limitation in all realms of social, intellectual, emotional, and linguistic life, Dickinson constructs poems that operate as holograms, containing in each particle the struggle for imaginative expression that typifies the whole. In her article "The Holographic Paradigm: A New Model for the Study of Literature and Science," Mary Ellen Pitts proposes that "privileging particularization" (80)—or what we have discussed as the tendency to confine meaning—derives from a mechanistic model that should be replaced by the hologram. She argues that whereas the machine paradigm allowed for the logical analysis of discrete parts in terms of a larger assemblage, the hologram "suggests wholeness through multiple perspectives" (81); this model implies that "all things are part of an interlinked web and are actually inseparable" (87). Pointing out that with the hologram "a single piece, rather than reflecting only a part of the image, will reflect the entire image" (81), Pitts touches on the most important application of the hologram to the poems of Emily Dickinson. If we think of the poems as defining loci where discontinuous speaking selves emerge though the dialogic play of centrifugal and centripetal forces, we need no longer look beyond the specificity of particular poems to find meaning. The whole is in this sense reflected in the details that communicate each poem's resistance to a totalizing system that progresses by means of exclusivity.

Once we understand that no voice exists in isolation, we can appreciate the way disjunctions invite readers to join speakers in the negotiation of specific linguistic environments. In terms Bakhtin applied to the work of Dostoevsky, we have a *"plurality of independent and unmerged voices and consciousnesses . . . with equal rights and each with its own world,* combin[ing] but not merged in the unity of the event" (*Problems* 6).

By creating such a plurality of speaking selves, each of which consciously or unconsciously challenges an exclusive and historically determined identity with an inclusive multiplicity of voices, Dickinson proposes an alternative to the "culturally monitored feminine community of expression" that Dobson states was designed "to screen out personal expression" (*Dickinson* xii). Indeed, "Estranged from / Beauty – none can be –" (P 1474 indicates that knowledge of a preordained identity can itself be understood as a potent stimulus for exceeding the confinement of a unified self:

> Estranged from
> Beauty – none can
> be –
> For Beauty is
> Infinity –   5
> And power to
> be finite ceased
> +Before identity
> was +creased –
> + When Fate
> incorporated us –
> + leased –
>   [ACL]

To be alive, the poem tells us, is to know that identity is a temporary state, something we "lease" as a departure from the reality it attempts to exclude.

That "lease" is a variant for "crease" points to the tension between a transient leasing and the permanence of a crease in one's face, the page of a book, or even an article of clothing that would have to be ironed again. Identity tries to deny infinity—here defined as Beauty—by means of hierarchic and exclusive forms of logic. The variant phrase about being "incorporated" by "Fate" enforces this latter position. Dashes that rupture the second and third lines emphasize the way that the phrase "none can / be –" immediately resists the finite, hierarchic state described in the phrase "Estranged from / Beauty." The middle lines then tell us that identity, the "power to / be finite," is an illusion. As in "Doom is the House without / the Door –" (*P* 475), this poem challenges romanticist assumptions that being alive means being alienated from infinity.

"Estranged from" is a discussion of identity that considers the possibility of estrangement. We witness conflicting voices set off by dashes in the second and third lines, followed by the consideration of a new premise: "Beauty is / Infinity –." This statement simultaneously denies the power of finite identity while affirming the fact that identity is an option that can be "leased." By contemplating a limiting and exclusive notion of the self, the speaker provokes the expression of alternative voices that exceed this concept without excluding it from the domain of possibility.

For Dickinson, the value of limitation is the way it functions to ignite the imagination in protest. In her clearest statement of this belief, Dickinson asks Otis P. Lord, "dont you know that 'No' is the wildest word we ever consign to language?" (*L* 617, #562). Implicit in this question is the understanding that, through language, limits are imposed that can stimulate wild responses. Kristeva accounts for the power of these responses when she argues that poetic language, when it violates the logic of the socio-symbolic order, "becomes a permanent struggle to show the facilitation of drives within the linguistic order itself" (*Revolution* 81). The violence inherent in this struggle threatens both the "unity of the social realm and the subject" (80). In Kristeva's terms, the subject who challenges the historical form of the symbolic enters a signifying practice within which "the strictly subjective" struggles with "all preexisting natural, social, scientific, and political systematicities" (204). This subject, who is simultaneously inside and outside objective social process, may reconstitute herself "within social process" or "reject all stasis and symbolize the objective process of transformation, . . . in which case [she] produces a revolutionary discourse" (205). As this theory predicts, Dickinson's poems frequently illuminate the moment speakers' imaginations lift them out of conformity. The voices that explode in these poems originate in social environments out of which speakers can emerge as creative subjects whose efforts point toward revolutionary forms of self-expression. In this sense, Dickinson's poetics departs from the Romantic vision of the solitary individual, suggesting instead a self that cannot exist in isolation from others.

By composing poems in which speakers either struggle to achieve a degree of imaginative freedom in their lives or open readers' eyes to the possibility of such a struggle, Dickinson gives voice to the forces that drive the mind toward exclusionary visions of the self. She pursues the implications of social identity in an effort to show how the mind too often submits to unacceptable restrictions. Suzanne Juhasz observes that "if the poet wishes for total experience, if she is daring and dedicated enough to pursue this quest, she can do no better than to explore, then write about, the place of the mind." Only by "journeying towards the farthest reaches of consciousness" can poets and readers "become most fully alive" (*Continent* 27). Once at these reaches, new voices and new speakers emerge as language is used to express new forms of experience. And the poem functions to urge perception beyond the confines of what is known.

Describing the writer in terms similar to those Dickinson used when advising her readers to "Tell all the Truth but tell it slant —" (*P* 1129, ACL), Bakhtin asserts that "the writer is a person who is able to work in a language while standing outside language, who has the gift of indirect speaking" (*Speech* 110). He writes that "any truly creative voice can only be the *second* voice in the discourse," because only a second voice expresses "*pure relation-ship*" and is not bounded by objectification. Speakers reflecting on their own material and spiritual conditions establish a creative influence over those conditions once they begin to voice alternative points of view, setting in motion dialogic relations (*Speech* 110). Such a practice necessarily involves refracting speakers' perceptions through language freighted with discourses that encourage conformity. To "tell it slant," then, requires speaking from the periphery or circumference of language; it means using language to say that which has never been said before.

Precisely because Dickinson's poetry seeks to expand the circumference of what is known, we as readers must attempt to enter the imaginations of her speakers as they knowingly or unknowingly confront limitation. Doing so requires that we consider alternatives to orthodox patterns of thought, replacing the exclusionary tactics of binary logic with inclusive and spatial possibilities that are not bound by the desire to achieve resolution. By acknowledging the authority of both the received knowledge of culture and the unique perceptions of individuals, Dickinson introduces us to the dialogic relation maintained among the voices that inform the thoughts of her speakers. As we participate in the experiences of speakers and imagine ways to assert independence without creating exclusive hierarchies, we enact primary struggles with limitation that are as visible in the dashes that separate individual words and lines as in the collective utterances of speakers. Throughout, we see her urging an imaginative life that cannot be contained within a single unified voice.

2

Playing with Elite and Popular Traditions

 WHEN EMILY DICKINSON REMARKS in an 1862 letter to Thomas Wentworth Higginson that "when I try to organize - my little Force explodes ‿" (*L*414, #271), she asserts that explosion accompanies her efforts to contain experience in language. Even acknowledging the probable weight of irony borne by this comment does not diminish the value of her metaphoric association of writing with explosion. This linkage of linear order and dispersion is especially useful in explaining the way Dickinson illuminates the reductive logic of cultural discourse in order to make statements about the spatial potentialities of artistic practice.

Beginning with an identification of cultural and artistic concerns as they are expressed in a very brief poem, I shall establish a foundation for more detailed readings of two well-known longer works. My aim is to demonstrate the richness of readings that highlight Dickinson's dialogue with popular and elite traditions in the creation of a self-conscious artistic language. Such readings explore the way Dickinson opposes the monologic exclusivity characteristic of patriarchal writing with her own dialogic and inclusive poetics.[1] Throughout this discussion I emphasize Dickinson's efforts to focus reader attention on the physical dimensions of both textual production and the activity of reading. By this means she encourages readers to take responsibility for their assent to primary assumptions crucial to the authorization of social values. Any desire for transcendence determined by social construction of an isolated self is thus challenged by poems that awaken readers to the limitless potential immediately available to a heterogeneous and unconfined self. Her poems show that no ontological duality separates individual perception from participation in more liberated states of being.

Central to dialogic readings that illustrate such heterogeneous selves is Dickinson's immersion in the discourse of her historical moment. The dialogue her speakers join arises through their engagement with the cultural currents of the day and their submission or resistance to dominant thought. "'Faith' is a fine invention" (*P* 185) typifies the way Dickinson's inclusive poetics makes use of conventional belief. The three versions of this poem demonstrate Dickinson's interest in magnifying and isolating key terms as a means of questioning the logic behind primary assumptions. Thomas H. Johnson's variorum uses the third version, from a letter to Samuel Bowles (*L* 364, #220); the first and second come from fascicles ten and twelve:

Faith is a fine invention
For Gentlemen who *see* -
But *Microscopes* are prudent
In an Emergency!
　　　　　[*MBED* 186]

"Faith" is a fine invention
For Gentlemen who *see*!
But Microscopes are prudent
In an Emergency!
　　　　　[*MBED* 230]

"Faith" is a fine invention
When Gentlemen can *see* –
But *Microscopes* are prudent
In an Emergency.
　　　　　[*P* 185]

The version of the poem sent to Bowles draws on the play with "'Faith,'" "see," and "Microscopes" that appears in the other two versions, plus it removes the exclamation point from the last line. Without going into the fascicle contexts for the first two versions, it is possible to conclude that Dickinson was devising means to emphasize the importance of these words as they contribute to a discussion of religious belief and natural sight as opposed to technically enhanced sight. The authors of *Comic Power in Emily Dickinson* see the poem as mocking "several aspects of conventional religious belief" through its suggestion that for many men sight is insufficient to sustain faith by itself; therefore it is "best to trust to science for clear vision" (18). I want to extend this observation in order to more clearly identify some of the logical extremes the three versions contemplate.

　　By placing "faith" in quotation marks in two versions, describing it as "a fine invention" in all three, and then juxtaposing faith to "Microscopes" (capitalized in all three, underlined in two, and italicized by Johnson) the poem suggests that belief inhabits a continuum running from religious faith at one extreme to trust in scientific technology at the other. In addition, the speaker tells us that the efficacy of these "inventions" hinges on the ability of "Gentlemen" to "see." To be safe, or "prudent," sight alone should not be trusted; instruments designed to extend and sharpen sight must be employed in emergencies.

The irony featured in what emerges as the poem's reductio ad absurdum treatment of objective verification represents Dickinson's darkly humorous commentary on the quest for certainty. Because the search for objectivity proceeds on the assumption that increased specificity will further affirm valid principles, each detail acquires the power to challenge the very foundation of thought. Each moment that perception itself becomes the subject of contemplation is potentially a crisis with enormous ramifications for science as well as for the identity of individuals. The poem asks: if faith is a useful invention when gentlemen can see, would it ever *not* be prudent to enhance vision? This question acknowledges an abiding instability between faith and sight by suggesting that sight precedes faith, rather than the other way around.

Whenever such a question is raised, the possibility of faith is paradoxically uncertain, inasmuch as faith of *some* sort is required prior to accepting the possibility of faith of *any* sort. Posing such a question, then, directs the focus of thought away from the truth that lies behind faith and directs it to the process of seeing and believing. This de-centering of the subject provides a basis for laughter by making the language conventionally used for the communication of spiritual and scientific truth opaque, transforming the conventional linguistic aim of transparency into the pleasurable play of language across the boundaries of discourse. Meaning is dispersed as opacity makes the material dimension of writing a more prominent feature of the reader's experience.

A complex of tensions consistent with those instigated by Charles Darwin's 1859 publication of "On the Origin of Species" appears in this 1860 poem. Having read Darwin in *The Atlantic* (Capps 133), Dickinson, who was raised on the natural theology of Edward Hitchcock (Wolff 342-43), was keenly aware of the unsteady union of science and religion implicit in Darwin's theories. By twisting and interweaving opposing discourses, she confuses the discrete logical trajectory of any line of reason in order to magnify the role of primary assumptions in the construction of meaning. The dash that falls after "see" at the end of the second line emphasizes the different assumptions at work in the two halves of the poem. The first two lines establish the limitations inherent in any invented faith; the second two lines then comment on the first two, troping on the notion that sight is a requisite for faith. The point is that the poem's language identifies its own propositional character by drawing attention to the way discourses derive from the presence or absence of primary perceptions. We can enter a discourse on faith and its application to experience once we accept the perception that gives rise to it, but if we cannot in some sense experience that perception, we instead turn our attention to the basis for vision itself. The discourse on faith initiated in the first two lines is thus abruptly replaced by a discourse on the technology of seeing.

Read from this point of view, the poem becomes a meditation on the meaning of faith at a time when the perception that should provide the basis for faith is missing. The last two lines introduce a different discourse, representing a new voice that gains strength as the desire for technological verification displaces trust in individual authority. In this case, natural theology, with its trust in the individual's apprehension of a divinely ordered universe, is challenged by an emergent science founded on laws consistent with a harsh and impersonal natural order. Yet, despite this distance and alienation, we find ourselves laughing as we imaginatively extend the logic of technology and visualize ever larger microscopes employed in absurd efforts to verify a solitary perception. Cristanne Miller usefully identifies this kind of humor as "humor of excess" that "issues from the poet's profound sense of displacement, or an imagination that has been prompted by repeated experiences of alterity to fantasize a world in which nothing takes its prescribed form" (*Comic* 105). The displacement Miller describes here correlates closely with Dickinson's perception of the poet's illocality and the experience of being homeless at home. Humor comes from seeing that experience defies containment in the prescribed forms we ourselves resist and by our resistance affirm as sources of power.

Our laughter comes not because we are entranced by the images we fabricate but because we delight in a polyvocal creation that does not invest words with the power to reveal truth; at the same time, we recognize that each image is grounded in language that aims at transparency. Because we are aware of a dialogism that eludes containment, we can laugh at the dissolution of serious truth claims that retain their seriousness even as they dissolve. In this regard, Dickinson's use of laughter corresponds closely to Mikhail M. Bakhtin's notion of carnival as "a suspension of all hierarchical precedence" (*Rabelais* 10) that evokes ambivalent laughter "directed at all and everyone, including the carnival's participants" (11).

This approach to the poem highlights the way Dickinson speaks to the material context within which she is working, while devoting attention to her craft as poet. It also throws light on the performative dimension of her poems, particularly as this dimension of her writing relates to professionalism and her use of enigmas. Simply stated, the language of individual poems moves in two different directions: one direction has to do with the consciousness of the speaker and the manipulation of that consciousness as cultural commentary; the other enigmatically turns language against itself to reveal the limitations inherent in any linguistic expression. These two interrelated dimensions of the poems generate a critique of elite and popular traditions at the same time that the poems assault conventional poetic practices. Clarifying the emergence of the subject through a process that Julia Kristeva describes as presenting "current historical processes . . . to the point of laughter," Dickinson produces a text that, in Kristeva's words, "is a practice assuming all positivity in order to negativize it and thereby make visible the process underlying it" (*Revolution* 233). This underlying process is the poem's non-symbolic physical status that emerges as readers encounter opacity. The self the reader discovers through the poems stands both in the symbolic and in the uncontainable semiotic that rejects unitary identity; the poems thereby point to the origins of identity in nonbinding primary assumptions. Because it constantly points beyond itself, the text becomes a celebration of freedom, identifying the limits of language rather than systematically resolving the questions it raises.

At the point that we as readers acknowledge the efforts of speakers to exceed the boundaries of linguistic containment, as when seeing and believing are absurdly conflated, we participate in the creation of new forms of language that depart from conventional representational and logical modes of expression. When this occurs, readers join in the poem's dance across and through discourses, participating in the performance of language rather than passively receiving a unified body of knowledge. As readers attentive to performative elements of the poems, we experience the poems spatially and not as coherent events constituted by the logic that governs discourse. Instead, we enter a hologrammatic event where the notion of parts in relation to wholes is replaced with the conception of an uncontainable totality revealed in a moment that stretches into infinity. This means that, through performance, reading becomes a nonlinear encounter with the space out of which poetic language arises.[2]

Our perception of language and the situation of the subject within language changes significantly when we move from the discussion of a specific meaning to concern with the language that gives rise to multiple discourse possibilities. Crucial to this change in perception is the redirection of reading, away from language as product to language as process that flows out of heteroglossia. Naturally, such a shift throws increased attention on the generation of meaning by a speaking and writing subject. Understanding the way Dickinson's poems negotiate both the intertextual dimension of multiple discourses and the intersubjective dimension of the speaking subject is for these reasons crucial to developing a complete picture of the way her poems operate.

If we discuss romanticist constructions of nature, for instance, and we concentrate on the containment of self implicit in romanticist discourses, we split our focus between the logic inherent in any specific discourse and the possibility of attaining a position not constrained by its own logic. As Mary Loeffelholz has argued, if the containment of women within patriarchal discourse is "a dominant male Romantic trope . . . shared among women writers themselves" (106), we must conclude that identity within a "'uniquely female tradition'" is "self-divided." Loeffelholz here draws attention to the plausibility of a "tradition" when individual writers are internally divided and thus undermine the possibility of generating the sorts of stylistic and thematic patterns essential to traditions. Betsy Erkkila siezes on this perception as a basis for her argument that women writers achieve political agency through participation in unresolved debate over definitions of self: "And thus this study [*The Wicked Sisters: Women Poets, Literary History & Discord*] proposes a model of women's literary history that engages the central paradox of feminism: it does its work even as it recognizes the instability and potential impossibility of its subject" (4). This discord enters Dickinson's poems through the dialogizing of boundaries that pushes against limits at the same time that limits are affirmed and therefore embraced.

As readers situated at the convergence of these contrary forces, we appreciate the explosive response to monologic containment so characteristic of Dickinson. We "see" that faith cannot be founded on material perception, technologically enhanced or not. Our awareness of this explosive dynamic serves as an indication that reading is proceeding on the level of performance. We recognize that the issue at stake in the faith poem is not the correctness of either personal authority or scientific validation but the release of energy possible when two opposing discourses are united. Reader sensitivity to dialogics helps clarify the speaking subject's release of unconscious energies in efforts to create language not confined by prior logic.

The voices that fuel such explosions depend for these reasons on reader familiarity with the sociohistoric contexts that give rise to specific linguistic expressions. Dickinson's manipulation of conventional language becomes a performative dance only if we identify the cultural traditions upon which various discourses depend. Following the lead of Barton Levi St. Armand and other critics who trace Dickinson's poetic engagement with popular and elite culture, I will examine the way "'Twas like a Maelstrom, with / A notch" (*P*414) and "I started early – Took my / Dog –" (*P*520) make use of conventions easily linked to both highbrow and lowbrow culture. My purpose is to read Dickinson as a writer whose treatment of contemporary writing not only places her within the artistic milieu Lawrence Buell describes in *New England Literary Culture* but shows that she is especially concerned with subjectivity and the speaking self. Buell argues that Dickinson and other late Romantics very deliberately extended the boundaries of literary practice by departing from established norms. While they accepted Romanticism's "protest against received forms," which they elevated to "the level of an anti-aesthetic impulse of protest against the constraints of art itself" (70), their artistic impulses were checked by a concern for the moral implications of their art. As a result, Dickinson's generation of writers was plagued by a sort of "self-division" (72) that, combined with the broadening horizon of professional opportunity in New England, prompted linguistic experimentation. These writers not only justified but assiduously pursued experimentation as members of an increasingly visible community of American professional writers.

Dickinson's decision not to publish publicly her poems does, of course, bear on assumptions that she had professional ambitions; however, practices Buell attributes to a certain group of professional writers effectively illuminate overlooked features of her poems, suggesting her participation in the community of publishing professionals even though her publishing was private and highly unconventional. Calling attention to Dickinson's professional concern with formal and thematic practices at a time of accelerated growth and change is useful because doing so introduces new ways of viewing her standing as a revolutionary artist. The terminology of literary revolution, in particular, allows readers to shift more easily from a concern with unitary meaning to the recognition of performance features that grow out of an unusually dialogized artistic environment. It was as a revolutionary artist that Dickinson magnified the physical dimension of writing, a strategy not available to writers whose primary concern was making a place for themselves in print culture. Only after that place had been secured could writers experiment in more narrowly artistic areas that for Dickinson included the physical substructure of writing as a symbol system.[3] Even though she did not enter the literary marketplace directly through broad publication of her work, Dickinson was responsive to opportunities offered writers in her day, and she acted on these as part of her extensive correspondence and through her preservation of poems in fascicles and sheets. The speaker of "Of

Bronze ⁓ and Blaze –" (*P* 290) may be expressing a sentiment akin to Dickinson's: while she labors for the moment in relative obscurity, her work will reach future readers:

> My Splendors, are Menagerie –
> But their Competeless Show
> Will entertain the Centuries
> When I ⁓ am long ago ⁓
> [*MBED* 269]

The maelstrom and mermaid poems were written in or around 1862, the year Dickinson was copying out poems at the rate of slightly more than one a day, completing approximately 366 poems in a twelve-month period. It was also the year that Amherst's first Civil War casualty returned home in a coffin, and the year Dickinson began her correspondence with Thomas Wentworth Higginson, after reading his article, "Letter to a Young Contributor," in the *Atlantic Monthly*. These details suggest important features of the context out of which she was writing: that she made time to write, despite household duties that were no doubt compounded during a period when a prominent family like hers would have been immersed in the political turbulence surrounding the Civil War,[4] and that she opened communication with a well-known literary figure—Higginson—in order to learn more about publishing.

Shira Woloska argues that through her family's "tradition of involvement in civic life" (34) and her correspondence with Higginson—"a colonel in the Union Army" and "an officer of its first black regiment when Dickinson was writing to him" (35)—"Dickinson in her room was better informed and closer to political circles than are most people under less constrained circumstances." More significantly, in seeming contradiction of her willingness to fulfill the domestic obligations customarily assigned women in the mid-nineteenth century, Dickinson composed poems that dramatically depart from both political debate and the values associated with the "separate spheres" ideology that clearly and narrowly defined not only the proper behavior but the thoughts and feelings appropriate to women.[5] Though she remained in her father's home and wrote about subjects considered proper for the "weaker sex," her treatment of these subjects was often far from orthodox.[6]

Beginning with readings of these poems that proceed on the assumption that language is transparent and monologic, I will move into readings more directly concerned with performative features. By this means, I hope to complement my discussion of Dickinson as artist who trades on cultural orthodoxies governing thought and behavior as a means of fashioning a unique artistic response. Though this reading chronology is avowedly artificial, given the complicated nature of cause-and-effect relations in works that self-consciously oppose linear logic, I think the procedure justified in the interest of clarity. Any reductive simplicity will, I hope, be countered soon enough through a discussion that aims to complicate the roles of speaker, author, and reader.

"'Twas like a Maelstrom" (*P* 414) is frequently read as an internal dialogue reflecting the speaker's psychological crisis. Without denying the force of such a reading, I choose to concentrate on the poem's external, material involvement with sentimental culture and its concern with the moment of death.[7] This interpretive stance admittedly muffles voices not attuned to the unified perspective I adopt, but it allows for an examination of voice proliferations that grow from a specific set of historical circumstances. In this way, my critical practice uses univocality to elaborate a cultural critique founded on polyvocality. This procedure acknowledges the necessity of assuming a specific critical identity in order to make concrete observations about the way writing speaks to culture, while never forgetting that such an identity is provisional.

The setting is one familiar to nineteenth-century American readers: a deathbed closely attended by a person we assume to be a friend or loved one who recounts what she has observed:

> 'Twas like a Maelstrom, with
> a notch,
> That nearer, every Day,
> Kept narrowing it's boiling
> Wheel 5
> Until the Agony
>
> Toyed coolly with the final
> inch
> Of your delirious Hem ˎ
> And you dropt ˊ lost, 10
> When something broke ˎ
> And let you from a Dream –
>
> As if a Goblin with a
> Gauge ˎ
> Kept measuring the Hours ˍ 15

Until you felt your Second
Weigh — helpless, in his Paws —

And not a Sinew ~ stirred ~
could help,
And Sense was setting numb ~   20
When God ⌐ remembered ⌐ and
the Fiend
Let go, then, Overcome ⌐

As if your Sentence stood —
pronounced —   25
And you were frozen led
From Dungeon's luxury of
Doubt
To Gibbets, and the Dead —

And when the Film had   30
stitched your Eyes
A Creature gasped "Reprieve"!
Which Anguish was the
utterest — then —
To perish, or to live?   35
                [*MBED* 313-14]

This speaker's fascination with dying builds from stanza to stanza, climaxing when she can no longer trust her own interpretation of what she has seen. Through her, Dickinson shows that consciousness is incapable of making the intellectual leap the speaker desires. This failure of consciousness directs attention to the speaker's language in order to expose the way assumptions she brings to the experience prevent her learning anything new about death.

The second poem also addresses a subject familiar to Dickinson's contemporaries: the individual's encounter with nature. As in the maelstrom poem, this poem introduces startling and unexpected innovations on a traditional theme—the Romantic discovery of the sublime—which serve to illuminate assumptions undergirding conventional practices. In this instance, the speaker recalls a sequence of events that begins with her going to view the ocean, moves to a description of her experience of the ocean, and concludes with her return to civilization.

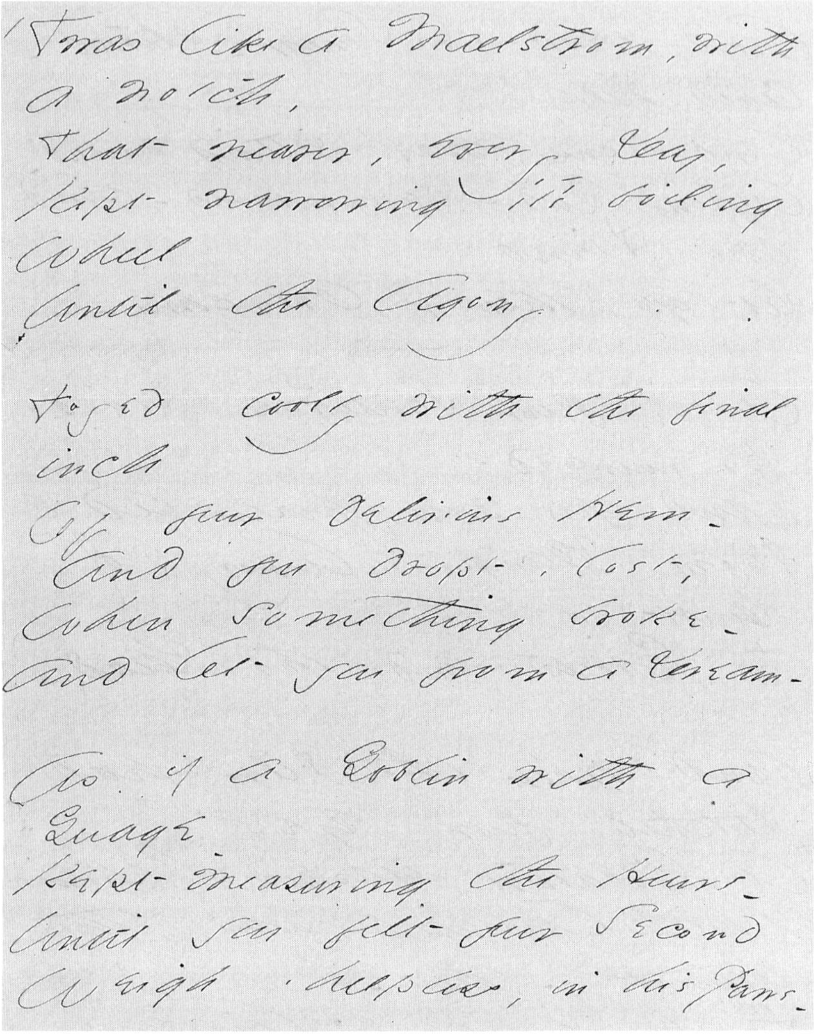

'Twas like a Maelstrom, with a notch,
That nearer, every Day,
Kept narrowing it's boiling Wheel
Until the Agony

Toyed coolly with the final inch
Of your delirious Hem —
And you Dropt, lost,
When something broke —
And let you from a Dream —

As if a Goblin with a Gauge —
Kept measuring the Hours —
Until you felt your Second
Weigh, helpless, in his Paws —

Figure 2. Poem 414, Fascicle 15. *The Manuscript Books of Emily Dickinson*, 313-14. © The President and Fellows of Harvard College. Reproduced by permission of Harvard University Press and the Houghton Library, Harvard University.

And not a Sinew - stirred -
could help,
And Sense was setting numb
When God - remembered - and
the Fiend
Let go, then, Overcame -

As if four Sentence stood -
pronounced -
And Prisoner was frozen. As
from Dungeon's Curving -
to Gibbets, and the Dead -

And when the Film had
stitched four Eyes
A Creature gasped "Reprieve"
Which Anguish was the
utmost - then -
to perish, or to live?

I started Early – Took my
Dog –
And visited the Sea –
The Mermaids in the Basement
Came out to look at me _   5

And Frigates – in the Upper
Floor
Extended Hempen Hands _
Presuming Me to be a Mouse _
Aground – upon the Sands _   10

But no Man moved Me –
till the Tide
Went past my simple Shoe _
And past my Apron _ and
my Belt   15
And past my + Bodice – too –

And made as He would eat
me up –
As wholly as a Dew
Upon a Dandelion's Sleeve –   20
And then – I started – too –

And He – He followed – close
behind –
I felt His Silver Heel
Upon my Ancle [*sic*] – then My   25
Shoes
Would overflow with Pearl –

Until we met the Solid
Town ⁻
No + One He seemed to know –   30
And bowing – with a
Mighty look –
At me – The Sea withdrew –

+ Bosom   + Buckle   + Man[8]
      [*P* 520, *MBED* 713-14]

This poem casts the speaker's journey in language designed to raise questions about her true intent. As readers question her motives, they become concerned with what her words say about *her* instead of nature. Reading then becomes a matter of weighing discourses rather than an experience of transparent language.

A comparison of the two poems reveals a number of striking similarities. Both describe actions that increase uncertainty instead of diminishing it: speakers leave and then return, having in the process infused with ambiguity their status or that of the character observed (if indeed the speaker in the maelstrom poem is not talking to or about herself). In one case, a reprieve from death is presented as a mixed blessing; in the other, the "Solid Town" provides protection from a threat about which the speaker had no prior knowledge, which may also be a mixed blessing. Both poems begin with familiar, quotidian events—a bedside deathwatch and walking the dog to view nature. Both poems address primary life changes: death or the near escape from death in one poem; and the birth of self-consciousness, possibly resulting from sexual awakening and a fear of the natural world, in the other. Both poems increase rather than decrease the uncertainty with which these major events are understood, and both poems raise questions that are unanswered. We do not know if dying is a greater anguish than living any more than we know that refuge from danger is preferable to fearless innocence. In short, the poems bind the familiar to the extraordinary, performing the traditional romanticist move of uniting material life with spiritual truth through the agency of individual perception.[9]

At the same time, however, the realm of the spirit is interrogated in a decidedly antiromantic manner that grants primacy to the multiple perceptions of a heterogeneous speaker rather than empowering a unified speaker through access to the infinite. In neither instance is the speaker encouraged to seek further contact with a divinity revealed through experience of anything resembling the sublime. Whether the sublime is defined as an alienation from nature overcome by intuition and reason, as outlined by Kant, or as the discovery of individuality in the midst of an infinite universe, as in Emerson (Horowitz 180-81), there is no evidence that the speakers discover such sublimity.[10] Quite oppositely, speakers demonstrate that the desire for unity that seeks elevated perspectives by means of abstract symbols is itself a source of alienation. Dickinson acknowledges the power and the necessity of the symbolic while simultaneously asserting a less clearly defined but more liberating immersion in material life where meaning proliferates.

Writing as she did from within a highly intellectual and socially prominent household at a time of great political upheaval, Dickinson was especially

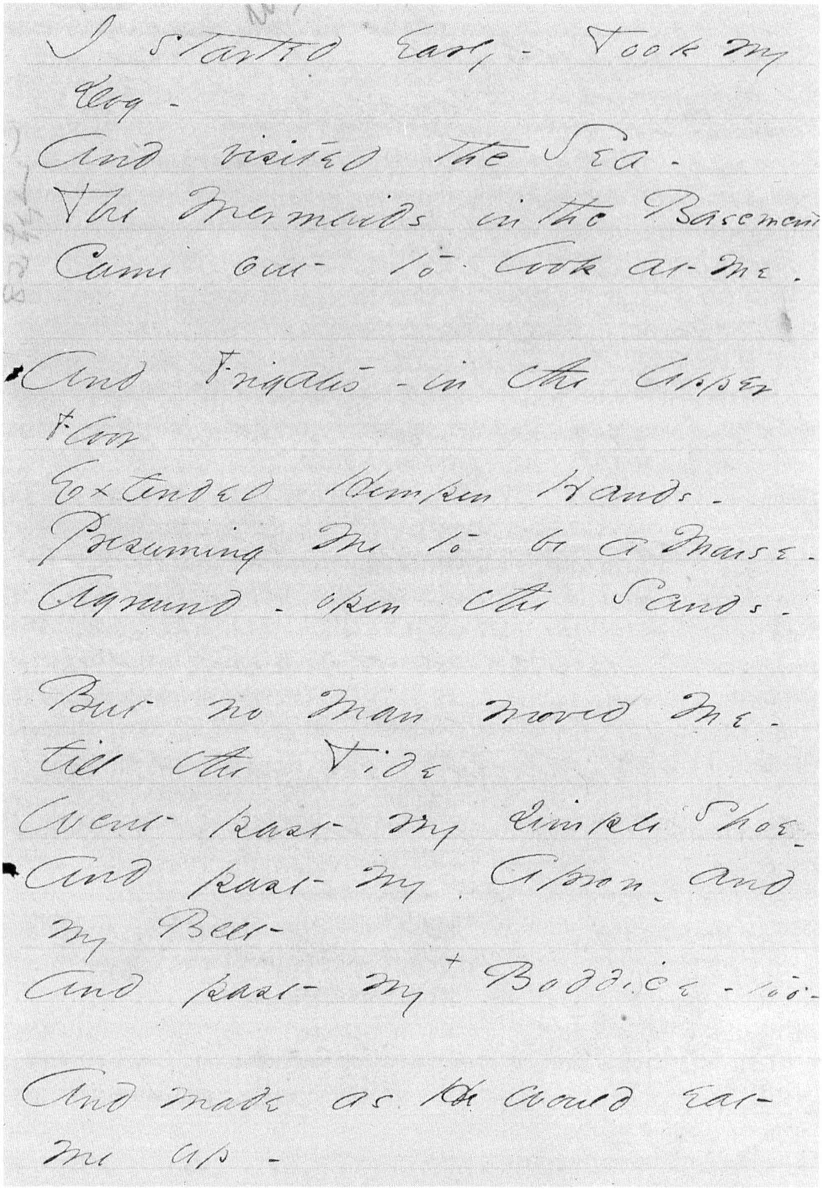

I started Early – Took my
Dog –
And visited the Sea –
The Mermaids in the Basement
Came out to look at me –

And Frigates – in the Upper
†Flow
Extended Hempen Hands –
Presuming Me to be a Mouse –
Aground – opon the Sands –

But no Man moved Me – till the Tide
Went past my simple Shoe
And past my Apron – and my Belt
And past my † Boddice – too –

And made as He would eat
me up –

Figure 3. Poem 520, Fascicle 30. *The Manuscript Books of Emily Dickinson*, 713-14.
© The President and Fellows of Harvard College. Reproduced by permission of Harvard University Press and the Houghton Library, Harvard University.

As wholly as a Dew
Upon a Dandelion's Sleeve -
And then - I started - too

And He - He followed - Close
behind -
I felt His Silver Heel
Upon my Ancle - then My
Shoes
Would Overflow with Pearl -

Until We met the Solid
Town -
No⁺ One He seemed to know
And bowing - with a
Mighty look.
At Me - the Sea withdrew.

+ Bosom + Buckle + man -

responsive to the forces Buell ascribes to the last generation of New England Romantic writers. Buell's point is that the uneasy tension between the individual artist's desire to flex his or her creative muscles and the fear of fomenting discord was exacerbated by the growth of writing as a profession (86-89). Writers like Dickinson wanted to push the limits of craft and promote experimentation because they perceived changes in the publishing industry that contributed to the social and economic standing of writers, suggesting that the literary arts in America had at last achieved maturity and that the time had arrived when aesthetic innovations were not only possible but necessary.[11] Dickinson's correspondence with Higginson is evidence that she was not inured to the general rush of adrenaline that seemed to be fueling the literary community. This professional concern, coupled with the general instability provoked by civil discord on a national scale, may account for Dickinson's extraordinary creative outpouring during the war years. Partly because of her knowledge of print conventions, Dickinson was unusually sensitive to the physical mutations coincident with standard editorial practice. As a result, one direction of her experimentation involved pushing the limits of coherence associated with reader expectations regarding content and visual form.

In the poems before us, questions about both the afterlife and the advisability of seeking inspiration in nature magnify conventional wisdom while simultaneously casting doubt on its accuracy. This inclusion of popular sentiment is one feature of Dickinson's writing that Wolff sees as resembling Walt Whitman's work inasmuch as both poets understood themselves as creating representative voices (141). Citing Dickinson's letter to Higginson in which she tells him, "When I state myself, as the Representative of the Verse — it does not mean — me — but a supposed person" (*L* 412, #268), Wolff reasonably attributes Dickinson's phrasing to Emerson's in "The Poet" where he states that "the poet is representative" (Emerson 223). Like Whitman in New York, Dickinson in Amherst sought to clarify the relation of the self to others in a uniquely American community at the same time that she insisted that any representative voice must speak out against mindless conformity. Jerome J. McGann describes the function of such representative voices in poetic texts that "display networks of human interests which are massively heterodox" for the purpose of challenging readers:

> They are not merely open to various "readings," they are inhabited by long histories of complex and often conflicted self-understandings. In this respect they hold a mirror up to the human world. But the mirror is held up as a challenge—like Ahab's doubloon—and not simply as a picture to be observed. That challenge is to imagine more than you

know, and to understand the imperative of such an act of imagining. Those who do not grasp this, who do not carry out the task of poetry, put their lives in the hands of men like Cyrus and Xerxes. . . . [9]

McGann's comments apply directly to Dickinson's use of speakers she wishes readers to question as part of their own processes of self-discovery. The imagination she hopes to awaken will enable readers to exceed the limitations of her speakers and the discourses they exemplify. In this sense, her writing communicates a distrust of any "I" and thus encourages readers to view their lives as exceeding the grasp of any temporal authority. So that while Whitman magnified the containing power of his omnivorous "I," Dickinson developed a plural "I" through which she repeatedly alerts readers to the personal assent necessary for containment.

My view of Dickinson's "I" shares Agnieszka Salska's sense that Dickinson introduces negativity into her version of Emerson's representational voice. Doing so allows speakers to voice political discourse without inscribing the self within a totalizing ideology:

> If, despite some objections, we can say that Whitman made his multifaceted, representative self adequately contain his private "I," Dickinson followed the opposite strategy. Self-acceptance and self-knowledge were the business of her life. She did not need the support of the representative role to ensure heroic dimensions to her innermost "I." Not only did she accept the private self as central, she claimed further that its greatness was not to be confirmed by the sublimity of any cause, nor did it rest in the security of any faith. For her the test of the self's stature was not in the noble rage of its ambition but in the actual performance in confrontation with experience. [20]

Though her response to Emerson differs from Whitman's, she is equally influenced by Emerson's desire for a new American poet. With Dickinson, however, "voice" becomes the "voices" of speakers who draw readers into language that interrogates the competitive and hierarchic objectives of ambition. And here it seems to me lies her strongest debt to Emerson. Her determination to extend experience through new language unconstrained by hierarchy establishes her credentials according to Emerson's own demands as he states these later in "The Poet": "The sign and credentials of the poet are that he announces that which no man foretold" (225). Dickinson's representative speakers demonstrate that all cultural maps, all logic that makes certain futures appear inevitable, depend upon shared assumptions. Once readers see that they agree to the terms of their own futures, they are in a position to consider alternatives and hence announce futures no other could have foretold.

If we think of Dickinson's poems as responses to both elite and popular literary traditions, we can see the way she exposes primary assumptions without reinscribing herself within systems of thought she sees as flawed. Her interrogation of prevailing perceptions of nature and the afterlife, for instance, initiates discussion of conventional beliefs without necessarily discarding those beliefs or replacing them with her own. As Gary Lee Stonum states in *The Dickinson Sublime,* she refuses to assume the authority necessary to dictate to others (8-9). Instead, she provides conflicting perspectives that the reader is then obliged to resolve, if indeed resolution is desired. The poems, then, come to represent the voices of the surrounding culture as these voices interact with alternative voices within the mind of the poet. In Salska's terms, Dickinson tests the "self's stature" (20) by opening multiple voice possibilities and offering readers opportunities to utter what has not been foretold or, conversely, to accept definition by preexisting voices. To hear these voices and by doing so to appreciate the conversation Dickinson creates, we must further familiarize ourselves with what the culture surrounding her is saying.

Popular culture, particularly in its manifestation as the Sentimental Love Religion that Barton Levi St. Armand identifies in *Emily Dickinson and Her Culture: The Soul's Society* and that Jane Tompkins describes as a source of sentimental power in *Sensational Designs: The Cultural Work of American Fiction, 1790-1860,* speaks loudly in the maelstrom poem. Because the poem focuses on the close observation of a dying person, it identifies a central feature of domestic life that fell within the woman's sphere. Jane Tompkins identifies the death of Little Eva in *Uncle Tom's Cabin* as a paradigmatic deathbed scene. After Little Eva has dispersed her curls to her servants and prepared herself for death, she enters a beatific state, her face acquiring "a high and almost sublime expression" (426). Then, when the end is at hand, her father leans over her, asking her what she sees:

> "O, Eva, tell us what you see! What is it?" said her father.
> A bright, a glorious smile passed over her face, and she said, brokenly,—"O! love,—joy,—peace!" gave one sigh and passed from death into life! [428]

According to Tompkins's argument, Harriet Beecher Stowe's careful construction of the death of Little Eva forms the center of the novel out of which an ethic of sacrifice radiates as a positive influence on the spiritual health of the other characters. The ultimate purpose is that of transforming the limited sphere of domestic life into a source of power achieved through emulation of Christ's sacrifice. Women become the vehicles whereby the kingdom of heaven is instituted on earth (141). And the spring from which this new dispensation flows is the behavior of dying people at the moment of death.

St. Armand links this concern with dying to Dickinson's poetry, writing that she had been well schooled in what he calls the "'science of the grave'" whereby

> deathbed behavior was taken as one of the barometers by which one could measure the rise or fall of the individual soul. If such behavior was characterized by calm acceptance and Christian composure, the chances were good that the soul could be sure of its election and that it was destined to join the Saints; if the dying person railed against death and abjured a hope of heaven, eternal hellfire and brimstone seemed equally imminent. [52]

Even though St. Armand does not go as far as he could in exploring Dickinson's critique of the "science of the grave," his is an accurate and careful explanation of the way her culture interpreted the scene of death. As the above passage makes clear, concern with the final moments of life quite naturally magnified the significance attributed to the dying person's last words and acts.

To further establish what he believes to have been a widespread idealization of the final moments of life, St. Armand introduces a passage by Lydia Huntley Sigourney, by far the most popular American poet in the middle of the nineteenth century (Buell 60). This passage, which appeared in her prose work *Letters to Mothers* in 1838, represents the same sort of smooth transition from mortality to immortality that Stowe later traded on in the death of Little Eva. In the Sigourney text, a devout Christian man interrupts his deathbed reading of scripture to ask his gathered family if they have noticed a sudden brightening in the room:

> Then, in a clear, glad voice, he said, "now, farewell world! and welcome heaven! for the day-star on high hath visited me. Oh, speak it when I am gone, and tell it at my funeral, that God dealeth familiarly with man. I feel his mercy, I see his majesty, whether in the body or out of the body. I cannot tell: God knoweth. But I behold things unutterable." And filled with joy, he expired. [Quoted in St. Armand 53]

How different this experience is from that related through the Dickinson poem! Read against the certainty and clarity of the Stowe and Sigourney passages, her poem undermines and exposes the socially constructed desire for resolution and peace that those authors took pains to affirm.

Dickinson's opening simile introduces death as a maelstrom, a natural phenomenon that generates fear and pain as the dying person is drawn inextricably into its funnel. Poe drew on the power of the maelstrom first in "MS. Found in a Bottle" in 1833 and Melville concluded *Moby-Dick* in 1851 with the Pequod disappearing into a whirlpool. The image was well known as a symbol of the mysterious and terrifying power of the natural world. Sharon Cameron writes that the whirlpool intensifies confusion about the "relationship between death and despair" (93-94). And the poem builds on the sense of fear engendered by the image. Instead of brightness and visions of heaven, we are given horrific images of "a goblin with a / Gauge" and a God whose sentence condemns the dying "To Gibbets, and the Dead" only to have the entire process reversed by an unidentified "Creature." On one level, then, the poem reads like a verse refutation of the science of the grave that was so central to the sentimental religion of popular culture.

But what about the precise wording and the step-by-step progress of the poem? Daneen Wardrop argues that this poem "exists without an identified first-person speaker, so that the action in the poem happens to an unnamed someone, in the guise of an uncomfortable 'you'" (45-46). I approach this "someone"—the "you" of the poem—as the subject of a deathbed watch like that which Dickinson experienced when her good friend Sophia Holland died in 1844 (Sewall 341-42). And Cameron is right in stating that death is very confusing for this speaker.

The opening simile turns on the nonspecific pronoun "it," for which no antecedent is given. We know that "it" has to do with death, because of what follows, but we cannot be certain that something even larger and more inclusive is not intended. Wolff suggests that "it" refers to an experiment that God conducts on humans, submitting us over and over to close encounters with death in order to observe our reactions (354-55). Such a reading is consistent with my conclusions so far and can easily be adopted as an alternative, for the time being. However, the maelstrom simile terminates at the end of the second stanza, to be replaced in the third stanza with a conditional "As if" that introduces the "Goblin with a / Gauge" that provides the controlling metaphor for the next two stanzas. Then, at the opening of stanza five, another conditional "As if" sets up a new sequence of images based on the notion that the dying person has received her "Sentence" from God. This sequence terminates after the word "'Reprieve'" in stanza six, at which point the speaker finally stops telling the sick person what her near-death experience was like and asks her which anguish would have been greater, living or dying. Ironically, the speaker never troubles to affirm the accuracy of her perceptions by weighing them against whatever account the recovering woman could conceivably provide.

Read as an internal dialogue, the poem represents a speaker whose deathwatch expectations characterize her inscription within the traditional woman's sphere, while her ongoing analysis of those same sentimental expectations is evidence of internal division. This internal struggle raises questions about the speaker's position inside or outside the woman's sphere at the same time that dialogue invests the oppositional poles of her debate with voice qualities that undermine simple binary opposition. The resulting multiplication of voice possibilities erodes the foundation for any masterful containment within a single dominant narrative. Instead, the speaker is democratically dispersed across a linguistic terrain where she and the reader negotiate meaning on an equal footing.

Given this reading, elements of the poem move beyond refutation of sentimental religion to an assault on its primary assumptions. The maelstrom, the goblin, God, and the final "Sentence" are revealed as ungrounded speculations made by the living about death and the process of dying. The gap separating the speaker's experience of dying from the actual perceptions of the dying person is never bridged. All we can know about death and dying, the poem tells us, is what we who live can formulate on the basis of personal assumptions we bring to the event. As far as this poem is concerned, at least, no certain knowledge of death is accessible to the living. This is the position E. Miller Budick takes in *Emily Dickinson and the Life of Language:*

> The maelstrom becomes the awesome reality that recalls the individual from the salvation that is death. The dream and the reality, the maelstrom and death, become interpenetrating currents in the vast ever-churning, ever-narrowing funnel of symbols that the poem describes.
> . . . Life becomes a process of eternal dying in which the "Anguish" never ceases, for "to perish" and "to live" are one and the same phenomenon. Both occur together within the self-contained, self-referential, self-created universe of the mind, a universe reduced from external cosmos to the internal world of the self. [154, 155]

Such a conclusion has the advantage of being consistent with other Dickinson poems, such as "Life _ is what We make it _" (*P* 698), in which the second line tells us, "Death – we do not know –" (*MBED* 853).

Even so, the poem does convey information about the afterlife, but not as that life exists in any objective external reality. The highly metaphorical and speculative nature of the poem introduces us to the way the speaker makes sense of an experience that defies verification and is therefore constrained only by her imagination. The subject of the poem is not limited to the afterlife or some experiment to which God submits human beings; it also embraces the horrors associated with the way the afterlife is imaginatively constructed. The speaker's envisioning of death is a reflection of the cultural emphasis on individual conduct during the final moments of life, identified by St. Armand. The inevitable outcome is a community of believers whose imaginary life is driven by fears of what eternity holds. And these fears are the basis for the poem's imagery. The reader can usefully think of the poem as expressing an unstable ground between the affirmation and the rejection of sentimental religion.

At the same time, the dashes that figure so prominently signal disjunctions that ultimately fracture each separate sequence of images, so that new narratives are required to continue the explanation. In Wardrop's words, "The reader dangles in the filaments of dashes that is a Dickinson poem, becomes entangled in the net of deforming and reforming words" (42). Each strand of imagery conceivably forming a critique is breached as different strands contribute to the discussion. An important clue to the fracturing process is given in the second line, with the mention of a "notch" in the maelstrom. In other Dickinson poems, reference to a notch indicates a check or dash flagging a passage in a book (*P* 360, *MBED* 745-46), the high-water mark of a flood (*P* 788, *MBED* 872-73), or a means of gauging the passage of time (*P* 269, *MBED* 154 and 874). In each instance, the notch records a past event and by doing so signals repetition. Here, the presence of a notch contradicts the apocalyptic finality connoted by "maelstrom." The presence of a fixed indentation in the otherwise rushing mass of liquid suggests some incongruity of the narrative within which it appears. Because the possibility exists that the notch will provide a means to escape the water and hence allow for a repetition of the experience, we conclude that the maelstrom narrative will not achieve closure and will ultimately give way to alternative accounts. And this is precisely what happens.

The dashes, then, enter the text as fissures in the logic of each sequence. The first dash appears when the "Agony" touches "your delirious Hem," and "you" is about to be swept away. Subsequent dashes emerge as the speaker pieces together equally defective accounts of the experience she imagines she is witnessing. Upward-or downward-slanted dashes, as well as their position above, on, or below the line, contribute to the tension felt by the speaker in addition to disrupting the syntax. For instance, the downward-pointing dashes that appear after "Hem," "broke," and "Gauge" visually capture the speaker's description of the dying person's progress downward into the funnel. Similarly, the higher, upward-slanting dashes after "God" and "remembered" signal the possibility of hope. The final sequence at last reveals the limitations of each preceding account by pointing self-consciously to its own flawed syntax, trading on the double meaning of the word "Sentence" in the first line of stanza five. It is not surprising that in this last stanza the dashes are flat, mid-level, noncommittal. No account receives a sentence; instead, each falls short of becoming a resolved syntactic unit, a sentence.

If indeed the "Sentence stood" as the speaker asserts, "you" would have been led "From Dungeon's luxury of / Doubt" into the certainty of death. Such a reading implies that what the deathbed observer who is our speaker really wants is not the survival of "you" so much as a resolution of gnawing personal doubts about death and eternity. When, frustrated, the speaker addresses the now recovering "you," she does so in words free of affection or sympathy. By asking, "Which Anguish was the / utterest," the speaker reveals her conviction that both life and death are at best bleak alternatives; the reader concludes that, for all practical purposes, heaven no longer exists for this speaker. Either that or the person to whom the speaker is talking is so heinous a being that eternity is inconceivable in any terms other than the most horrific.

But this concern with what the speaker thinks and how her thinking comments on traditions like the Sentimental Love Religion is only one facet of the poem. At the point its language identifies its complicity in the multiple cul-de-sacs it has enumerated, we can begin to trace an alternative, performative dimension. When the word "Sentence" enters the poem, to be precise, we see a new subject introduced: the process of writing, of using language to push the imagination beyond binary limits. There is no "Sentence," the poem tells us—all that falls under the rubric of the sentence is conditional—and we cease to place our trust in the speaker's search for resolution, even though that search continues. Suddenly, all the dashes in the poem stand out like notches that disrupt each sequence, revealing and perhaps mocking both the monumental ambition of the speaker and the inadequacy of any discourse to fulfill the speaker's purpose.

We read the poem's cultural commentary at the same time that we acknowledge its self-conscious admission that all discourse is flawed; therefore, we finally perceive the poem's performance. The poem's movement across and through the speaker's earnest attempts to understand and contain death becomes the poem's dance. To see, hear, and participate in such a dance, we must activate that dimension of the poem that de-centers the speaker and allows us access to the speaker's efforts to create. Otherwise, we remain passive, observing the speaker as a unified, aloof ego. Our active engagement is possible only when we cease to concern ourselves exclusively with either the speaker or the social critique and observe the dialogic movement that includes all discourses the poem engages.

From this perspective, purely physical features of Dickinson's writing achieve special power. In addition to the dashes that both echo and undercut the speaker's hopes and fears, certain words become particularly significant. The word "Toyed" that opens the second stanza barely sustains the pattern of marks that qualify it as a word; the "y," especially, pushes the word in the direction of a cartoon face that rather sternly confronts the reader. The material marks in this way capture visually the poem's "toying" with the socially determined wish to contain death within the discourse of sentimentality. By staring at readers, the word acts as a mirror reflecting the serious visages readers bring to texts that deal with this subject. As such, it humorously reminds us that grim demeanors are the products of constructed perceptions and that even death yields to the playful imagination.

In treating Dickinson's writing as a species of cartooning, I am extending the argument Martha Nell Smith makes in her chapter, "The Poet as Cartoonist," in *Comic Power in Emily Dickinson*. Smith presents a succinct overview of the history of cartooning and the kinds of cartoons with which Dickinson would have been most familiar. I have acted on her speculation that "the scope of [Dickinson's] holographic textual production" can be diversified by "the possibility that her comic drawings and layouts might best be counted as cartoons" (66). Particularly relevant to my discussion of the way words take on the properties of cartoons is Smith's observation that "since they present a whimsical world in which anything can happen and from which audiences expect the outrageous, cartoons offer a forum in which the unsayable or unthinkable can be voiced with impunity" (64). In the maelstrom poem, the word "toyed" successfully violates the sanctity of the deathwatch and becomes a mocking reflection of the reader's solemnity precisely because it trades on readers' anticipations of outrageousness. Absence of prior commentary on the humorous dimension of this poem reflects cultural resistance to comedy in otherwise grim treatments of death and a tendency among readers of Dickinson to view her approach to death as characterized by a profound sense of awe that leaves no room for levity. Additional work with manuscripts will no doubt significantly expand our appreciation for the scope of Dickinson's cartoon humor.

One of the greatest artistic achievements of Dickinson's dance is that it successfully integrates comic and tragic elements. The dance laughs at itself because its efforts are sincere and therefore filled with the pain that comes with failure and frustration. If it were not for this element of pain, the tension that is released through the explosions of laughter would not exist.

Aware that the speaker is more concerned with the accuracy of her own thought than with the survival of her acquaintance, we can question the need to continue thinking of the "you" as an additional person. However, coming to such a reading *after* considering a dialogue with another person magnifies the sense of the speaker's entrapment. Read as a conversation the speaker conducts with herself, the poem takes as subject the impossibility of liberating the imagination from the confines of a unitary body, anchored to a specific point in space and time. Both the speaker's questions and her play with different logical sequences affirm the use of language to direct attention beyond itself, beyond containment. When the speaker at last asks which is the superlative form of anguish, her request for a hierarchy, albeit a very grim one, represents her frustration with the slipperiness of language that *appears* to be going somewhere but never gets there. Witnessing this desperate wish to terminate uncertainty, we experience a peculiar form of personal freedom that results from our observing a desperation that need not implicate us. Once we understand the choices that may in fact not be so clear to the speaker, we can choose to affirm life. The cool toying that at first may have seemed cruel, can now be read as an invitation to delight in our own power to discover and affirm meaning.

Because we are aware of the speaker's seriousness in attempting to achieve certainty about death, we become sensitive to the limitations of each explanatory strategy and position ourselves in the process of selecting voice possibilities. The number of voice options marshaled by the end of the poem makes understandable the speaker's wish to force the final morbid question about which anguish is "utterest." From "Maelstrom" to "Goblin" to "Sentence," the speaker's effort to discover a transcendent metaphor fails, and we are left with the knowledge that the sentences do not hold. Because we are faced with this knowledge, we can answer the question about the utterest anguish by rejecting the binary logic that opposes life and death. We are capable of accepting our encounters with limitation as a dance that brings joy even as it reiterates the frustration inevitable in the pursuit of any specific discourse. Hence, the performance becomes the experience of including voices that together fail in their stated aims but through their articulation allow for an immersion in the act of creating through language.

The poem questions the possibility that language can account for anything but immediate bodily experience. As a physical embrace of various voices, the poem celebrates the richness of the moment. Consequently, one of the problems with discussing anything so grand and extrapersonal as death is that language simply fails to provide the necessary linkage with reality. Through its performance, the poem proves that pleasure is afforded by the movement of language itself and not by unitary meaning. Maybe a linkage with God was possible in a more homogeneous past, but not now; at least that is what the speaker of "Those – dying then" (*P* 1551) asserts:

> Those – dying then,
> Knew where they went –
> They went to God's Right Hand –
> That Hand is amputated now
> And God cannot be found –
>   [ACL]

Proceeding on the understanding that Dickinson is more interested in the possibilities for linguistic play than in unchanging truth, I want to contrast Dickinson's notion of language with that expressed by Emerson in his 1836 essay *Nature*. There Emerson writes the following: "The world is emblematic. Parts of speech are metaphors, because the whole of nature is a metaphor of the human mind. The laws of moral nature answer to those of matter as face to face in a glass" (35). What is more, he tells us that "that which intellectually considered we call Reason, considered in relation to nature, we call Spirit. Spirit is the Creator. Spirit hath life in itself. And man in all ages and countries embodies it in his language as the Father" (32). The poet, then, is that person who uses language correctly, "who turns the world to glass, and shows us all things in their right series and procession" ("The Poet" 230). In these passages we are given a very clear sense of the optimism for which Emerson is so famous, an optimism that urges the exploration of language and the continual discovery of new bonds uniting the individual with the godhead.

Dickinson responds to this urging in the mermaid poem only to arrive at a different, considerably darker, vision of the individual's relationship to deity and of the poet's vocation. Loeffelholz writes that "Dickinson's account of the human eye and its workings is distinctly different [from Emerson's]"; in particular, "she denies the eye's distance *from* nature and foregrounds its workings *on* nature . . ." (13). A brief analysis of the poem about the mermaids intimates that Dickinson may well have had Emerson's well-known transparent eyeball passage in mind. Because this particular passage in Emerson became so famous as a paradigmatic moment in his work, I am using it as an epitome of the elite tradition that flows through Emerson and the Transcendentalists into the Saturday Club and the *Atlantic Monthly*. As Joan

Shelley Rubin writes in *The Making of Middlebrow Culture,* Emerson was "the figure who, perhaps more than any other individual, both typified and defined the cultured person for mid-nineteenth-century Americans" (8).

Emerson includes this event in the opening pages of *Nature,* stating that he has experienced the vanishing of "all mean egotism" while "crossing a bare common, in snow puddles, at twilight, under a clouded sky" (24). "I become a transparent eyeball," he writes, "I am nothing; I see all; the currents of the Universal Being circulate through me; I am part or parcel of God." Like Emerson, the speaker in the Dickinson poem is recalling a past experience that awakened her to a new and deeply moving vision of the world she inhabits. Also like Emerson, she feels currents circulating through her, only with her the currents are tides whose movement she finds alarming.[12]

Dickinson's play with Emerson gains force through its exaggerated innocence and implicit questioning of Emerson's credulity. The diction throughout her poem is youthful, unsophisticated, composed mostly of one-syllable words. The rhyme, consistently masculine and regular up to the last two stanzas, wavers at that point and becomes imperfect, dramatizing the confused shock felt by the speaker. These features of the poem work in conjunction with a narrative that advances by means of parataxis, piling one "and"-initiated phrase upon another to engender a breathless quality, intensified by the dashes, so that the entire piece reverberates with a childlike innocence. As Judy Jo Small points out, the pronounced narrative presence in the poem combines with its meter to produce resonances with the ballad rather than with the hymn (45). This sets the stage for a message more secular than spiritual.

The first two stanzas establish the setting and the tone: a young girl goes to view the ocean with her dog. She seems no more self-conscious than Emerson says that he was. Through her eyes we see the sea as a house where mermaids live in an underwater basement and frigates on the upper floor or surface extend their "Hempen Hands" to her. Here the poem departs from the Emerson model. Because the speaker recollects a troubling past experience, the narrative is structured to emphasize her efforts to tell calmly what happened even though doing so is difficult. The dashes tell us this, acting as they do to resist final resolution or fusion of the narrative. At the same time, they hint at growing suspense by dropping from the neutral midline position to rest on the line of inscription after "Hands," "Mouse," and "Sands" at the ends of lines 8 through 10. When the dashes fall below the line after "Shoe" and "Apron" in lines 13 and 14, we see the speaker's agitation in marks that trace declining confidence. This movement of the dashes enforces the sense of nervousness elicited by the words alone as the speaker remembers the hempen hands, and we begin to wonder very early about where her dog, her protector, has gone.

But can we trust such a picture of vulnerability? And what about the threat implicit in the hands that come toward her from the ships, as if Stephen King were infusing an otherwise romantic setting with malevolent spirits? We may presume the frigates are moored and the hands are massive rope hawsers, but it is difficult to think of the speaker as a mouse and not be disturbed by what we know of the traditional enmity between mice and ships.[13] I will shortly come back to this mouse as a figure for "hidden power" and "Dickinson's poetic vocation" (Anderson 86).

The third stanza brings sex into the poem, and we think again about mermaids and frigates. No man "moved Me," she says, and we know she must mean the men or one of the men who work on ships. And she tells us that though she has never been moved before, she is now, by a "Tide" that we don't for a minute think of as composed of seawater—not now that she has been moved by a man. Then we get a reverse blazon, where this tide moves from "Shoe" to "Apron" to "Belt" to "Boddice" and then behaves as if "He" would eat her up. Readers must think of Mercutio in *Romeo and Juliet* when he attempts to elicit a response from Romeo by describing Rosaline's "fine foot, straight leg, . . . quivering thigh, / And the demesnes that there adjacent lie" (II, i, 21-22). Even the innocent-seeming speaker senses the significance of the tide's movement, quickly shifting the focus of the narration by introducing an elaborate simile comparing herself to "a Dew / Upon a Dandelion's Sleeve." How innocent and unsophisticated is she, we wonder. Is she a simple girl or does she have more in common with the sea-dwelling mermaids who "Came out to look at [her]" than she is letting on?

Her seemingly instinctive reserve vanishes as she returns to the narrative that by this point has metamorphosed into a melodramatic chase, the damsel fleeing before a ravening tide of drives she may know only too well. As Anderson points out, after line 21, where the speaker "started – too –," she seems to be in control: she is "followed" (line 22) rather than eaten. Is she running away or leading? Why do her shoes suddenly overflow with "Pearl" (line 27)? Are her feet churning nightmare fashion in piles of shucked oyster shells perhaps, or is she admitting to an experience, a sensation, that strikes her as improper and therefore unacceptable though pleasurable? Surely we must acknowledge the sexual connotations of pearl that can "overflow" shoes. There has been so much metaphoric sexuality already that something physical and, for the narrator, unspeakable must be connoted by the shoes. Besides, the rhyme falters with the word "Pearl" that falls out of sound with "Heel" (line 24).

By the time we enter the last stanza, the seamlessness of perfect rhyme is gone. And the speaker meets the "Solid / Town" (lines 28 and 29) where he or it, whatever it is that accompanies her, recognizes no one but appreciates the dominant conventions nonetheless, and bows before withdrawing. All we know for certain is that the companion the speaker acquired during her walk is not at home in the town, where she remains. As in the maelstrom poem, we are left with uncertainties rather than the resolution we might have expected. But because we are considering this poem in the context of Emerson's eyeball passage, we see some purpose at work, even if that purpose is no more redeemable than to point out the duplicitous character of subjective experience that Emerson trusts so implicitly. Not only do we as readers distrust the speaker's report, filling in the parts she is either cloaking or leaving out, but we also appreciate the ease with which nature deceives and seduces innocents, creating such confusion that we are relieved when the speaker gets to the town. And we are pleased when at last the speaker desists in her efforts to account for experiences we are convinced either defy her descriptive powers or leave us vulnerable to her rhetorical manipulations.

Readers may question the account Dickinson's speaker has provided of herself; can we accept the disingenuous voice of the speaker? Certain features of the poem, like the elaborate simile about the "Dandelion's Sleeve" and the fall from perfect rhyme as the speaker dashes toward the safety of "the Solid / Town," may strike us as a touch too contrived to allow for any easy trust in the speaker's veracity. Because we are ourselves self-conscious readers, alert to Dickinson's careful staging of speakers, we recognize that she strains the limits of narrative coherence. Is there a true story somewhere in the fragmented narrative of the speaker, or are we confronting the reductio ad absurdum we spotted in the faith poem?

Asking these questions directs reading to the poem's performative dimension. This time, instead of dialogizing the discourses of religious and scientific certainty or the afterlife, we confront a mix of vocabularies linked to nature and personal experience. The more closely we scrutinize the language of the poem, the more distant the possibility of resolving our initial concern becomes. We conclude that in addition to describing a girl's walk to the beach, the poem parodies Emerson's eyeball experience, critiques the transcendentalist view of the individual, and rejects the notion that either language or eyeballs are transparent.[14] We also recognize that the authority for assessing the various discourses of the poem inevitably passes into our hands as readers. By dialogizing these discourses, the poem challenges the characteristic patriarchal desire to impose hierarchic order with a feminist desire to embrace a full range of dialogized discourses. Rather than single-mindedly desiring an elevation of the self achieved through a process of exclusion, the self we experience is equally capable of wishing to exceed conventional boundaries. As a result, like other Dickinson poems, this one presents a challenge to established literary codes at the same time that it exposes the efforts of elite and popular traditions to contain the centrifugal force of language.

Given this awareness of the multiple language systems at play in the poem, it becomes possible to interpret it as an affirmation of the speaker's initiation into her vocation as poet. The mermaids that come out to see the speaker at the end of the first stanza express a sympathy with the speaker that touches on one of Dickinson's central metaphors of poetic illocality—the sea. Their coming out to view her could represent their welcoming of the speaker into the community of women poets. Like her, they have learned to take the sea inside, to make the sea their homeless home. For it is a matter of taking the sea inside that enables the speaker to wrest power from the masculine forces that threaten to "eat / [her] up" (lines 17-18). The "Tide" that had assaulted her as an external force in stanza three is conveyed by her to the "Solid / Town" mentioned in the final stanza. In this way, the speaker proclaims her power to straddle boundaries that define the voices of social discourse and secure the fealty of the sea. As poet, she incorporates the masculine as well as the feminine; no longer cowed by an autonomous male force, she takes it within herself, exacts a bow and a "Mighty look" (line 32), then dismisses it as a Queen would a member of court. This final gesture also establishes feminine dominion over the sea that throughout the poem has been described as masculine. We sense Dickinson the artist reclaiming for women the whole domain of poetry—the "serious" as well as the popular—that, like the sea, has been masculinized by the hierarchic practices of patriarchy.

3

Dash and Voice in the Letters

 SUSAN HUNTINGTON GILBERT DICKINSON'S obituary notice for Emily Dickinson wonderfully captures the poet as she was known by her primary correspondent. These public remarks are worth examining in connection with Dickinson's letters, because in them Sue describes the accomplished artist whose development I want to trace in the letters. In particular, I wish to show that Sue shares a metaphoric language with the experienced older poet that links poetic illocality to the unsettling of readers. With that sense of the mature poet firmly in mind, we can read Dickinson's early letters as the first stages of an artistic journey from childlike innocence to the queenly confidence Sue describes. The path of development indicated by her use of the dash clearly shows that she had formed an artistic relationship with language by the late 1840s. Examination of her writing during the forties, or what might be considered her artistic prehistory, suggests that Dickinson adopted features we now consider central to her mature style during a period when she may have had inklings of her future as a writer but was not yet certain of her vocation.

Sue's 18 May 1886 notice in the *Springfield Republican,* "Miss Emily Dickinson of Amherst," describes Dickinson's "swift poetic rapture" as "the long glistening note of a bird one hears in the June woods at high noon" (H Box 9).[1] But this relatively commonplace figuration of the poet as bird is transformed with language that associates the bird with the explosive potential of the phoenix—a bird that, as we shall see, is central to Dickinson's own self-representation in her letters. For this whistling bird is, elsewhere in the obituary, glimpsed "'in the light of her own fire'" and described as a "'soul of fire in a shell of pearl,'" both allusions that suggest the eternal phoenix in its defining act of deconstruction.

The juxtaposition of these two birds—the "glistening" singer heard in a summer's day, the self-immolating phoenix—couples a benign and homey simplicity with apocalyptic profundity. This yoking together of opposites is echoed in what Sue describes as the simultaneous unease and delight that Dickinson's poetry created in its readers:

> Like a magician she caught the shadowy apparitions of her brain and tossed them in startling picturesqueness to her friends, who, charmed with their simplicity and homeliness as well as profundity, fretted that she had so easily made palpable the tantalizing fancies forever eluding their bungling, fettered grasp.

Here Sue implicitly asserts that Dickinson's coupling of "homeliness" with "profundity" made readers fret at the ease with which newly awakened understanding exposed their prior limitations. By making Dickinson's synthesis of the mundane and the extraordinary an undercurrent of *her* obituary, Sue is in sympathy with Dickinson's attempts to unfetter readers by making "palpable" their habitation of homes more "profound" than they had ever imagined.

Sue's use of language is intriguing for two reasons: it shows us the sensibility of a woman who, as Martha Nell Smith has shown, was a partner in Dickinson's life as author; and in the obituary Sue comments publicly on the poet she knew so long and so well.[2] For these reasons, it is especially intriguing to note how prophetic was Sue's forceful exhortation that future Dickinson readers *not* reductively translate the eccentric features of Dickinson's life as deviations born out of weakness:

> Not disappointed with the world, not an invalid until within the past two years, not from any lack of sympathy, not because she was insufficient for any mental work or social career—her endowments being so exceptional—but the "mesh of her soul," as Browning calls the body, was too rare, and the sacred quiet of her own home proved the fit atmosphere for her worth and work. All that must be inviolate. One can only speak of "duties beautifully done"; of her gentle tillage of the rare flowers filling her conservatory, . . . of her tenderness to all in the home circle; her gentlewoman's grace and courtesy to all who served in house and grounds; her quick and rich response to all who rejoiced or suffered at home, or her wide circle of friends the world over.

In Dickinson, Sue describes a woman who performed the domestic duties required of her with grace, while simultaneously inhabiting a universe that extended far beyond the confines of her father's home in Amherst. Sue attempts here, futilely, to stem misinterpretations of Dickinson's seclusion by transforming the public perception of deviance into awe before an artistic genius that blazes phoenixlike within the nest of convention.

Sue's obituary reuses imagery Dickinson used to describe herself, here in a riddling, "early January" 1881 letter to Elizabeth Holland:

> I knew a Bird that
> would sing as firm
> in the centre of
> Dissolution, as in it's [*sic*]
> Father's nest –
> Phenix [*sic*], or the Robin?
> [over, and sideways on the page]
> While I leave you
> to guess, I will take
> Mother her Tea –
>   [HCL H56,[3] *L* 687-88, #685]

With these words Dickinson defines two poles of identity—the robin pole, where the "song" emanates from a fixed, domestic home, and the phoenix pole, where the bird sings from the "centre of Dissolution." These lines elaborate Dickinson's preceding description of herself as leading a "Gymnastic Destiny," "prancing between" Lavinia's "ideal 'Irons' in the ideal 'Fire'" and her mother's illness. Not only has Sue picked up the imagery of two oppositely significant birds, this "prancing" illocality, simultaneously domestic and cosmic, conveys the same view of poetic identity Sue seized on in coupling the homely and the profound.

The frequency with which riddling remarks like these to Elizabeth Holland appear in the letters encourages the view that Dickinson used her letters to explore the concept of identity—an entirely appropriate avenue of exploration given the generic expectations of letter-writing that presume language emanates from a single "self." The playfulness expressed in this letter to Elizabeth is a device Dickinson frequently uses to draw readers into the tensions that inform her poetic self. The letters show that for several years in her early life, Dickinson tried to obey social conventions, both grammatical and conceptual; these letters create the impression of a unitary self existing in an orderly world, and they can be very serious in tone. But by the early 1850s, as Dickinson is rejecting convention—after her departure from Holyoke and while she is resisting the religious fervor that has swept up Sue and her father—the letters register a very different sense of identity, one that is not unitary but polyvocal, characterized by homelessness in space and time.

and me, prancing
between - a Gymnastic
Destiny -
Tails of Kamtchatka
clip the Rose - in
my Puritan Garden,
and as a farther
stimulus, I had an
Eclipse of the Sun
a few Mornings
ago, but every Crape
is charmed -
I knew a Bird that
would sing as firm
in the Centre of
Dissolution, as in its'
Father's Nest -
Phenix, or the Robin?

Figure 4. Letter 685, *The Letters of Emily Dickinson*, 687-88. Harvard College Library, H56. Reproduced by permission of Harvard University Press and the Houghton Library, Harvard University.

While I leave you
to guess, mother for tea will take
Smith

Dickinson's communication of this self is accompanied by, or perhaps accomplished through, stylistic shifts to the style we know from her poetry: the increased use of the dash; nonlinear thinking; the emergence of many voices in single letters; a greater demand for intimacy with the reader.[4]

My purpose in this chapter is to clarify the way Dickinson deliberately broke from conventional writing practices in the early fifties, so that by 1862, and the first letters to Higginson, she is already managing voices and engaging in the visual play characteristic of her poetry and later letters. Rather than attempt an analysis of all manuscript graphics, I will here focus on portions of texts that best exemplify Dickinson's commentary on poetic identity. I work directly from manuscripts whenever my discussion requires examination of the chirography; in instances when my concerns are more general—as in an analysis of semantic content alone—I work from the standard print versions of the letters. Although much still remains to be explored about what Susan Howe calls Dickinson's "polyphonic visual complexity" (*Birth-mark* 141), here I make the broad argument that the decade of the fifties was the period when Dickinson formalized choices about style that would characterize her writing for the rest of her life.

Dickinson's earliest letters give the distinct impression of the nascent poet reining herself in to comply with the conventional expectations of her readers. The letter to Austin of 18 April 1842—the first of the Thomas H. Johnson and Theodora Ward *Letters* collection—predates this self-control. Here, Dickinson rapidly skips from subject to subject, relating seemingly random bits of news about roosters and the health of acquaintances:

> William found the hen and Rooster after you went away that you could not find we received your letter Friday morning and very glad we were to get it you must write oftener to us the temperence dinner went off very well the other day all the Folks Except Lavinia and I there were over a Hundred there the students thought the dinner too cheap the tickets were a half dollar a piece and so they are going to have supper tomorrow Evening which I suppose will be very genteel. . . we have very pleasant weather now Mr Whipple has come and we expect Miss Humphrey tomorrow – Aunt Montague – has been saying you would cry before the week was out Cousin Zebrina had a fit the other day and bit his tongue into – as you say it is a rainy day and I can think of – Nothing more to say. . . .
> [*L* 3-4, #1]

The same randomness is evident in her second letter, written thirteen days later. In neither does she use any form of punctuation but the dash.

Curiously, by the time Dickinson writes the fourth extant letter, in the autumn of 1844, the dashes have all but disappeared, the language is more controlled, and the tone formal. Instead of addressing Austin as "My Dear Brother," a practice she followed in the salutations of her first two letters to him, Dickinson now drops the possessive pronoun and introduces his name: "Dear brother Austin." Never again does she write to her brother without using his proper name.

Along with distance of formality comes syntactic unity, both of which suggest Dickinson's desire to conform to social pressure and consummate an identity. She no longer communicates to her brother through the associative ramblings so prominent in this excerpt from her second letter:

> I am glad you took the Latin lexicon – if it can be of any use to [you] because I have had good luck in borrowing one – your Clothes came – safe by Mr Pr[?]er and we were very glad to hear that you were well and in good spirits – the hens get along nicely –.
>   [HCL L54,⁵ *L* 4-5, #2]

In contrast, the 1844 letter is distinctly detached and controlled:

> As Mr Baker was going directly to where you are I thought I would write a line to inform you that if it is pleasant day after tomorrow we are all coming over to see you, but you must not think too much of our coming as it may rain and spoil all our plans.
>   [ACL, *L* 8, #4]

Here Dickinson has replaced associative descriptions with a coherent linear narrative; at the same time, she focuses on the probability that her hopes will be frustrated. Her use of conventional syntax that logically unites subject, verb, and direct object underlines the causal relationship suggested by the content: if it rains, it will spoil our plans. This reasoned perspective conveys an adult's understanding that life is confined by external events. Dickinson's desire to prove that she could responsibly inhabit the linguistic home dictated by convention left little room for the disruptive influence of the dash.

During the eight years that include this 1844 letter and extend to a 3 April 1850 letter to Jane Humphrey, while Dickinson seems to submit herself to the authority of grammatical and logical rules, the content of her letters include a related subservience: to conventional notions of time. The letters she wrote to her good friend Abiah Root during this period communicate an intense fascination with mutations in personal and private life that she attributes to "Old Father Time" (*L* 13, #6). In a dashless letter of 7 May 1845, Dickinson reports that "Old Father Time has wrought many changes since your short visit." She then lists these changes in an order that progresses from the most pleasant to the most disturbing. First she mentions that two female acquaintances were married, then she describes moves to new homes by three Amherst residents, and she concludes with a humorous rendering of a friend's departure from Amherst:

> but the worst thing old Time has done here is he has walked so fast as to overtake Harriet Merrill and carry her to Hartford on last week Saturday. I was so vexed with him for it that I ran after him and made out to get near enough to him to put some salt on his tail, when he fled and left me to run home alone . . . .
> [*L* 13]

In this instance, Dickinson's efforts to deal with time involve not only inscribing her perceptions in language but the use of comedy to impose an additional measure of order. The seriousness of Harriet Merrill's removal is couched in language designed to extend Dickinson's authorial power by reducing the threat posed by Father Time. We sense that the familiarity engendered by personification is also part of her effort to protect herself from an alien force that threatens her happiness. Personification acknowledges the unique discourse time authorizes; once time ceases to function as a human creation—a means of measurement—time can be metamorphosed into Time, a force unto itself.

Dickinson's comic treatment of the Old Father figure persists through many letters of this period, registering her growing alarm at the terrible potency of Time. In a 25 September 1845 letter to Abiah, Dickinson writes of the swiftness of Time's passage, commenting that "some one must have oiled his chariot wheels . . . for I don't recollect hearing him pass" (*L* 20, #8). As she elaborates further, we see how her concern with the threat posed by Time is now less effectively cloaked by humor:

> But I will not expatiate upon him any longer, for I know it is wicked to trifle with so reverend a personage, and I fear he will make me a call in person to inquire as to the remarks which I have made concerning him.

Immediately preceding this passage, Dickinson tells Abiah of her mother's decision that she should not return to school this term and that instead she is "going to learn to make bread." She speaks with great confidence of her "grace" in the kitchen and she predicts her future ability to "keep house very comfortably." She even alludes to scripture (James 2:17, paraphrased as a comment on "faith without works") in an effort to authorize her behavior: "Excuse my quoting from Scripture, dear Abiah, for it was so handy in this case I couldn't get along very well without it." Her awareness of a much more serious discourse on time—one that admits none of the limited playfulness possible with Father Time—leaves her feeling increasingly vulnerable as she contemplates the conventional belief that scripture conflates woman's time with domesticity.

Dickinson's admission that Time may turn on her for having trifled with him in her "remarks" is particularly revealing. The letter tells us that she has left the circumscribed domain of gender-appropriate behavior and transgressed in a manner not in keeping with her social and sexual status. Dickinson's use of humor here injects distance from troubling events, reflecting her distress at not feeling comfortable in her assigned role as a woman. The sense of danger so clearly registered in her fear that time will punish her is not sufficiently diluted with irony to dissipate its seriousness. As a result, the letter presents us with a highly structured, hierarchic world where any violation of the rules is dangerous.[6] Were she able to understand time as cultural construct rather than as ontological given, she could conceivably interrogate her assumptions and gain control over them. Dickinson does ultimately achieve an astonishing measure of control over her experience, but first she has to face her fears more directly.

In her 8 September 1846 letter to Abiah, Dickinson has noticeably reduced the levity with which she addresses the influence of Time. Once again, she comments on his fleet passage, but in this instance we detect an adult concern with the prudent management of life:

> Does it seem as though September had come? How swiftly summer has fled & what report has it borne to heaven of misspent time & wasted hours? Eternity only will answer. The ceaseless flight of the seasons is to me a very solemn thought, & yet Why do we not strive to make a better improvement of them?
> [*L* 37, #13]

In place of the potent speaker who would chase Old Father Time with a pinch of salt, we encounter a reverential if not meek or even chastened voice, full of remorse over her inability to make constructive use of her hours. The solemnity so evident in these lines coincides with the Christian view that life stretches from birth to eternity. Dickinson's expression of sorrow in the final sentence conveys the extent to which at fourteen years of age she has internalized the values of the adult world.

Speaking directly to Abiah in the next paragraph, she recommends that they "strive together to part with time more reluctantly, to watch the pinions of the fleeting moment until they are dim in the distance & the new coming moment claims our attention" (*L* 37). Even though she has acknowledged the brevity of life, Dickinson proposes what amounts to a strategy for impeding time. This glimmer of rebelliousness demonstrates her determination to oppose personally the impersonal force of time that has replaced Old Father Time. We are not surprised when we learn two sentences later that she has "not yet made [her] peace with God" (*L* 38). Full entry into the adult world of terminal events demands a measure of surrender Dickinson is unwilling to provide.

In the letters to Abiah Root, we can clearly see how Dickinson struggled to adopt the socially acceptable, adult view of experience. This effort required that she silence all but the monologic voice attuned to Christian values and social expectation. Her concern with syntactic unity suggests that Dickinson accepted as givens the rules of logic and social conduct that fix the world in the grid ordained by prevailing social, temporal, and linguistic expectations. Fortunately for us, this effort failed and Dickinson began once again to acknowledge the power of alternative voices. Not surprisingly, the reentry of voices coincides with the earliest stages of Dickinson's artistic use of language to manipulate time and her employment of the dash as her primary form of punctuation.

In *Lyric Time: Dickinson and the Limits of Genre,* Sharon Cameron links syntax to time in ways directly applicable to the renewed use of dashes that now begin to reappear in Dickinson's letters. Cameron suggests that Higginson (and most other editors of Dickinson) overlooked an important component of her writing when he "did not think to explain the disjointed syntax of her utterances or the reluctance of the words to totalize themselves in a concrete situation by their author's pull away from time" (10). This "pull away from time" is presented two ways in the letters: through a thematic reconceptualization of time, and through the reasserted syntactical and grammatical disjointedness of the earliest letters.

The dashes begin to surface again in the letters of 1849, after Dickinson has declared her resistance to religious conversion and returned home following her second and final term at Mt. Holyoke. Starting with a Valentine's Day letter to William Cowper Dickinson, we see a steady increase in confidence along with a corresponding dependence on dashes. At this point, her decision to construct a style strikingly similar to that of her first letters demonstrates both her rejection of social conformity and her affirmation of the self that spoke so openly in the 1842 letters. In spite of the fact that William had recently lost his sister, Dickinson's Valentine's Day letter is decidedly upbeat, focusing on renewal. Part of her enthusiasm for life can be attributed to the celebration of Valentine's Day, but there is a specific reference to the book *Picciola,* by X.B. Saintine, that marks a change in Dickinson's outlook. In that story, a prisoner transforms his view of life as a result of watching a plant grow in the prison courtyard. Dickinson appears to have taken these events to heart, writing of the book, "I fancy that it whispers pleasant things to me – of freedom – and the future" (*L* 75, #27).

This optimistic view of the future contributes to her sense of humor and an increased self-confidence easily observable in her January 1850 letter to Joel Warren Norcross. She opens that correspondence with reference to a dream in which an uncle who lied to his niece suddenly ages and descends to the depths of hell. In this parody of a jeremiad Dickinson situates herself in the position of God's prophet. Her description of the dream exhibits all the exuberant play of the earliest letters while reclaiming potency she had forfeited to such external authorities as the weather, time, and logic. Dickinson asserts her own authority by hurling curses at her uncle:

> I call upon all nature to lay hold of you –[7] let fire burn – and water drown – and light put out – and tempests tear – and hungry wolves eat up. . . . Any other afflictions which now slip my mind shall be looked up and forwarded to you immediately.
> [ACL, *L* 78, #29]

Dickinson's irony and exaggerated rhetoric suggest that she has established herself as an equal of the adult recipient of the letter. The playfulness itself implies the freedom of expression possible between equals. This tone, together with a consistent use of dashes, remains a prominent feature of her letters from this point forward, in spite of objections raised first by Austin and later by Higginson.[8]

Having asserted her authority to address adults as equals in her own terms, Dickinson proceeded to develop a unique understanding of time as an extremely flexible medium, comprehensible by degrees rather than by lifetimes. In her 3 April 1850 letter to Jane Humphrey, she treats time as an uncertain quantity closely linked to the emotions: "How long does it seem since you left me, has the time been fleet, or lagging – been filled with hope, and the future, or waste and a weary wilderness – and no one who knew the road?" (*L* 95, #35). The next sentence—one increasingly disrupted by dashes—hints at the courageousness of Dickinson's activities over the previous winter: "I have dared to do strange things–bold things, and have asked no advice from any – I have heeded beautiful tempters, yet do not think I am wrong." The humor and the irony so much in evidence in previous letters is replaced by an aggressive confidence that belies more troubling undercurrents. Her admission that she is engaged in "strange things," that her life is solitary, and that she has yielded to temptation, betrays an acute sensitivity to the prominence choice and responsibility are acquiring in her life. Instead of fearing that her difficulty conforming to social expectation results from a constitution over which she has no control, she now assumes responsibility for conscious decisions.

Dickinson communicates her concern to Jane in the closing lines of her letter:

> Be strong Jennie in remembrance, dont let "bygones *be* bygones," – love what you are taken from, and cherish us tho, so dim. Dont put us in narrow graves – we shall *certainly rise* if you do, and scare you most prodigiously, and carry you off perhaps! This is the end of earth!
> [*L* 95-96, #35]

These words represent more than just encouragement or humorous overstatement; they suggest instead the sort of prophetic formula we saw in the 1849 letter to William Cowper Dickinson. Jane is advised to ignore conventional wisdom as expressed in the cliché about "bygones" and cling to what she is "taken from," to fix her gaze on the fleeting moment. And lastly, she is exhorted not to place "us in narrow graves," not to consign the memories of acquaintances to the oblivion of a forgotten past. The comic threat that both promises a horrific resurrection and parodies itself with a qualifying "perhaps," is extended into more obvious parody by a mocking reiteration of the familiar prophecy of the end of the earth. As was the case in previous letters, humor acts as a means of dissipating her fear of losing what she holds most dear. We are meant to take seriously her exhortation to resist time by clinging to memory and, by that means, resist confinement in any chronological moment.

This writing—that uses dashes to further her aim of disrupting time and de-centering the self—offers strong evidence that by 1850 Dickinson had begun to define herself through an artistic use of language that already drew on the broadest elements of her mature style. We can also see that her early efforts to govern her thought by submitting to conventional writing strictures ultimately clarified her sense that standardized rules of grammar could not accommodate the self she sought to express.

Dickinson increasingly defines the artistic self now beginning to take shape in her letters through metaphors of birds and the sea, both of which convey temporal and spatial illocality. As we have already seen in her letter to Elizabeth Holland, Dickinson adds the explosive power of the phoenix to the traditional association of birds and poets, in order to merge the seasonal, timebound bird with the timelessness of apocalypse. Out of this unstable mix of predictability and disruption comes a new sense of the poet's voice as fluctuating, discontinuous, multitudinous.

All the tropes and images with which Dickinson alludes to her poetic voice have in common the sense of illocality consistent with being homeless at home. For Dickinson, the poet's homelessness in space and time means that the true poet has no stable linguistic "home." Dickinson's practice of occupying and then vacating a variety of voices becomes her means of demonstrating that within the house of language exist many mansions, none of which can accommodate the polyvocal self. That self dwells in the shifting vastness of the sea—the most frequent of the images Dickinson uses to convey poetic illocality. As Barbara Antonina Clarke Mossberg has noted, Dickinson "can 'sing' even while her mind or brain is supposedly inoperative": "she is able to function as an artist despite, or perhaps because of, the dysfunction of her brain, her mind, and even her soul" (29). However, the letters recommend conclusions quite different from Mossberg's: where she asserts that Dickinson was unavoidably "detached from her informing consciousness" and therefore "trapped in a plural identity" (30), the letters propose that Dickinson used language to claim plural identity and in that way elude entrapment in monologic consciousness.

Though her most sustained commentary on writing and reading appears in correspondence with Susan and Higginson, references to poetic identity often appear in letters dedicated to other topics. An example closely related to her comments to Elizabeth Holland appears in a November 1881 letter to Frances Norcross. There she observes that "Home is the riddle of the wise – the booty of the dove" (*L* 717, #737). While ostensibly addressing the physical homes of Frances and Louise, the comment extends its field of reference to link "home" to the dove of Genesis that brings evidence of land to Noah while he drifts on the flood. By doing so, Dickinson indicates the complexity of her sense of home: the dove is not physically in the location designated "home" but acquires the "booty" as a result of having been there; conversely, Noah has not been anywhere but acquires the "home" signified by the dove's "booty." "Home" then is a sense of locality that can be experienced through a message delivered and received at sea. Because Dickinson associates birds with poets and repeatedly refers to herself as at sea, we can interpret the "riddle of the wise" to mean that poets and readers must be gymnasts who can deliver or read the language of home while living the non-language of the sea. Such riddling treatment of "Home" implies the necessity of multiple voices for gymnastic poets.

Many of the best-known passages from Dickinson's letters illustrate the extent to which she dances away from containment in specific linguistic locales. In 1862 she writes Higginson that when she tries to organize her thoughts her "little Force explodes" and "All men say 'What'" to her (*L* 414-15, #271). In 1866 she first observes to Sue that she lives "in the Sea always" (*L* 441, #306), then informs Higginson that "Immortality" is the "Flood subject" (*L* 454, #319). Perhaps she had already tasted "Eternity in Time," the paradoxical writer's home that she attributes to George Eliot in 1881 (*L* 689, #688) and applies to herself in 1882, writing the Norcross sisters that "Eternity . . . sweeps around me like a sea" (*L* 750, #785). In the context of Dickinson's statements about the essential homelessness of the poet we can better understand the crucial question Dickinson apparently asked Higginson during his first visit in 1870: "'Could you tell me what home is?'" (*L* 475, #342b).

And it is in the context of Higginson's probably responding "What?" that we must consider Dickinson's telling him in 1876 that "Nature is a Haunted House – but Art – a House that tries to be haunted" (*L* 554, #459a), a remark that she echoes in a letter-poem to Sue the following year when she describes Sue as possessing a "Haunted House" and a "Ghost" (*L* 598, #530). When she then sends a note of thanks to Sue in 1881, asserting that "The Competition of Phantoms is inviolate" (*L* 699, #707), we sense that she and Sue have worked around the bafflement of men like Higginson. She appears to share a logic with Sue that follows from repeated assertions that art and those who create it exceed containment. To accommodate ghosts is to make the next world part of this one, to be at sea while on land is to flood the familiar with an overwhelming vastness, and to explode language is to oppose referential specificity with dialogic possibility.

Dickinson also makes the unsettling power of the poet's voice the subject of an 1884 letter to Helen Hunt Jackson in which she speaks as one poet to another, wishing Jackson speedy recovery from a broken leg and urging her to follow the example of "the convalescing Bird" whose first note stunned the universe:

> As was said
> of the convalescing
> Bird, And then
> he lifted up
> his Throat
> And squandered
> such a Note _
> A Universe
> that overheard
> Is stricken by it
> yet –
>   [BPL,⁹ *L* 840, #937]

Here Dickinson appears to be speaking very directly to a fellow poet; that is, to one who understands personally the true poet's power to disrupt the comfortable habitations of readers.

Dickinson's deservedly famous letters to Higginson enact her ideas about the ineluctable nature of identity both in their deployment of multiple voices, which range from the voice of the child to the voice of the monarch, and in their overt statements about the nature of identity, voice, and poetry. Reliance on the dash varies in these letters according to the frequency of voice shifts and the degree to which Dickinson grants or challenges Higginson's authority at any particular moment. In all her correspondence, Dickinson is sensitive to her readers' willingness to dance between the phoenix and the robin, but with no reader does she so frequently mix audaciousness and respect as with Higginson.

Not until the first correspondence with Higginson in 1862 do the letters show that Dickinson could employ distinct voices as strategic attempts to elicit certain responses or test reader acuity. The first Higginson letter speaks with the innocence and potential we associate with the child's voice, a voice already registering in the poems. In this letter, dashes predominate, the whole gist of the message is directed to the future—"Are you too deeply occupied to say if my Verse is alive?" (BPL Higg 50, *L* 403, #260)—and Dickinson does all she can to be deferential. She chooses to represent herself in this way despite her being capable not only of directness but imperiousness; her letters to Samuel Bowles show that she was already addressing literary men of power and influence with all the playfulness of her letters to childhood friends.[10] The tone of the first letter to Higginson is unwavering and the message brief; it begins with the request for Higginson "to say if my Verse is alive" and ends on a note of vulnerability, beseeching Higginson not to "betray" her.

Dickinson's complicated response to Higginson's criticism in her third letter (June 1862) demonstrates both her growing trust of Higginson and her confident deployment of a repertoire of voices. The letter invites us to experience the shifting voices that constitute the continuum[11] between the child and the Queen. As the letter opens, the speaker is an adult: she tells Higginson that his "letter gave no Drunkenness / because I tasted Rum / before" and that "I have / had few pleasures so / deep as your opinion" (BPL Higg 52, *L* 408, #265). She then writes of a tutor who died before she became a poet and

> when far afterward ⌣
> a sudden light on
> Orchards, or a new
> fashion in the wind
> troubled my attention ⌣
> I felt a palsy,
> here - the Verses just
> relieve -   [b][12]

How differently she presents herself here than in the previous letter, where she had made "but one or two" (*L* 404, #261) verses before the past winter. Suddenly, the poet is a woman with a considerable past who studied with a tutor.

By the fourth paragraph, a new voice surfaces that does not speak in the past tense of the adult:

> I smile when you suggest
> that I delay "to pub-
> lish" ‒ that being foreign
> to my thought, as
> Firmament to Fin –   [c]

Now the speaker deports herself with all the condescension of a monarch, smiling at the importunities of inferiors and radiating the power of a poet content to be at sea. Placing the infinitive "to publish" in quotation marks, and then breaking the word "publish" into two parts on separate lines visually enacts her distance from the activity signified, as well as marking her rejection of the honorific status Higginson attributes to conventional publication. From this point, the letter retains the present tense until the child asks for help, declaring herself unobtrusive as "the Mouse, / that dents / your Galleries –," and shifting the discussion into the future as she asks Higginson if he will be her "Preceptor."[13]

The careful manipulation of voices in this letter reflects Dickinson's cautious guiding of Higginson into the haunted house of art. She treats *him* like the timid soul she pretends *she* is when she withdraws into her mouse persona. She wants him to delight in pursuit of the speaker's elusive presence; she wants him to enjoy discovering the phantoms of prior expectations. This is the deliberate encounter with disorientation she hopes he will learn to welcome by the time he sees her face-to-face eight years later. Then she will want him to take pleasure in her asking him "what home is" when, sitting in her living room, he might expect her to clarify the issue for him. Dickinson seems to hope Higginson will discover that part of her art lies in deftly derailing expectations; sadly, he either does not see this, or he is unable to acknowledge consciously what he imperfectly perceives. However, that he is sensitive to her power though not fully appreciative of the aesthetic she has presented him is evident in his confession to his wife that "I never was with anyone who drained my nerve power so much" and "I am glad not to live near her" (*L* 476, #342b). Higginson's response to Dickinson is instructive, as it points to the way that in her house—or the house of her father—Dickinson displayed little of the traditional hospitality we associate with being "at home." This comes as no surprise to us because, unlike Higginson, we have access to a vast body of work through which Dickinson repeatedly states that she is not at home, and glad of it.

In her fifth letter to Higginson, Dickinson explains some of what she has learned about freeing herself from containment within a single voice. She writes:

> I had no Monarch in
> my life, and cannot
> rule myself, and when
> I try to organize, my
> little Force explodes ﹏
>   [BPL Higg 55, *L* 414, #27]

This statement accompanies Dickinson's admission that her writing has not always satisfied Higginson. She wonders if the poems enclosed in this letter are more "orderly," and she announces her intent to "observe" his "precept" though she doesn't "understand it always" (415). She even records her mystification at his inability to understand her words:

> you say "Beyond your
> knowledge". You would not
> jest with me, because I
> believe you - but Preceptor ⌣
> you cannot mean it?
> All men say "What" to
> me, but I thought it
> a fashion –   [d]

That she is having fun with Higginson is clear; the two poems that accompany this letter are "Before I got my Eye put out ⌣" and "I cannot dance upon my Toes –," both highly ironic comments, one on physical disability and the other on the need for male instruction. When the letter is read in conjunction with these poems, we hear Dickinson adding a mocking undercurrent to her apparent obsequiousness in order to tell Higginson that fashion and other prevailing cultural discourses too severely house meaning and deserve to be exploded.[14]

Dickinson shows that she is the true jester when on the previous page of this letter she teasingly alludes to Higginson's constrained imagination. After defending her reclusive behavior by stating that other people talk of "Hallowed things, aloud" that "embarrass my Dog," she proceeds to link Higginson to her dog Carlo and a chestnut tree:

> . . . I think
> Carl[o] would please
> you – He is dumb ⌣ and
> brave – I think you
> would like the Chestnut
> Tree ⌢ I met in my walk.
> It hit my notice suddenly ⌣
> and I thought the Skies
> were in Blossom –   [c]

Dickinson insinuates that Higginson would be more pleased by a dumb and brave dog than by an articulate and perhaps disobedient woman. After all, she has just responded to his charge that she "confess[es] the / little mistake, and omit[s] / the large – Because / [she] can see Orthography ⌣ ." Her reference to the chestnut tree that caught her attention by dropping a nut on her head is meant to show that objects as obvious as trees can go unnoticed just as easily as orthography.

Dickinson uses the tree illustration to tell Higginson that *he* has mistakenly applied hierarchic standards to writing that purposefully thwarts such hierarchic expectations. Her alteration of perspective followed a discomforting knock on the head that drew her gaze heavenward, opening her eyes to blossoms that filled the sky—a beauty she did not know was there. But because Higginson refuses to question his assumptions about poetic form, he is impervious to the chestnuts Dickinson drops on him through her orthographic innovations. The low, downward-pointing dash after the capitalized word "Orthography" visually captures the way she deliberately elevates seemingly insignificant marks: capitalization suggests importance, and the mark points down and away to signal the lowly status of that which she seeks to magnify. This use of visual effects parallels Dickinson's use of graphics when she points the dash upward after "Tree," as if representing the height of the tree, then turns down the low dash after "suddenly" to signal the downward plummet of the nut that strikes her head. As long as Higginson remains oblivious to these sorts of visual signals, he cannot fully appreciate the beauty Dickinson offers him through her poetry.

In this letter, Dickinson uses multiple means to show Higginson that by penetrating beneath his preconceptions he can embrace life more completely, if less conventionally. To make this point as clear as possible, she follows the descriptions of Carlo and the chestnut tree with a similarly allegorical description of childhood experience in the woods:

> When much in the Woods   [d]
> [next page]
> As a little Girl, I was
> told that the Snake
> would bite me, that
> I might pick a poisonous
> flower, or Goblins kidnap
> me, but I went along
> and met no one but
> Angels, who were far
> shyer of me, than I
> could be of them, so I
> hav'nt [*sic*] that confidence

in fraud which many
exercise.   [e]

More than anything else, this anecdote clarifies the mental and imaginative disposition of a young girl who "went along" in the woods despite warnings of danger. This poet questioned convention from the beginning, acting on curiosity rather than on a logic founded on fear. After all, fraud is possible only if the supposed victim subscribes to the same system of logic employed by the deceiver, and Dickinson's exploding force suggests a most unsystematic organization. However, Dickinson's concern here lies not so much in the girl's negative rejection of warnings as in showing Higginson the positive benefits available to a mind not confined by prior discourse.

Interestingly, this narrative stands apart from the rest of the letter as a normalized (dashless) narrative, as if Dickinson is telling Higginson that she can command the conventions when she wants to, and that she departs from them only for good reasons. Her next words to Higginson bring the child's voice into the poem by shifting to future tense ("I shall observe"), acknowledging his authority ("observe your precept"), and protesting ignorance ("I don't understand / it, always"). Deployment of the child's voice here indicates Dickinson's sensitivity to having pushed Higginson about as far as she feels she can. It may also indicate that such a sustained effort at conventional syntax has brought her to the limits of her power to contain the force that repeatedly explodes into voices.

The letter's early mention of an exploding force suggests explosions occur when Dickinson attempts to subordinate her thought, and that she is unable to do so because she has no "Monarch." Though much of the letter reads as if it were a request that Higginson become her monarch, we can credit such a request only if we assume that she is unhappy about the explosions. But if the childhood reminiscence says anything, it is that freedom from the authority of monarchs has enabled her to visit angels. By flooding the monologic voice of warning with her own sense of dialogical possibility, she is able to release voices latent in the language designed to contain her.

Of all the many letters that address the relation of homelessness to voice, none display Dickinson's creativity more effectively than the one she sent Higginson in January 1874, a month after his second and final visit. In it she introduces the topic of "home" to express the loss she felt following his departure and to describe once again the active involvement of readers in the creation of meaning:

I always ran
Home to Awe
when a child,
if anything   [a]
[next page]
befell me.
He was an
awful Mother,
but I liked
him better
than none.
    [BPL Higg 84, a-b; *L* 517-18, #405]

Dickinson's coupling of "Home" with "Awe" brings to her understanding of home the sense of amazement and unpredictability that we are acquainted with from her previous phoenix references. To underscore the quality of disorientation she hopes Higginson will see as home's illocality, she playfully mixes orthodox gender associations: the "Awe" linked to "Home" becomes a "He" immediately transmuted into an "awful Mother."

Once Dickinson has established this sense of fluctuating locality, she can describe the way readers who inhabit such unstable homes necessarily authorize voice qualities that reflect their unique perspectives. She first tells Higginson that she would rejoice in his return, then she narrates her poetic appreciation of the process by which listeners (readers) attach meaning to sensation (texts):

Death obtains
the Rose, but
the News of
Dying goes
no further
than the Breeze.
The Ear is the
last Face.   [c]

By stating that sight and smell can be more immediate sources of information than the ear, Dickinson informs Higginson that hearing is part of a complicated procedure with plenty of room for the imagination. Her synecdochic use of "Ear" for auditory perception synesthetically asserts every listener's power to create visual effects from auditory sources; we can assume that the same would hold for the reverse, as when a reader invests written words with the sounds of speech.

Dickinson immediately clarifies for Higginson the metaphoric import of what she has just written by translating it into plain language:

> We hear after
> we see –   [c]

And with her next words she chidingly declares her frustration at not having successfully communicated this message to him:

> Which to tell
> you first is
> still my Dismay –

Dickinson is dismayed presumably because she had to explain what she hoped Higginson would have figured out on his own.

As in so many of her letters to Higginson, Dickinson follows blunt imperiousness with more respectful language. This time, she uses a highly allegorical anecdote that appears to shift subjects but actually extends her discussion of the poet's relation to language:

> Meeting a Bird
> this Morning,
> I began to flee –
> He saw it and
> sung.   [d]

The bird who sings after seeing represents the poet who gives voice to her perception, and the speaker who hears after seeing performs like a reader.

Dickinson's concluding comments to Higginson come through language that describes the reader's power to counteract authorial disdain—perhaps of the sort she has expressed through her blunt language. As she continues the anecdote of the bird, she shows that readers who act on the power they possess to invest sounds with voice properties can detect multiple voices in any utterance:

> Presuming on
> that lone result

His infinite
Disdain
But vanquished
him with my
Defeat –
'Twas Victory
was slain.   [d]

Dickinson's point here is that poets who found disdain on monologic unity ("lone result[s]") presume a mastery that polyvocal readers can see and even hear—not as authoritative, however, but as one voice among many, none of which has the power to determine ultimate meaning.

At the end of this passage, Dickinson may be admitting her own propensity to wield the club of disdain and hence to presume power that restricts its user within the hierarchy of victor and vanquished. When she writes Higginson, "I shall read / the Book," she seems compelled to show him that she can speak as a Queen without falling into exclusionary habits. She commends his book *Oldport Days,* reflects on his writing, and asks, "Was it you / that came?" Authors, she suggests, always exceed the construction of their words and open readers' minds to vaster habitations. Before such infinite potential, we are all become as little children.

Dickinson's closing words are written as Higginson's scholar, as a child whose respect for her preceptor is renewed, as if her letter had taken her full circle:

Restored in
Arctic confidence
To the Invisible.   [e]

She withdraws to the wings, leaves center stage to Higginson; her words express anew her determination to respect his dignity and ensure the continuation of their correspondence.

What Dickinson has described for Higginson is the gymnast's experience of writing that takes her to the centrifugal heart of linguistic expression, not away from it. Far from soliciting a solution to an unfortunate situation, she is stating a condition that yields power. The robin and the phoenix require an uncertain locality; they celebrate the force that explodes any clear sense of home in the here and now. Dickinson states the situation succinctly in an 1881 letter consoling Mrs. Holland for the recent loss of her husband:

"Here!" There are typic "Heres"
Foretold Locations –
The Spirit does not stand –
Himself – at whatsoever Fathom
His Native Land –
[*L* 715, #733]

By questioning "home" as defined by nineteenth-century American culture,
Dickinson eroded primary assumptions about the locus of the self and opened
new possibilities for poets. A single, recognizable, and distinctive poetic voice
has been traditionally understood as a distinguishing feature of poetic maturity. Denis Donogue effectively sums up the traditional view of voice and the
relation readers seek to establish with such as voice:

> The question of voice is always a question of authority. When we refer
> to a young writer as finding [her] voice, we mean that [she] has devised
> a style such that, [her] sentences once uttered, we recognize a voice and
> distinguish it from other voices. There is no reason why we should cele-
> brate this achievement, except that we want the writer to have that
> degree of authority among [her] works, and we want to obey [her].
> [118]

As Gary Lee Stonum has demonstrated, however, Dickinson rejects this
"dominant myth of American literary culture," according to which "the great
writer is an isolato, who retreats from the uncaring or impure realm of public
discourse in order to create a world elsewhere, the artistic sanctuary in which
[she] is the lord of meaning and form" (192). For Dickinson, the notion that
one voice could make a poetic home proved as constricting and inadequate a
habitation for her aesthetic self as the domestic and sentimental definition had
proven for her social self.

The letters of the 1850s show that Dickinson's independence becomes
an increasingly prominent feature of all she writes, emerging most forcefully
as she confronts the expectations of adult life and defines alternatives that
allow her to sustain contact with childhood moments. In the letters that
she wrote when most absorbed in fascicle creation—during 1862, 1863, and
1864—Dickinson increasingly associates freedom and the passage of time
with the voice of the child—the voice that, as we have seen in her earliest letters, naturally and unself-consciously rejected grammatical strictures.[15] The
decade leading up to her most productive years shows an increasing disregard
for any exclusive hold the present might exert on her conscious thoughts.

Concrete experience provides her only the slenderest of holds on reality, as this 1853 letter to Dr. and Mrs. Holland suggests:

> If it wasn't for broad daylight and cooking-stoves, and roosters, I'm afraid you would have occasion to smile at my letters often, but so sure as 'this mortal' essays immortality, a crow from a neighboring farm-yard dissipates the illusion and I am here again.
> [*L* 264, #133]

By 1858, her association of childhood with eternity is more pointed:

> I meet some octogenarians – but men and women seldomer, and at *longer* intervals – "little children," of whom is the "Kingdom of Heaven." How tiny some will have to grow, to gain admission there! I hardly know what I have said – my words put all their feathers on – and fluttered here and there.
> [*L* 336, #190]

Dickinson's expression of illocality in this letter goes about as far as might be hoped in unraveling the mystery surrounding her advancing seclusion. When words can fly like birds and like birds acquire voice, is there further need to alter one's habitation materially?

Ironically, more than any other nineteenth-century American writer, Emily Dickinson made the house in which she was born, spent most of her life, and died the locus of scholarly fascination both about herself and her poetry. The physical fact that she inhabited a clearly defined and still standing dwelling would seem to provide a wonderfully concrete referent for questions about the poet and her work. Some evidence, we would like to think, must have sifted through the net of family and personal censorship. However, the tangibility suggested by physical specificity proves increasingly elusive the closer one approaches. In her own day Dickinson received guests and wrote in the house while also exciting curiosity about it—by lowering baskets from its windows, speaking from behind its doors, listening from the top of its stairs, seldom departing from it, and making it the object of local legend.

Though her poems and letters are much more the product of her physical touch than the house she lived in, they are nonetheless houses of sorts and therefore invested with all the complexities we attach to her being at home in physical structures. It seems clear that Dickinson kept a portion of herself remote from any of the habitations through which she passed as writer, daughter, sister, lover. She did this not because she feared upsetting the conventions of her day but because she was determined to give voice to the totality of her experience. Doing so required that she build into her writing evidence that any discourse affirmed by her speakers was provisional and contingent. The letters best exemplify this because in them we most clearly see the way that, even when she addressed herself to specific audiences, she still danced away from containment within established discourse.

4

Listening to the Child

"WHAT ONCE WAS 'HEAVEN' / Is 'Zenith' now!" objects the speaker in "'Arcturus' is his other name ⌣" (*P*70, *MBED* 83-84).[1] Such anger at the scientific insistence that precise terms replace general words like "'Star'" and "'Heaven'" reflects the frustration Dickinson's child speakers feel when adult terminology restricts their imaginative engagement with language. This speaker, who refers to herself as a "little girl," objects to the intrusive presence of science: "It's very mean of Science / To go and interfere!" she states. But this interference is symptomatic of a more pervasive adult intrusion that consistently diminishes the child's authority. In recognition of this adult intrusion, the child enters language to voice objections to authority that she refuses to accept. For this reason, adult discourse provides the historical consciousness against which the child defines herself.[2]

When, late in 1850, Dickinson writes to her friend Abiah Root, she hints at the close relationship between early adulthood and childhood. She speculates that another friend, Abby Wood, has not visited her because "she is more of a woman than I am, for I love so to be a child" (*L* 104, #39). Specifically, she separates herself from Abby's acceptance of social codes that, in her guise as child, do not yet apply to her: "Abby is holier than me – she does more good in her lifetime than ever I shall in mine – she goes among the poor, she shuts the eye of the dying – she will be had in memorial when I am gone and forgotten" (*L* 104-05). For Dickinson, knowledge of adulthood prompts the desire to retain a hold on childhood; once she understands the adult requirements for success, she can choose to prolong a stage of life that she no longer inhabits fully. Just as the "Faith" poem exposed scientific precision as a mask for absurdly digressive logic, here adult authority exemplified as scientific terminology is presented as a product of self-denial rather than power.

By saying that "Abby is holier than me," Dickinson establishes a point of view resistant to the adult authority she knows well as a woman educated in the social expectations of her day. According to Gerda Lerner, learning what constituted acceptable adult behavior was essential to a nineteenth-century woman's education: "For girls the subduing of the will, the acceptance of self-subjugation, and the development of excessive altruism were the desired educational goals" (3). Dickinson recognizes the loss of personal authority this process demands, and she decides to emphasize the childhood that she sees all the more clearly for having encountered the forces that separate her from it. Cynthia Griffin Wolff has appropriately described Dickinson's child voice as signaling an "epoch of 'no'" that "marks the beginning of autonomy and effective action in the world and the relinquishment of the illusion of absolute power" (188). The distance granted by this separation from personal omnipotence paradoxically enables Dickinson to voice the child's limitlessness in her poems.

As is clear in Dickinson's letter and the poem about "'Zenith'" replacing "'Heaven,'" the child's disregard of personal and cultural limits outlines the way social codes impinge on individual freedom. Because history is foreign to the child, the child's speech collides with that component of language that insists on conformity. The concept of "heteroglossia," as defined by Bakhtin, illuminates this opposition by explaining that each utterance reflects a unique context at odds with a text that carries its own independent history. In Dickinson's poems the voice of the child speaks out of an eternal present within which context is everything. This infinite present magnifies the centrifugal movement of language that inevitably meets a centripetal counterforce that seeks to stabilize the meanings of words. Michael Holquist provides a definition of "heteroglossia" (in the glossary he appends to *The Dialogical Imagination*) that is useful in understanding how the term applies to Dickinson's use of child and adult voices:

> The base condition governing the operation of meaning in any utterance. It is that which insures the primacy of context over text. At any given time, in any given place, there will be a set of conditions—social, historical, meteorological, psychological—that will insure that a word uttered in that place and at that time will have a meaning different than it would have under any other conditions; all utterances are heteroglot in that they are functions of a matrix of forces practically impossible to recoup, and therefore impossible to resolve. Heteroglossia is as close a conceptualization as is possible of that locus where centripetal and centrifugal forces collide. [428]

In the previous chapter, I concentrated on the way Dickinson uses the child's voice in the letters to express an infinitely expandable sense of the present that can take the form of wishing for greater future fulfillment. An example would be her request that Higginson be her preceptor. The future orientation of this voice reflects Dickinson's use of the child as a tactical retreat from regal imperiousness as well as a means to assert the paradoxical blend of humility and limitlessness so characteristic of the child. This chapter concentrates more narrowly on the way the child's voice points to infinite potential unknowingly surrendered upon entering discourse.

The child speaking in these poems triggers a retroactive appreciation for the limitless centrifugal potential of prevocal language so frequently at odds with the stabilizing language of the adult—that voice whose authority depends on conformity within the social order. The child, not yet constrained by history or identity, defines for the reader a space within which language and the speaking subject articulate a potential never fully realized but most evident just prior to the subject's entering history. For an instant, the child speaks the language of pure potential.[3] To hear this voice, we must listen for unencumbered utterances.

Wolff's comments are again useful in clarifying the proximity of voices that "are not always entirely distinct from one another: the child's [v]oice that opens a poem may yield to the [v]oice of a young woman . . . the diction of the housewife may be conflated with the sovereign language of the New Jerusalem . . ." (178). Thus, even in a poem like "I'm ceded – I've stopped / being Their's –" (*P* 508, *MBED* 363-64), in which the speaker is determined to sever all bonds to childhood, the advance into adulthood is not clear. What we see instead is the hierarchic, rule-bound adult consciousness opposed to the child's assumption of supreme authority. Dickinson shows us the tension that complicates and binds these very different discourses as a means of challenging the notion that the child is subsumed by the adult. Within her formulation, abstract social codes and the artificial demarcations of class and age are all adult means of confining the child's limitlessness.[4]

> I'm ceded – I've stopped
> being Their's –
> The name They dropped upon
> my face
> With water, in the country   5
> church
> Is finished using, now,
> And They can put it with

my Dolls,
My childhood, and the string   10
of spools,
I've finished threading – too –

Baptized, before, without the
choice,
But this time, consciously,   15
of Grace –   +
Unto Supremest name –
Called to my Full $_+$ – The Crescent
dropped – + ·   Eye
Existence's whole$^+$ Arc, filled up,   20
With $^+$ one small Diadem -

My second Rank – too small
the first –
Crowned $^\pm$ Crowing – on my
Father's breast $\smile$ 25
A $^+$ half unconscious Queen $\smile$
But this time $\frown$ Adequate –
Erect,
With $^+$ Will to choose,
Or to reject,   30
And I choose, just a
$^+$Crown $\frown$

+ term   + ~~surmise~~   + ~~Rim~~
+ just one   + whimpering   + dangling
+ too unconscious   + power   + Throne
+ An insufficient Queen –

Because the speaker retroactively recalls an authority she surrendered unknowingly, we can hear the voice of that earlier authority in her present determination.

    When the speaker puts her dolls behind her and proposes for herself
a new baptism ("But this time, consciously, / of Grace –"), she founds her
achievement on a historically based perception of self—all sense of accomplishment depends on the perception that change is possible only if she clings
to what she has been in the past instead of becoming what she hopes to

be. Her insistence that there be a new baptism shows her intent to improve upon what happened "before, without the / choice." The poem reads as a prelude rather than an entrance into new consciousness; the last line suggests a state about to be entered and not a presence already achieved. The speaker sees herself as having been a "half] too unconscious Queen ⌣ / But this time" things will be different, this time she possesses the "Will to choose . . . just a Crown ⌃." And here the poem leaves us: in a place somewhere between the child and the adult.[5] The speaker's dismay at having been named and baptized without the knowledge that she was subscribing to an external authority opens her mind to the infinity of her experience as a child. An upward-pointing dash after "Crown" counters the downward-pointing dash after "Queen" as a way of underscoring the speaker's overly simplistic belief that she can correct the error of her earlier "unconscious" station.

Dickinson's considerable use of visual effects like these dashes alerts readers to the constructed nature of language that the speaker wades through in an effort to reassert her independence. Through lineation, in particular, Dickinson further disrupts culturally determined continuities already undermined by dashes. Separating "being Their's" from the first line magnifies the speaker's detachment from her parents, a violation of conventional notions of physical, emotional, and spiritual connectedness that is extended to her face in line 4 and the church in line 6, and concludes with "Crown." The collective impact of this fragmentation is first an increased awareness of the centrifugal force that dismantles the ritual of baptism and second a heightened sense of the speaker's struggle to make the now disassembled ritual come together and serve her ends.

The first stanza concludes with a powerful visual comment on the unraveling of logic that is extended through the second stanza and countered in the third. Dashes that frame "too" at the end of line 12 combine with the misplaced horizontal cross of the manuscript "t" to effectively reduce the symbolic coherence necessary to see "too" as a word and not as a meaningless cluster of marks (see fig. 3, page 48).[6] We "read" the word as a cartoon enactment of the speaker's determination to cease her "threading" of adult logic; now she will take advantage of her power to act as she believes adults do by making symbols serve her authority.

This illustration of the way readers must consent to symbolic meaning by making raw data conform to anticipated patterns sets the tone for the next stanza's interrogation of the highly symbolic ritual of baptism. When Dickinson situates three crosses in the spaces between lines 18 and 20 and then writes in the word "Eye" on line 19, she seems to be commenting on the way readers actively exercise their eyes to gather all the physical data that must be processed before discerning meaning. The combination of three crosses simultaneously suggests a pun on "eye" and "I" that positions the speaker among three crosses, as if her earlier baptism corresponded to Jesus' mortification on Golgotha—a humbling experience over which she will ultimately achieve Christlike triumph. Ironically, the poem so effectively demonstrates the reader's role in the construction of meaning that it erodes the speaker's efforts to turn ritual authority to her own ends. Though she may not be conscious of what she has done, her deconstruction of baptism has emptied it of the very power she wishes to employ.

By introducing a speaker who rejects a known past and is about to enter an imagined but undefined future, the poem establishes a link connecting past and future at the instant that the speaker's anticipation of change is greatest. Thanks to visual signals and the disjunctive power of dashes, we see the speaker's entrapment in circular reasoning, where all she imagines of a more liberated future—a future in which she has "stopped / being Their's"—is what she has learned from adults. As readers, we see more than she does: that in order to achieve her aim of discarding all that she now finds burdensome and oppressive, she must step outside of herself, creating what Kristeva describes as "an area of chance" that makes possible the discovery of a new semantic and ideological self: "a localized chance as condition of objective understanding, a chance to be uncovered in the relationship of the subject of metalanguage to the writing under study, and/or to the semantic and ideological means of constitution of the subject" (*Desire* 98). We contribute to the makeup of this "area" by reading the poem's visual commentary on meaning construction and setting it in dialogue with the expectations we attribute to the speaker.

This participation in the speaker's desire for change increases our awareness of a primary instability that de-centers the subject. Our activity as readers parallels that of Dickinson who, as poet, reads what she has written and responds by creating new text based on her experience as a reader of her own words. The visual signals built into the poem are our clearest indication that she wants readers to participate with her on this level.[7] If the voice that emerges is allowed to register the many shifts in perspective that inevitably occur as the writer grasps the implications of a particular stance or attitude, the resulting poem is necessarily made up of many voices, not a single unified voice. As the poem's interplay of thought and perception proceeds, each voice is subjected to the same destabilizing process, and each voice acquires new form as new choices occur to the writer and the readers. The area of chance defined by the repeated rupturing of logical sequence feeds a growing realization that the self is far greater than any linguistic manifestation. In this sense, Dickinson's child speaker surfaces through a voice that dissipates once it enters language, making the child the least stable of all Dickinson's speakers. Listening to the child, therefore, is always a matter of hearing a voice that mutates in the direction of adulthood even as it speaks. If we as readers decide that the speaker who claims that she has already "ceded" in the first line is the same speaker who is in the act of choosing in the last line, we do so as a matter of choice, not because the poem commands such a reading.

In order to consider the broader dimensions of the poem, as readers we must consider the poem's overall coherence. At the outset we know only that the poem inhabits a space created by the writer, the speaker, and the reader. As we read the poem in its entirety, we notice shifts from present to past as the speaker aggressively denies the objects and actions of her past and struggles to define a future she lacks the language to describe in concrete terms. We can immediately see how concrete and abstract language correlate with the speaker's movement from past to present and future tenses. "They dropped" water on her face in the past, but she is "ceded" now; she was "Crowned – Crowing – on [her] / Father's breast" before, but now she is "Adequate – / Erect."

We can see also that the longest continuous syntactic units occur in the first stanza, where the greatest attention is given to the past. Dickinson chooses not to use a period that would close the door on the ordered and concrete past that has taken up so much of the speaker's life and dictated so much of the poem's form. When in the second stanza we are told that "Existence's whole Arc" is now "filled up, / With one small Diadem"[8] we hear a voice mocking the linear progression of historically grounded sentences. Following visual effects that assert the role of the "Eye" (and "I") in constructing meaning, the speaker's words communicate her refusal to accept as sufficient a diminished perception of self and world: a "small Diadem" fills "Existence's whole Arc."

In the final stanza, the speaker dismisses the past, reducing all recollections to impotent fragments no longer able to impose order on the poem's form. The "Will to choose" is finally "will" in the service of a speaker struggling to assert her power "to choose, / or to reject" and who decides to "choose, just a / Crown ⌐." We are left with a speaker who, by assuming the crown, claims dominion over time and identity. The inconclusiveness of the last line, as signaled by the disjunctive dash, reminds readers of the discrepancy between pure potential and the certainty of limited existence. The poem shows us that the crown symbolizing the speaker's achievement of personal authority is incapable of fulfilling the child's expectations because its power depends on conformity within established symbology. Situated at the threshold of a present that is about to unfold, the speaker approximates as closely as possible the limitless potentiality that characterizes the child.[9] Our efforts to imagine the experience the speaker seeks to recapture take us back through heteroglossia to the materiality that predates and surrounds even the most potent symbols.

"I'm ceded – I've stopped / being Their's –" demonstrates that the child's voice must be thought of in dialogue with other voices. To hear the child is also to hear the voices that instruct, curse, comfort, and punish an innocent, unformed consciousness. These voices represent social discourses on parenting and religious belief, for instance, that enter poems as verbal distillations of the environment readers must interpret according to their understanding of prevailing conventions. Speaker, writer, and reader construct meaning through a process of affirming or denying values perpetuated in these discourses. Consequently, speakers define themselves in terms of voice properties perceivable within the reader's horizon of expectation. Because the child trusts adult authority, the child articulates conventional social expectations in the baldest terms imaginable and in this way informs the reader's horizon. When Dickinson writes, "I prayed ⁻ at first, a little / Girl, / Because they told me to –" (*P* 576, *MBED* 665-66), she magnifies the trust a child instinctively feels for the words of adults:

> I prayed ⁻ at first, a little
> Girl,
> Because they told me to –
> But stopped, when qualified
> to guess   5
> How prayer would +feel – to me –
>
> If I+ ∽ believed God looked
> around,
> Each time my Childish eye
> Fixed full, and steady, on   10
> his own
> In +Childish honesty –
>
> And told him what I'd
> like, today,
> And parts of his far plan   15
> That baffled me –

The + mingled side
Of his Divinity ⌐

And often since, in Danger ⌐
I count the force 'twould   20
be
To have a God so strong
as that
To hold+ my life for me

Till I could+ take the Balance   25
That+ tips so frequent, now,
It takes me all the while
to poise ⌐
And then – it doesn't stay –

+ sound   + supposed   + solemn –
+ under – further +   the light +
Catch my +   slips so easy +
It is'nt [*sic*] steady – tho' –

Through this speaker we hear the commands implicit in the deepest levels of
trust as an older, more experienced person recollects when she ceased to obey
without question ("Because they told me to –"). As a result, we readers are
positioned at that point in the speaker's history when she first acquires sufficient self-awareness to affirm or deny the dictates of authority. We can hear
the adult speaker reliving a past moment, and we can hear the innocent voice
of the child who turns to God and tells him of the "parts of his far plan" that
"baffled" her. The presence of these voices contributes to what Stonum calls
Dickinson's "ambivalence about authorial mastery" (15). In *The Dickinson
Sublime,* he attributes what I have been describing as the dialogue of adult
and child to the sensibility of a poet so "acutely sensitive to relations of domination and submission . . . that she tends to measure all bipolar phenomena
for their resemblance to the structure of mastery" (18). I would augment
Stonum's remarks by suggesting that integral to Dickinson's concern with
avoiding mastery is her conviction that identity is predicated on binary logic
and hence demands a move toward mastery.

We can see resistance to language in the speaker's comment that
she stopped praying "when qualified / to guess / How prayer would feel]
sound – to me –." The speaker's naive assumption that God's perceptions

can best be understood by sympathetic participation reflects childlike wonder at the infinite expanse of deity. However, the isolation of "to guess" on a separate line communicates an alienation from prior innocence that follows the speaker's imagining herself as arbiter of such auspicious and specialized language as prayer. This imaginative act takes her away from the phase of life that preceded her breaking off prayer. "And often since," she says in the last two stanzas, "I count the force 'twould / be / To have a God so strong / as that" who could "hold my life] the light for me," a life "That tips so frequent] slips so easy, now." Again, the lineation that sets apart "be" and "as that" emphasizes the speaker's suspension of her "being" between what she was and the "that" she is contemplating. As in "I'm ceded –," the certainty of earliest childhood yields to the discovery of a linguistic universe that alters with each effort to imaginatively participate in it.[10] And each alteration introduces the possibility of a new voice, suggesting a speaker whose ambitions and desires are anything but static.

Dickinson situates the child in poetic contexts where adult voices predominate in order both to assert the presence of the child within adult experience and to magnify the extent that the adult has submitted to social authority. Placing the child within such an adult-dominated narrative enables Dickinson to clarify the concrete nature of childhood pursuits when compared with the abstract objectives of grown-ups:

> +nearest
> The +maddest dream – recedes –
> unrealized –
> The Heaven we chase –
> Like the June Bee – before
> the Schoolboy –   5
> Invites the Race –
>
> Stoops to an Easy Clover –
> Dips — Evades –
> Teases – deploys –
> Then – to the Royal Clouds –   10
>   +lifts
> +Spreads his light pinnace –
> Heedless of the Boy –
>   +bewildered
> Staring – +defrauded – at the
> mocking sky –

Homesick for steadfast Honey –   15
Ah ⌐ the Bee
Flies not – that brews
That rare variety!
      [*P* 319, *MBED* 285][11]

The middle lines of this poem approximate the immediacy of a childhood experience further removed from adulthood than the voices in either "I'm ceded –" or "I Prayed." The voice that expresses only the specific sensations of a boy in single-minded pursuit of a bee is the voice of an eternal present, not yet touched by time. He sees the bee as it "Dips — Evades – / Teases –," but he is not confused or troubled by the uncertainty these alternatives suggest to the adult controlling the narrative structure of the poem. The opening and closing lines frame this immediacy with a receding "maddest] nearest dream" and an impossibly "rare" bee that together embed the simplicity of childhood in the adult's consciousness.

We must, however, resist the temptation to read these poems as monologic commentaries on childhood filtered through the memories of adults. A distinctive feature of Dickinson's inclusive poetics is her creation of voices that are not subsumed within larger binary oppositions. The same dialogizing practice that establishes tension among the various voices in the poems ensures that each one is full and complete in itself. Sharon Cameron's comment in *Lyric Time* that lyric speech "is not a remembrance of the diverted or altered presence, but a distinct contradiction of the reality from which it diverges" (207), emphasizes the extent of this disjunction. In the case of the boy chasing the bee, the child is not absorbed by the adult who interprets bees as dreams. What we hear is not the voice of the man or of the author; Cameron's identification of contradiction rests on her recognition that a new reality emerges through distinct voices: "At the center of the contradiction rises the lyric's choral voice, however disguised under the cloak of a customary first-person speaker . . . ." The chiastic framing that positions the sensations of the boy in the thoughts of the man also emphasizes the differences that forever hold the boy and the man apart.

Rather than presenting a smooth progression from limited to expanded vision, the poem magnifies the rupturing of childhood innocence by external observations fundamentally at odds with naive trust. The adult point of view limits potential instead of helping to realize latent powers. We would not have a sense of the speaker's alienation from other voices if a single unified consciousness dominated the poem. Were a single voice to pervade the poem, the child would be subsumed in the hierarchy of time and abstraction determined by the adult. As it is, the poem does not move toward transcendence but instead achieves what Kristeva describes as "a modality of transformation" in her description of Bakhtinian dialogism: "[Dialogism] does not strive toward transcendence but rather toward harmony, all the while implying an idea of rupture . . . as a modality of transformation" ("Word" 58).

In Bakhtinian terms applicable to these Dickinson poems, the child converses with the adult in an environment that dialogizes language. Generally speaking, the utterances we hear as we encounter the words of the poem and the ways these words appear on the page establish the poem's treatment of adult conventions. And here the presence of dashes is crucial. Dickinson's use of dashes in lines 8 and 9, then in lines 13 and 14, isolates first the bee's action as seen by the boy and then the man's attempt to place the boy in his own past. The bee that "Dips — Evades –/ Teases — deploys" is presented as raw action that eludes definition. Does it merely "dip" or is the bee a conscious entity that can "evade" or "deploy"?

Line 10 at once poses and defers the inevitable question about the resolution of such uncertainty: it opens with the word "then," followed immediately by a dash. This dash magnifies the separation of the desire for an explanation from the metaphorical assertion, "to the Royal Clouds / Spreads] lifts his light pinnace –." By focusing on the movement of the bee, these lines make possible the voice in line 12 that underscores the movement of the poem away from the direct perceptions of the boy. The heedlessness of the bee complements the indifference of the universe and the inappropriateness of the boy's perceptions. Again, the dash separates "staring" from "defrauded] bewildered," indicating the movement from neutral action to a value-laden interpretation that serves the aims of adult consciousness.[12] The final four and a half lines of the poem introduce phrases that grow into independent clauses as the adult exerts increasing degrees of control. When at last the concluding voice says, "Ah ⌐ the Bee / Flies not – that brews / That rare variety!" one detects an air of relief and triumph, as the adult distances the bee and the boy's thoughts from adult knowledge.[13]

Sensitivity to Dickinson's deployment of voices helps clarify her fascination with "degree" and her use of dashes to signal potential shifts of voice. Even though the voices entering the poem sometimes seem like shades of a single consciousness rather than discrete selves, we should treat them as separate because of the inclusive, centrifugal movement within the poem's language. Our desire to reduce the field of reference held by specific terms and situate them in the isolated consciousness of a recognizable mind is a part of the poem too, but only the adult part. Writing in "We talked as Girls do –" that "When Girls to Women, softly / raised / We – occupy] recollect –

Degree –" (*P* 586, *MBED* 427-28), Dickinson asserts the correspondence of measurement with time, social and political station, and adult consciousness in general. Her use of the variants "occupy" and "recollect" points directly to central tensions between the child's timelessness and the adult's identity in time. The discovery of external coordinates signals each alteration of self that makes possible the adult submission to history:

> We talked as Girls do –
> Fond, and late –
> We speculated fair, on
> Every subject, but the Grave ‿
>   Of ours, none affair –   5
>
> We handled Destinies, as cool ‿
> As we – Disposers – be –
> And God, a Quiet Party
> To our Authority –
>
> But fondest, dwelt upon   10
> Ourself
> As we eventual ‐ be –
> When Girls, to Women, softly
> raised
> We – + occupy – Degree –   15
>
> We parted with a contract
> To +cherish, and to write
>
> + recollect ‐   + too ‐ partake –
>
> [last lines on a separate page]
>
> But Heaven made both,
> impossible
> Before another night.

Not by coincidence, the girls who here contemplate their adult lives consider all subjects but death, unself-consciously wielding power commensurate with God's simply by viewing life as pure potentiality. As in "I prayed," sympathy with the universe is assumed.

Only by stepping away from the immediate encounter with childlike omniscience is the adult voice able to diminish the girls' authority. Characteristic of many Dickinson poems where an adult attempts to circumscribe a child's experience, use of the past tense contributes to the sense of adult domination. Here, the first and fourth stanzas are in the past tense, thereby placing in perspective the infinite present of the child indicated by the present-tense verbs in the second and third stanzas. If we read the whole poem with special attention to the descent into history demanded by the adult, we discover a reversal of the *New England Primer*'s mnemonic for the letter "A": "In *Adam's* Fall We Sinned All" (quoted in Watters 198). Dickinson tells us that we each fall into history on our own, not prior to birth but at the moment we cease to believe in our own omnipotence. It is this realization that most troubles the adult and explains her determination to fix the past, once and for all.

Like "The maddest] nearest dream – recedes –," this poem reflects the tension that separates the adult, who wants to place the events of childhood in perspective, from the immediate power of the child's perceptions. Notably, the child's full participation in the present differs from the adult's determination to fix experience in a language of rules and external authority. The adult voice of the final stanza attempts to dismiss childhood fantasies and the "Authority" mentioned in line 9 by disposing of them in a remote past. The dashes that mark the child's imperfect grasp of adult discourse predictably disappear as the adult assumes control in the dashless final stanza. Given this adult desire for containment, Dickinson's positioning of the final three lines on another page acquires special significance both as a visual enactment of the adult's desire and as an ironic commentary on the way adult desire corresponds to discomfort with the child's potency. To say that "Heaven" prevented her fulfilling the childhood commitment "to write" is the speaker's way of denying responsibility for behavior (or lack of behavior) that still troubles her.

Most striking is the intensity with which the adult wishes to distance herself from the perceptions of the child. Any empathy we feel for the child's loss of power is the result of our own construction of events; the language of the poem does not express the child's sorrow. To appreciate this feature of the poem we must accept the possibility that the adult fears loss of self-identity if she does not constrain the language her memories of childhood call to mind. We must see that the children who "handled Destinies" and were "Disposers" capable of subordinating God to the position of "Quiet Party" might threaten an older woman who accepts the dictates of a "Heaven" that has "made . . . impossible" the contracts of childhood.

From line 1 to line 15, the voice of the child increasingly pulls the poem into a present that acknowledges no superior power. As the third stanza closes, the girl describes the woman, inverting the power relationship that opens and closes the poem. When the child's voice says, "When Girls, to Women, softly / raised / We – occupy] recollect - Degree –," she tries to extend the authority claimed in line 12 by presuming the power both to assert her sovereign "Degree" and to share it with other women. The ascendancy of voices that unite to affirm inclusivity and deny the authority of historical context by claiming "We" first, then "occupy," and, finally, "Degree," forces the adult to interrupt and terminate the recollection. By introducing the variant "recollect" for "occupy" in line 15 the poem effectively suggests the growing uneasiness between the child's present and the adult's memory.

The power struggle enacted in this poem traces the way that the adult dominates by force rather than by persuasion. An adult speaker opens and closes the poem but does so through correspondence with an external system of values that authorizes proper behavior. Just as in "The maddest] nearest dream – recedes –," this poem begins with the sort of straightforward declaration we all know well: "We talked as Girls do." Originating in this commonplace experience, voices shift as the child acquires a more precise individuality and the adult fights for dominance. Beginning with a simple clarification of affection and time, "Fond, and late," we jump suddenly into a clause and two phrases that suggest an increasingly compulsive voice, one that races to assert the inescapable bondage of the individual to time. Then the child's voice resurfaces, clarifying the lack of concern the girls felt for "the Grave." But here the stanza ends, as if to impede the galloping meter of lines 3 and 4 that line 5 failed to heed properly.

A calmer and more controlled adult voice opens the second stanza, a voice that imposes distance through reassertion of the past tense, so that the girls only "handled Destinies" and have no present business with them. But the next line counters this attempt to impose distance, introducing a voice that increases in power and force as it urges the discussion back into the present: "As we – Disposers – be –." The momentum gained by this assertion of the child's unrestrained present enables the child next to utter three phrases in the acceptable metrical order of six- and eight-syllable lines: "And God, a Quiet Party / To our Authority –." When compared with the first stanza, the second stanza evinces a clear gain in the girl's power to wrest control from the hands of the adult.

In recognition of this increase in power, the adult voice dominates the first three lines of the third stanza. Placing a special emphasis on the past tense, the voice speaks with the kind of insistence we associate with patient teachers. But before the third line is completed, the impetuous voice of the child redirects the words of the adult, bringing the force of what has just been said into the present. The insertion of a single syllable where two would have filled out the line magnifies the child's increasing impatience with the adult. Declaring through "be" her existence in the present, the child dominates the rest of the stanza by speaking in a voice that registers no subordination to external force. Instead, they are "Girls, to Women, softly / raised" *now;* they "occupy – Degree –" because they say they do this instant.[14] The child's voice does not coincide with the "recollect" variant that instead foreshadows the concluding stanza of the poem, where the adult voice eliminates any opportunity for the child to speak further by encasing that voice in memory. The forcefulness and determination that motivate the adult voice register in the length of her statement, the equivalent of a lecture a parent might deliver to an unruly child.

Our expectation of closure indicates our sympathy with the adult rhythms of maturation rather than reflecting anything explicitly conveyed in the poem. The imaginative energy that dialogizes the conversation between adult and child clearly derives from the child's language. Speaking on behalf of unformed consciousnesses with no historical identity, the child triggers a fundamentally conservative reaction from the adult. Acting to contain and control, the adult represents the socializing force of culture that seeks to stabilize the mode of expression. If we approach the poem as a discussion instigated by the adult's recollection of a moment in childhood, we can see how the child's language threatens to displace the adult, not by questioning adult authority, but by expanding the range of meanings attributable to any word. The tension in the poem grows as the voice of the child maximizes the potential meaning of words at the same time that the voice of the adult diminishes the field of reference for particular words by stressing the ways words participate in larger syntactic and cultural contexts: the hierarchic world ordained by God ("Heaven") ultimately displaces pure potentiality.

Dickinson's creation of this tension makes impossible any clear separation of the monologic adult voice from the dialogic interplay of voices in the poem. By showing how language loosed from history increases immediacy, the poems demonstrate that the present of the child perpetually challenges the adult's sense of elapsed time. Seen as artistic statements, these poems suggest that the difference between adult and child depends on the way each perceives time. Rupturing one voice with the entrance of another, the poems provide an interplay of voices that are distinct components of a unique linguistic entity. Any pleasure we experience is the result of the arrangement, duration, and intonation of the voices sculpted into satisfying patterns. Time contracts and solidifies as the phrases and sentences of the poems grow longer; conversely, time expands beyond all sense of proportion as dashes fracture syntactic unity. As readers, we observe the interplay of centrifugal and centripetal forces in language that both pulls the speakers toward a definition of identity and pushes them into assertions of omnipotence.

The primary difference between the letters and the poems is the amount of space Dickinson allows for each voice within the text. In the poems, the movement from voice to voice can be abrupt and even competitive, acquiring speed as the language is compressed and the dashes become more pivotal as marks of ruptures or shiftings. Poems like *P* 762, "The Whole of it came / not at once – / 'Twas Murder by degrees –" (*MBED* 517) set up the destructive genesis Kristeva describes, while extending the moment of change by expanding it into degrees. The poems that most dramatically oppose the timelessness of the child to the rules of adult life are frequently accounts of startling disjunctions. In the following passage, the adult voice or conscience intrudes into the thoughts of a speaker, who winces as she contemplates punishment for violating convention:

> Who is it seeks my Pillow Nights –
> With plain inspecting face –
> "Did you" or "Did you not," to ask –
> 'Tis "Conscience" – Childhood's Nurse –
>
> With Martial Hand she strokes the Hair
> Upon my wincing Head –
> "All" Rogues "shall have their part in" what –
> The Phosphorus of God –
> > [*P* 1598, no published ms.]

The opening stanza of "Abraham to kill him" (*P* 1317, ACL) communicates the antipathy the child feels for the adult. Here, God's manipulation of adults is described as a violent assault on the child:

> Abraham to kill him
> Was distinctly] directly – told –
> Isaac was an Urchin –
> Abraham was old –

Similarly, "A loss of something" (*P* 959, *MBED* 1113-14) opens with an expression of the child's vulnerability. In this instance, the speaker recalls the sense of loss that initiates the child's passage into early adulthood:

> A loss of something
> ever felt I −
> The first that I
> could recollect
> Bereft I was −

The second stanza of "A Door just opened] there opened − / on a Street ‿ "
(*P* 953, *MBED* 1048) makes clear the way dashes that expand the present
illustrate the exclusion of the child from the closed logic of the adult world:

> The Door as ⁺ instant shut ‿
> And I ⁓
> I ‿ lost ‿ was passing by −
> Lost doubly − but by
> contrast − most −
> ⁺Informing − misery −

> + Sudden   + Enlightening − Enabling ‿

These poems may represent some of the most disturbing encounters with the
structured world of the adult, but they are important to bear in mind because
they provide in relatively pure form the voices of the child that we hear in diluted or fragmentary form in a great many poems.

One of the best-known Dickinson poems, and one of the few to
have been published during her lifetime, was "A narrow Fellow in / the Grass"
(*P* 986, *MBED* 1137-39). In the variorum, Johnson notes that there are two
fair copies of this poem: an 1865 version that he selects and an 1872 version
that Dickinson included in a letter to her sister-in-law, Sue. Johnson's prefer-
ence for the fascicle version in this instance suggests that he was willing to
consider Dickinson's stated objections to the print version of the poem.

The version sent to Sue replaces the dash following "Him" in line 4 with
a question mark. As Johnson shows, Dickinson's decision to replace the dash
results from the alteration performed by the editorial staff of the *Springfield
Daily Republican*. When the poem appeared in the 14 February 1866 edition
of the *Republican*, a comma was inserted at the end of the third line (Dickinson, *Poems* 712-15). Dickinson wrote Higginson in 1866 that she was
"defeated . . . of the third line by the punctuation" (*L* 450). By inserting a
question mark, she emphasizes the pause within the line and asserts her determination not to punctuate the end of the line. When she sent the poem to
Susan, she did so in the context of a misreading that she wanted to correct.

The question mark, therefore, makes sense in the context of prior readings and does not indicate Dickinson's rejection of her initial punctuation.

I find the history of the poem's punctuation particularly interesting in that it demonstrates both the difficulty contemporary readers had making sense of Dickinson's dashes and Dickinson's sensitivity to editorial alterations of her text. Her own changes in the letter version represent her response to an expanded context—including her original poem and the *Republican* version. For that reason, I see her action as predicated on her initial composition *in addition* to the published poem. Her writing in this sense acknowledges the poem's participation in a public discussion. More than anything else, Dickinson's determination to combat misreadings may account for her reluctance to publish poems she knew editors would alter.[15]

Part of this poem's enduring appeal is the apparent simplicity of its language. It opens by describing a snake in terms so familiar that the mythic associations normally allied with the snake are kept at a distance. But questions about who the speaker is become more pressing as we read on and discover that the force driving the poem comes from a primordial fear predating the snake's participation in the speaker's personal history. Only when we reach the end of the poem do we understand that the distancing effect of homely figures of speech is not so much for the benefit of the audience as for the adult who struggles to contain the child still captivated by what the speaker describes as "Zero at the Bone −."

> A narrow Fellow in
> the Grass
> Occasionally rides −
> You may have met Him −
> did you not   5
> His notice sudden is −
>
> The Grass divides as
> with a Comb −
> A spotted shaft is
> seen −   10
> And then it closes
> at your feet
> And opens further on −
>
> He likes a Boggy
> Acre   15

A Floor too cool
for Corn
Yet when a Boy, and
Barefoot ⌣
I more than once at   20
Noon
Have passed, I thought,
A Whip lash
Unbraiding in the Sun
When stooping to secure   25
it
It wrinkled, and was
gone —

Several of Nature's
People   30
I know, and they know
me —
I feel for them a
transport
Of cordiality ⌣   35

But never met this
Fellow
Attended, or alone
Without a tighter
breathing   40
And Zero at the Bone —

As we listen for the voice of the child in this poem, we hear not the child speaking directly but the muffled efforts of a child attempting to speak from within an adult. The casual atmosphere of the first two stanzas cloaks a subtle manipulation of time that alters the relation of voice to reader and suggests the speaker's inability to focus clearly on his subject. The snake "Occasionally rides," we are told, as if we are about to hear a discourse on zoology, then suddenly the voice moves from the ahistorical moment of science into the subjective experience of the listener: "You may have met Him." But instantly we are back in the authoritative context of the speaker's own knowledge. The stanza ends and we have heard the speaker's voice shift twice: from the opening declaration to the interrogation of the audience and back to the speaker's assertion of authority.

The second stanza advances in the present tense, producing events in strict chronological order that never move closer to the snake than metaphor allows. The insecurity evident in the voice shifts of the first stanza intensifies with each effort of the speaker to provide description without increasing his proximity to the object he describes. The stanza ends with the snake moving away.

The third stanza drops into an even more detached voice ("when a Boy") that conceals layers of fear in blankets of detachment. Tension mounts as the stanza extends itself into fifteen lines. The longest syntactic unit of the poem—the longest sustained voice—is that which takes the speaker closest to the snake. The lines that would ordinarily split on the page to acknowledge the beginning of a new stanza are bound tightly together, refusing any pause until the speaker once again describes the snake as leaving his immediate presence: "It wrinkled, and was / gone."

Now that the worst is over, a cooler voice speaks at the opening of the fourth stanza. The immediate encounter behind him, the speaker talks first of his knowledge of nature and then of the emotion he feels for every natural being except the snake. That admission requires a separate stanza and five dashless lines. When dashes do appear, after "me" and "cordiality," they signal first the speaker's uneasiness about being known, even by "Nature's / People," and second, relief at putting the language of snakes behind him. The low dash visually suggests the bow appropriate to the mood the speaker aims at with "cordiality" in an effort to replace personal anxiety with suave gentility.

The final stanza extends this voice in an effort to make it clear that, while the speaker wants to believe that he has contained and dismissed the snake, he has not done so in a convincing manner. With perfect concentration, the speaker makes the confession that has hovered beneath the surface in everything that preceded it. Now the voice of the child is closest to the surface of the poem, but even here raw experience is cloaked in metaphor. Zero at the bone is never experienced directly—the degreeless eternity of the child remains at arm's length. Visually, the "Z" of "Zero" is drawn so that it stands apart from the line in semblance of a snake, signaling the reader that the speaker has not succeeded in translating raw experience into a manageable symbolic context. As if to drive home the falseness of the adult's confession of fear, a dash appears as the last syntactic marker. We are left with the sense that the speaker will approach the snake again, that he will have to do so until he allows the child to speak directly and the horror we never see but sense from the beginning of the poem to the end is finally expiated.

Perhaps the most useful reading of "A narrow Fellow in / the Grass" comes from our sensitivity to the evasive movement of the adult voices that betray fragmentation and fear. Seen in this light, the poem reads like an object lesson in the necessity of allowing the voice of the child to enter the speech of adults. Doing so would accomplish two of the goals that Dickinson values most: it would challenge the terminal nature of adult time by making the timelessness of childhood a more prominent feature of adult life, and it would provide a means to sustain the child's faith in personal potential while conforming to social conventions. As in all of Dickinson's poems, the aim is to maximize the voices and include the full range of possibilities available to the imagination at any given moment. What finally makes Dickinson's poetics inclusive is her effort to push the level of dialogization to the point that her words become triggers for their liberation from predetermined logical and cultural grids. In accomplishing this end, the voice of the child is crucial because through the child the "destructive genesis" of the poem begins.

5

The Community of Self

DICKINSON'S POEM "Finding is the first / Act" (*P*870, *MBED* 1043) describes and enacts a deeply troubling failure to resolve key stages in life:

> Finding is the first
> Act
> The second, loss _
> Third, Expedition for
> The "Golden Fleece"   5
>
> Fourth, no Discovery –
> Fifth, no Crew ﹏
> Finally, no Golden
> Fleece _
> Jason ˏ sham, too ⁀   10

In the first five lines, the poem exposes myth as a tool that culture uses to replace the power of childhood ("Finding") with fame and fortune ("'Golden Fleece'"). Crucially, the speaker's frustration hinges on her belief that life organizes itself in meaningful sequences—six consecutive "acts." But even though the poem focuses on losses of identity and direction, the message may not be all negative. Dashes in the last line, which begin beneath the word "Jason," rise through the comma after "sham," and point upward from mid-line after "too," rupture the speaker's depressing catalogue of failures while visually suggesting upward progress. The speaker's final observation that "Jason" is a "sham" suggests that she has been freed from the discourses that have directed her life since the "loss" in line 3. With her queenly abandonment of cultural myth, the speaker can achieve a measure of liberation from the predetermined sequences that attempt to contain her, returning to the childhood perception of a limitless self.

Read in this way, the poem outlines two primary losses that appear to cancel one another: the loss that constitutes the second "act" and the final denial of the power of myth. Three voices are demarcated by these losses—the first, "finding," voice of the limitless child; the second voice, a participant in conventional cultural discourse, who pursues the fame and fortune of the "'Golden Fleece'"; and the third, queenly voice, which has returned to the child-self with a new measure of mastery and control. Instead of privileging one voice over the others, the poem in its entirety suggests a heterodox self composed of these three speakers, introducing the possibility of multiple voices in dialogue with the singular voice of myth.

Many other individual poems by Dickinson chart this cyclical move from omniscience to dependence and back to omniscience. "I never lost as much but twice ⌣" (*P* 49, *MBED* 48) and "My life closed twice before its close –" (*P* 1732, no ms.), for example, both trace the experience of speakers who assume personal power after passing through childhood and the pressure to conform that is most pronounced in young adulthood. It is my contention in this chapter that these voices, and the multiple self they together constitute, can be heard throughout Dickinson's poetry. In some cases a single voice will take over entire poems; more often, voices fence with each other within single poems, acquiring and relinquishing dominance alternatively. The first voice is the voice of the limitless child, explored in the previous chapter. Here I will explore the second and third voices, which I call the "bride" and the "Queen." After arguing that the relationship between these voices suggests that a self is made up of multiple core speakers, I will explore the way each of these two voices represents and challenges dominant cultural conventions. As in "Finding is the first / Act," hearing these different voices depends on recognizing Dickinson's use of dashes to signal the dialogic nature of experience.

THE MANY INFLECTIONS OF THE PEN

In an 1853 letter describing the marriage of her friend Emily Fowler, Dickinson suggests an idealized vision of marriage as the perfect union with another, the final escape from loneliness: "Dear Emily, when it came, and hidden by your veil you stood before us all and made those promises, and when we kissed you, all, and went back to our homes, it seemed to me a translation, not any earthly thing . . ." (*L* 277, #146). The letter clearly invests great significance in the power of social convention to elevate and transform those who conform to its dictates.

Dickinson here is speaking in what I will call the voice of the bride. A speaker's actual marital status is irrelevant to my identification of bride voices; indeed, I here extend the bride's symbolic function beyond her anticipation of marriage to suggest a more general confidence in the potential of socially authorized discourse to confer personal power. The bride's poems originate in the present and often oppose social expectation with the evidence of actual experience, expressing the speaker's ambivalence about the role she imagines herself assuming; a distinguishing feature of these works is the freshness of the speaker's discovery that self-fulfillment may not coincide with social conformity. Poems like "A Wife – at Daybreak – / I shall be –" (*P* 461, *MBED* 781)[1] and "The World – stands – solemner – to me –" (*P* 493, ACL) reveal how the reality of marriage falls short of the "girlish dream" engendered by society. At once exalted and despised, wifehood promises power while devaluating the role of independent thought, so that the speaker often finds herself conforming in ways she senses are unnatural.[2]

Out of the welter of conflicting impulses that typifies the bride's state of mind, a confident voice emerges, speaking with regal authority. I call this speaker the Queen, as she was so designated by Dickinson in numerous poems, notably "I dreaded that first Robin, so," where the speaker refers to herself as "The Queen of Calvary" (*P* 348, *MBED* 355-56) and "I'm ceded –" where the child describes herself as "A half unconscious] too unconscious Queen" (*P* 508, *MBED* 363-64). In her speech there is no uncertainty about a future identity and no wish for a respite from the demands of solitary existence. She reclaims the pure potential of early childhood: "I dwell in Possibility –" and "For Occupation" spread "wide my / narrow Hands / To gather Paradise –" (*P* 657, *MBED* 495). The Queen proclaims her own domain; she issues decrees. For her the future is irrelevant, as there is no way for her to imagine a greater fulfillment than that she experiences as she speaks.

One basis for Dickinson's employment of so many voices is her conviction that "a Pen has so many inflections and a Voice but one" (*L* 559, #471). The physical presence of a speaker can cloak the conflicting thoughts and feelings that are always close to the surface in writing. Within the mind of any speaker, innumerable voices articulate a wide range of perspectives on any given issue, so that fully representing the whole person in writing is possible only if these voices acquire some form of acknowledgment on the page.[3] Reading the poems as voices inhabiting a speaker's mind at different stages of a growth process culminating with the Queen, we can view all phases of that process that cycles from child to Queen as creations of the author who declares that she has "no Tribunal" (*L* 409, #265). Dickinson asserts this interdependence of voices in the last stanza of "Like Eyes that looked on Wastes" (*P* 458, *MBED* 775):

> Neither – would be absolved –
> Neither would be a Queen
> Without the Other – Therefore –
> We perish – tho' We reign –

In this passage dashes disrupt each line's linear advance, challenging the terminating power of death while reiterating the poem's argument: "We perish – tho' We reign –." So long as the self is discontinuous and polyvocal, death is absorbed within the individual as a natural component of the mind's weighing of alternatives. Once again, Bakhtin is useful in explaining the mind's capacity to witness termination only if it regards the terminating entity as external or other: "The other, all of him, is totally *in* time, just as he is altogether in space"; whereas, "I myself am not, for myself, altogether in time—not *all* myself. . . . As the *subiectum* of the act that postulates time, I am extratemporal" (*Art* 109). So it is that the speaker of "My Life had stood – a / Loaded Gun –" (*P* 754, *MBED* 825-26) is able to state the apparent paradox death poses for the conscious mind: "For I have but the power] art / to kill ⌣ / Without – the power to die –."

One of the greatest challenges Dickinson set herself was that of discovering a speaker whose voice could express limitless power and at the same time not perpetuate a hierarchy that dismisses other voices as inferior. This voice had not only to admit the speech of other voices but also to grant them authority equal to her own. The primary difference between the voice of the Queen and those of the child and the bride is that the Queen confers power on others, whereas the child asserts only her own, and the bride is tentative about her status. Seen in this light, the bride's is the least confident of the voices. To escape the trap of relegating childhood and youth to memory, the Queen grants each the freedom to speak openly in her poems. Thus we can hear the voice of the conventional wife saying "'My Husband'" and "Stroking the Melody" in "Title divine – is mine!" (*P* 1072; ACL; HCL H361; no fascicle ms.), even though the poem simultaneously undermines faith in the transformational power of marriage.

The more clearly we hear these conflicting voices, the more we come to see the struggle that Stonum positions at the heart of Dickinson's ambivalence about the just distribution of power. Addressing her "ambivalence about authorial mastery," he concludes that while "she by no means always rejects mastery . . . she also never remains comfortable with that role for long" (15). I go further than Stonum on this point: it seems to me that, while Dickinson's *speakers* may strive for or assume mastery, the *poems* consistently dialogize hierarchic discourse. The voices Dickinson incorporates in her poems express contrary views on specific issues in order to suggest the subject's potential liberation from any single point of view. Thus, certain but by no means all of Dickinson's speakers may assert their willingness to perish, precisely because they see their extinction as part of an inclusive vision: "We perish – tho' We reign –."

Dickinson's verbal artistry enables her to focus this struggle, limiting it to the barest of essentials. As the prominence of the first person plural "We" indicates, the artistic manipulation of conflict is often conducted with deadly seriousness because the subject is not a single unified speaker but a community. By itself, survival can become a form of triumph when any single moment encompasses all voices contributing to the complete event. The Queen who elevates other speakers to her level by including them in her aesthetic embrace, "selects her own Society _/ Then – shuts the Door –" (*P* 303, *MBED* 450).[4]

Here readers begin to sense the magnitude of Dickinson's ambition. By creating an inclusive poetics, she affirms all features of human experience through an aesthetic based on historical circumstance while resisting historical limitation. Dickinson believed that "'No' is the wildest word" (*L* 617, #562), as she said in an 1878 letter to Judge Otis Lord, because she repeatedly translated limitations into stimuli for the imagination, so that any experience of limits could simultaneously illuminate a prior self free of such limits. Dickinson claimed ownership of the power she was able to create as a result of overcoming the limitations of "'No'"; whatever her imagination brought to her conscious mind was hers to do with as she chose. The voices that constitute stages in her growth toward poetic omnipotence become members of her community of self. In terms that apply directly to Dickinson's project, Kristeva argues that poetic language represents an attempt to deny the finality of individuation: "some therefore even contend that one can find in poetry the unfolding of this refusal" (*Revolution* 50). As we shall see, Dickinson attributes to her Queen the power of an omniscient creator entirely capable of doing what she pleases with whatever she imagines.

THE BRIDE

Each of Dickinson's speakers reiterates the struggle to establish an acceptable position within the discourses that structure the environment she inhabits.

Coming to terms with authority is a central feature of this process, just as it is for the author and the reader. In the case of the bride, the poems record various degrees of sensitivity to the threat to selfhood that marriage poses. "All that I do" (*P* 1496, ACL) presents an extreme example of the extent to which Dickinson's speakers can communicate unquestioning acceptance of external authority. In this instance, the speaker is a woman who so completely interprets herself as the subject of the male gaze that her only source of meaning comes from imagining how her lover sees her:

> All that I do
> Is in review
> To his enamored mind
> I know his eye
> Where e'er I ply   5
> Is pushing] roaming/plodding/staring/ambling close behind
>
> Not any port
> Nor any flight] Pause
> But he doth there preside] Where he does ~~first~~ not preside
> What omnipresence lies in wait   10
> For her] one to be a Bride] For an impending Bride

As I have already remarked, one of the outstanding features of this poem is its absence of dashes, an absence that provides a syntactical complement to the speaker's conformity within social convention. When considered in the context of other Dickinson poems dealing with marriage, this speaker appears remarkably detached from the experience she describes. The regular pulse of the iambs suggests that Dickinson chose to emphasize the speaker's immersion in rhythms that shape and direct her life. This is emphatically the case in line 6, where word variants magnify the "plodding" and almost bovine "ambling" of the line. As a final coda expressing her submission to larger forces, the speaker concludes by referring to an unspecified "her" or "one" who will enjoy the benefits of being a bride. Through these words, the poem provides a final glimpse of the speaker not in the approving terms she deliberately presents but oppositionally, as a generic functionary within a society where her significance depends upon gaining another's approval.

Dickinson was not alone in her determination to counter the myth that girls become women through marriage. Letters like the one Harriet Beecher wrote to her good friend Georgiana May on the "eve of her marriage to Calvin Ellis Stowe" in 1863 (Lerner 58), express similar sentiment: "Well, my dear, I have been dreading and dreading the time, and lying awake all last week wondering how I should live through this overwhelming crisis, and lo! it has come, and I feel *nothing at all*" (59).

Sarah M. Grimké also acknowledges such a disparity between the anticipation and the reality of married life. In her 1856 essay "Marriage," she links expectations about marriage to the way nineteenth-century women perceived themselves as incomplete: "O! how many women who have entered the marriage relation in all purity and innocence, expecting to realize in it the completion of their own halfness, the rounding out of their own being, the blending of their holiest instincts with those of a kindred spirit, have too soon discovered that they were unpaid housekeepers & nurses, & still worse, chattels personal" (Lerner 95-96).

In one of the most frequently quoted of all Dickinson's letters, that to Susan Gilbert written in June 1852, when Dickinson was twenty-one, she expresses a like concern with the immediate and long-term disappointment too often encountered in marriage:

> Susie, we must speak of these things. How dull our lives must seem to the bride, and the plighted maiden, whose days are fed with gold, and who gathers pearls every evening; but to the *wife*, Susie, sometimes the *wife forgotten*, our lives perhaps seem dearer than all the others in the world; you have seen the flowers at morning, *satisfied* with the dew, and those same sweet flowers at noon with their heads bowed in anguish before the mighty sun; think you these thirsty blossoms will *now* need nought but – *dew?* No, they will cry for sunlight and pine for the burning noon, tho' it scorches them, scathes them; they have got through with peace – they know that the man of noon, is *mightier* than the morning and their life is henceforth to him. Oh, Susie, it is dangerous, and it is all too dear, these simple trusting spirits, and the spirits mightier, which we cannot resist! It does so rend me, Susie, the thought of it when it comes, that I tremble lest at sometime I too, am yielded up.
> [*L* 210, #93]

All three of these women express disappointment at the failure of married life to fulfill the bride's expectations, but only Dickinson speaks of marriage as a frightening ordeal, a necessity women must endure regardless of their personal inclinations.[5] In Vivian R. Pollak's words, Dickinson "emphasizes" the "inauthentic, antiprogressive, and antinatural state" of institutionalized marriage (163). Throughout the preceding passage, Dickinson questions the role nature plays in compelling women to marry and accept a lifelong dependency on "spirits mightier, which we cannot resist." Is there nothing, she asks her friend, that women can do to prevent this terrifying eventuality?

Part of the attraction marriage exerted on women, aside from its obvious economic and social benefits, derived from the belief that through marriage women achieved a union within themselves that allowed for fuller and richer lives. Once conditioned to view themselves as incomplete, women perceived men as bearers of superior strength—as the "men of noon"—through whom they could be completed. The Grimké passage, with its comment that women quite naturally expected "to realize . . . the completion of their own halfness," demonstrates that even well-educated women accepted this perception. Dickinson acknowledges this idea, but challenges it by calling attention to the insidious way the feminine pursuit of self-fulfillment was doomed by a culture that at once insisted on unitary identity *and* sexual difference. As Monique Wittig points out in "The Straight Mind," "the concept of difference between the sexes ontologically constitutes women into different/others. Men are not different, whites are not different, nor are the masters" (29). Sexual difference, according to Wittig, is treated as ontological and primary, when in reality it is political and contingent.[6] Because proper behavior is predicated on the basis of sexual difference and therefore implies an unbridgeable chasm separating "men" and "women," "women" can never achieve the unified identity they are urged to pursue. The natural outgrowth of such a logical impasse is ritualized belief in a mysterious transformation whereby these "women" will paradoxically cease to be themselves.

Dickinson avoids confusing ontology with historical contingency by focusing attention on the boundaries that establish binary opposition and promote the perception that women are incomplete. As Mary Loeffelholz argues, Dickinson's focus on boundaries makes "the border itself, not the supposed integral essence of the territory contained, the place of definition" (110). In this way, "the border might be seen deconstructively, not as irreducibly 'primary,' but as the effect of its own undoing" (111). Approaching Dickinson's discussion of marriage with the assumption that she is challenging fundamental boundaries serves two ends: it calls into question the perception of sexual difference that informs social convention, and it encourages the consideration of alternative versions of selfhood.

In the poems that deal most directly with marriage, women speakers attempt to work through the various phases of attraction and resistance that Dickinson has more painfully (and playfully) outlined in the letters. Poems like "I'm 'wife' – I've finished that –" (*P* 199, *MBED* 171) and "A Wife – at Daybreak – / I shall be –" (*P* 461, *MBED* 781), which explore a speaker's true feelings about marriage, are typical of Dickinson's more than forty wedding poems (Pollak 157). Both poems open with speakers who confidently assert their marital status, only to conclude abruptly as doubts undermine their initial declarations. In "I'm 'wife' – I've finished that –," the speaker moves from a declaration of regal triumph to the admission that what she has gained through marriage is a "comfort" not available to mere girls. But as the speaker presses the favorable comparison with girlhood, her words falter and she finishes by saying, "But why compare? / I'm 'Wife'! Stop there!"

"A Wife – at Daybreak –/ I shall be –" similarly begins by stating the triumph that comes to the bride, but in this case the anticipated transformation does not materialize, and the speaker is confounded by a "Face" she has seen "– before –," deflating her expectation that a "Master"/husband would transport her to another plane. We immediately see that the speakers in both poems use language that reflects the myth of marriage. At the same time, however, this language is challenged by experience that does not conform to the myth.

The resulting poems rupture the social construction of marriage and offer the possibility that speaking subjects can exceed the boundaries of sexual difference even while appearing to affirm them. Bakhtin describes speakers who experience such homelessness at home; that is, he refers to speakers who acknowledge and yet refuse containment in dominant discourse as "unconsummated" (*Art* 13). Without ignoring the obvious pun on "consummation" unavoidable in the present context, I want to stress the value of Bakhtin's concept as it applies to Dickinson's examination of boundaries. As she stated in her letter to Sue, Dickinson regretted the loss of self that seemed so central to the process of becoming a "wife." Her regret was founded on the belief that her life would be transformed for the worse and that, for all practical purposes, she would cease to exist: she would be "yielded up" like other "trusting spirits."

Instead of continuing to trust blindly or powerlessly, Dickinson separated herself from what Bakhtin calls "a world which derives its value, independently of the yet-to-be meaning of the event of lived life, purely from the concrete manifoldness of its already existing makeup" (*Art* 12-13). For both Bakhtin and Dickinson, perception must remain responsive to the unanticipated, the "yet-to-be-meaning," if the seeing and feeling subject is to grow and hence sustain life. "If I am consummated and my life is consummated," Bakhtin writes, "I am no longer capable of living and acting. For to live and act, I need to be unconsummated . . . I have to be . . . someone who does not coincide with his already existing makeup" (13). Through her chirography, as well as through her creation of speakers who embody the marriage mythos of her day, Dickinson introduces into her poems the richness and the uncertainty of the "yet-to-be" world necessary for continued life. In doing so, she directs reader attention to the dialogic plenitude of heterglossia that antedates role stratification in social discourse.

"I'm 'wife' – I've finished that –" (*P* 199) demonstrates Dickinson's deft introduction of multiple discourses that counter the monologizing text of the marriage myth. Again, Dickinson uses the language of the marriage myth in order to explode it from the inside. Because of the distortions that characterize Dickinson's publication history, we can see that the earliest published versions encourage a straight reading of these myths. By altering her written text, editors gave the first published version of the poem a form that promotes belief in a unified self significantly complicated by Dickinson's manuscript. This posthumous publication replaces her dashes with more conventional punctuation, producing a syntax that does not register the centrifugal, dialogizing disjunctions signaled by the dashes; instead, the syntax affirms meanings that the dashes pointedly interrogate. Reading the 1890 version therefore helps clarify the extent to which Dickinson employs the diction of the very discourse she wishes to dismantle.

Here, in the first published version, regularized punctuation suggests contentment on the part of the speaker:

> I'm wife; I've finished that,
> That other state;
> I'm Czar, I'm woman now:
> It's safer so.
>
> How odd the girl's life looks   5
> Behind this soft eclipse!
> I think that earth seems so
> To those in heaven now.
>
> This being comfort, then
> That other kind was pain;   10
> But why compare?
> I'm wife! stop there!
>   [*Collected* 44]

In this version, the speaker consistently asserts the regal glory of her new "state," implying that her current experience is a prelude to heavenly bliss. She terminates her comments with a complacent self-satisfaction—she loses interest in extending the comparison with her past state because she now finds her previous life odious.

The manuscript version of the poem encourages readings that depart radically from so conventional an assertion of the wife's dominion.

I'm "wife" – I've finished that –
That other state –
I'm Czar – I'm "Woman" now –
It's safer so –

How odd the Girl's life looks   5
Behind this soft Eclipse –
I think that Earth feels so
To folks in Heaven – now –

This being comfort – then
That other kind - was pain –   10
But why compare?
I'm "Wife"! Stop there!

Though the quotation marks around "wife" and "Woman" could conceivably emphasize the power of these words, succeeding text urges simultaneous alternative readings. The disjunction signaled by the dashes impedes the momentum that allowed the speaker to dismiss any further comparison with her prior "Girl's life." Does she think that her feelings resemble those of risen souls in heaven, or does the analogy collapse as she stumbles in her attempts to identify the benefits she supposedly enjoys?[7]

Given this uncertainty, the first two lines of the last stanza read like a forced effort to impose logic on an unruly and rebellious collection of perceptions. We no longer know whether she is denying pain by projecting it onto an abandoned state or simply trying to recollect her previous state in order to appreciate her present bliss. In either case, the movement of the poem is significantly retarded by dashes and the degree to which the reader must sort through options without obvious authorial direction. As a result, the poem illuminates seams in the discourse on marriage that the regularized version conceals.

If we read the poem dialogically, we can respect both the power of the originating view of marriage and the strength of the poem's resistance. By reading inclusively, acknowledging the conventional unified reading while stretching to imagine the readings provoked when resolution is disrupted, we can more fully respect the heterodox character of the speaker who appears to have recently entered wedlock. Approaching the poem in this way also allows us to discover a speaker who eludes containment within a unified identity, and hence escapes falling victim to the irresistible attraction of male power.

As her poems and letters attest, Dickinson invested considerable time and energy examining pervasive nineteenth-century myths of marriage. The doctrine of "halfness" Sarah Grimké alludes to is an essential part of these marriage myths because it denies the possibility of a female self autonomous from men. By questioning this denial of self, Dickinson moves from examining the supposedly miraculous transformations of marriage to analyzing the boundaries that constitute sexual difference. Contrary to popular belief, these issues were not academic ones for Dickinson; all too often, Samuel Bowles's reference to Dickinson as the "Queen Recluse" (quoted in Sewall 474) has obscured the poet's vital involvement with the larger world by casting her as an eccentric spinster. In fact, Dickinson had numerous close relationships with men and might well have married Judge Otis Lord late in life had her mother's fatal illness in 1882 not commanded her full attention. Dickinson's pointed yet passionate examination of the marriage myth reflects a mind resisting the oppressive social paradigms of her time by analyzing, interrogating, and exposing assumptions she believed contrary to her own best interests as a woman.

Stonum's assertion that Dickinson finds unacceptable the binary opposition of master and slave at the heart of most power relations (15) is key to understanding how Dickinson secluded herself in her home while writing poems that expand the scope of her personal freedom. "I tie my Hat – I crease / my Shawl –" (*P* 443, *MBED* 553-55) shows how concealment of an alternate self or selves is necessary, even if it is painful:

> To simulate – is stinging work -
> To cover what we are
> From Science – and from Surgery _
> . . . .
> 'Twould start them –
> We _ could tremble –   5
> But since we got a
> Bomb –
> And held it in our Bosom
> Nay – Hold it – it is calm –

Therefore – we do life's   10
labor -⁸

The speaker's shift in tone from frustrated anger to confident assurance shows that she had to free herself from subservience to an external identity before she could assume control over her experience. Once freed from subservience, the speaker can choose conformity as a guise, as the temporary house for a homeless self whose power to explode convention is meted out selectively. The constant need to be vigilant could account for the expressions of fear in the letter to Susan in which Dickinson considers the attraction of male power. Self-preservation similarly requires that the older poet temporarily accept her spinster status as a familiar and unthreatening social mask that affords her the invisibility to wield unrestricted poetic power.

THE QUEEN

When the reader approaches the poems of the Queen after having listened to the voices of the child and the bride, a striking difference immediately surfaces: this voice either speaks with the first person plural, "we," or it establishes the speaker's personal power in terms she comfortably conflates with the prerogative assigned the royal "We." Instead of imposing conformity, however, such a Queen acquires power by embracing opposing views as part of a dialogized linguistic domain founded on heteroglossia. As the monarch of inclusion, she demonstrates her sovereignty by acts of invitation that expand fields of reference rather than confining them.

In her June 1869 letter to Higginson, Dickinson writes, "When a little Girl I remember hearing the remarkable passage and preferring the 'Power,' not knowing at the time that 'Kingdom' and 'Glory' were included" (*L* 460, #330). Stonum's illuminating discussion of this statement points out that Dickinson treated power as something to be cherished and not as a force one individual wields to subdue or master another (53). As "Mine – by the Right" (*P* 528) shows, the voice of the Queen declares its power by affirming many kinds of authority:

Mine – by the Right of
the White Election!
Mine – by the Royal Seal!
Mine – by the Sign
in the Scarlet prison –   5
⁺Bars – cannot conceal!

Mine – here – in Vision – and
in Veto!
Mine – by the Grave's Repeal –
Titled – Confirmed ⌐   10
+Delirious Charter!
Mine –+ long as Ages Steal!

+ Good affidavit ⌐   + while
+ Bolts

[*MBED* 452]

Election, royal seal, a sign in a prison, and the Christian implications of "the Grave's Repeal" are all presented as confirmations of the speaker's power. Indeed, this is a most "Delirious Charter!" Systems of government and symbols of authority spanning the whole of human history are here gathered as evidence of the timeless power the speaker declares is hers "long as Ages Steal." No wonder men said "What" to her (*L* 415, #271); no wonder she considered their confusion a matter of fashion. How could their thinking be perceived as anything but narrow and provincial when she was speaking out of such a broad understanding of tradition and thought?

The mention of "Veto" in line 8 indicates that Dickinson is not categorically opposed to the possibility of denial. In her 31 December 1861 letter to Louise Norcross she acknowledges that it is "Odd, that I, who say 'no' so much, cannot bear it from others. Odd, that I, who run from so many, cannot brook that one turn from me" (*L* 386, #245). Taken together, the poem and the letter imply that Dickinson recognizes the apparent inconsistency in her behavior. At the same time, we must bear in mind that she is the woman to whom all men say "What," the woman who considers such expressions of befuddlement inevitable. As was the case in her decision to reject the diminishment of self implicit in conventional marriage, Dickinson conflates the notion of self-preservation with the removal of herself from situations that threaten to diminish her freedom. She aims to expand personal choice by acknowledging voices that define power as the ability to impose conformity. Any inconsistency produced by this practice marks her willingness to authorize voices that are at odds with each other.

A central strategy implicit in Dickinson's use of the royal "We" comes from her recognition that the term always denotes plurality, even while employed by a single speaker. She sees the convention of the royal "We" as evidence that culture does sanction a plural construction of the self in a special circumstance. Her innovation comes through her expansion of the specialized "We" to encompass the generic "I," so that in her poems the "We" displaces the conventional practice of conflating self with a singular, unified identity. Where the royal "We" supersedes the orthodox "I" in the speech of royalty, Dickinson's speakers assume that the self is plural to begin with; a unified "I" represents for her an unfortunate decline in stature, founded on a social practice that mistakenly views self-definition as a means of acquiring rather than surrendering power. For Dickinson, "We" is the norm, not the exception.

She makes use of this reconstruction of "We" and "I" in "Much Madness is divinest Sense ⌣" (*P* 435, *MBED* 680), where she argues that sanity hinges on accepting a "We" that is always plural but not necessarily more than a single person. By trading off ordinary and specialized functions simultaneously, Dickinson demonstrates that whether her speakers are part of a majority or not depends entirely on the way they view themselves:

> Much Madness is divinest Sense ⌣
> To a discerning Eye –
> Much Sense – the starkest
> Madness –
> 'Tis the Majority   5
> In this, as All, prevail –
> Assent ⌣ and you are sane –
> Demur ⌣ you're straightway dangerous ⌣
> And handled with a Chain -

Despite the playfulness with which these lines revolve the question of sanity, a hard edge lies beneath the surface. The almost placid opening that overlooks the horror of madness by assuming a cosmic perspective is dramatically opposed by closing lines that define the poem's subject not as the speaker alone but as the reader and the author included in the "you" of line 6. We readers, then, potentially enter that community of people who are "handled with a Chain" should they "demur."

The progression of the poem follows an implacable logic whereby the reader is interrogated and forced to react as if living a parable. If as readers we possess "a discerning Eye," we will understand that madness can be "divinest Sense" and that much sense is "the starkest Madness." We can also perceive the precariousness attributed to any lack of balance, any slip in the direction of absolute certainty. The middle two lines tell us that "the Majority / In this, as

All" prevails; and instantly we understand that success in avoiding the chain depends on our ability to determine the majority. The key to sanity and control is our "Assent." We understand the parable if we enter it and assume that we are the majority, the voice that demands "Assent" and the voice that speculates about the relative character of the cosmos. Containing these voices requires that we situate the spectacle uniting relativism and autocratic decree within a single instant. That way, the voices of dissent can speak without representing demurral. As long as we are both the voices that conform and the voices that stray, we can speak freely. As long as we accept a fundamental homelessness, we can make a temporary home in whatever discourse serves our immediate needs.

The Queen establishes her dominion by defining the community over which her majority presides. Because this majority is always contained within the Queen, the number of citizens is irrelevant; what matters is the Queen's knowledge that homelessness affords her dominion over whatever discourse she employs. The only danger the Queen faces is that of mistaking the provisional house of a specific discourse for a preexisting and enduring home. "The Soul selects her own Society –" (*P* 303) makes abundantly clear the Queen's understanding that language is her vassal, that her personal interests are primary, whatever they may be, regardless of what other alternatives may appear to observers unaware of her concerns.

> The Soul selects her own Society –
> Then – shuts the Door –
> +To her divine Majority ‿
> +Present no more –
>   [*MBED* 450][9]

Here the speaker outlines the procedure the Queen follows in establishing her authority: first she selects, then she shuts a door, and finally what is outside ceases to impinge on her experience. As Suzanne Juhasz observes, "Traditional ideas about power are reversed here. Not control over vast populations but the ability to construct a world for oneself comprises the greatest power, a god-like achievement, announces the opening stanza" (*Undiscovered* 15). The speaker in this instance appears to find the Queen's potential denial of her existence troubling, but need she actually be concerned? Is the speaker's anxiety about position justified? Need she see herself as either inside with the Queen, benefiting from her indifference to others, or outside, "Present no more"? The dilemma posed by such clearly drawn binary oppositions reflects the confusion queenly behavior produces in observers who do not appreciate the illocality of homelessness. In this case, the speaker's bafflement demonstrates her inability to read the Queen accurately.

The second stanza suggests that the speaker is trying to resolve the question of exclusion, and not succeeding:

> Unmoved – she notes the Chariots ⌣ pausing ⌣   5
> At her low Gate –
> Unmoved ⌐ an Emperor be kneeling
> +Upon her Mat –

By stressing the "Unmoved" quality of the Queen, the speaker magnifies the inscrutability of "her" behavior and the mystery surrounding her power. Even as the presentation becomes more concrete, citing particular instances of the Queen's indifference, the role of exclusion remains uncertain. Does the presence of "Chariots" and "an Emperor" imply an aristocratic exclusivity, or does the Queen's lack of concern represent a denial of hierarchic authority?

The last stanza situates the subject within the speaker's mind, establishing the speaker's aim as that of understanding the basis for the Queen's action:

> I've known her _ from an ample
> nation –   10
> Choose One _
> Then ⌣ close the +Valves of
> her attention ⌣
> Like Stone -

> + On   + obtrude   + On   + Rush mat   + lids –

At this point the speaker desires nothing less than to control those actions that have an influence over her but which elude her comprehension. She is like one of the men who say "What." At the same time, the speaker is both included and excluded by the actions of the Queen. Her uncertain position irks her to the point that she must push for a resolution of her perplexity. Lastly, we recall the conflation of the Queen and the "Soul" in the first line, so that what unfolds is the struggle of a minority voice to discover logic in a series of events that defies logical interpretation. Thus the mind of the Queen takes shape as a place where binary oppositions fundamental to conventional social order are present but not dominant: the anxious speaker defines the il-locality of the Queen's homelessness at home.

We can read the entire poem as the efforts of a conformist speaker to understand the Queen's illocality. In the first stanza the voice traces a simple chronology as a means of determining causality, but the effort fails. No foundation for the soul's selection is discernible. The second stanza explores specific instances of the Queen's selection only to conclude that she is "Unmoved," that she reveals nothing in the way of an observable standard for judgment. And in the last stanza the speaker's personal experience also fails to yield a rationale for the soul's choice. At no point does the speaker discover an underlying logic through her efforts to research the soul. As readers we are impressed not by the speaker's failure to discover certainty but by her tenacity. The one value that emerges as central to the speaker is her resolve. She proceeds as if driven by a secular doctrine of works, whereby the formal procedures are more important than any unanticipated information. Even though the speaker is unable to unite her observations in a coherent explanation, she remains steadfast in the attempt to do so. She slips only at the very end, when she has at last resorted to personal experience and falls into figurative language. She creates "Valves" for the soul's "attention" that she says close "Like Stone." The variant "lids" for "Valves" magnifies the way the speaker's struggle has been conducted within her mind, behind the eyes / I's of the Queen.

These shifts in the speaker's use of language suggest the future course of her thought, implying that she could begin to authorize personal constructions of events rather than continuing to rely on external systems for interpretations that forever pose but never answer questions about origins or personal motivation. But the poem does not give us the speaker's emergence from "What"; it requires instead that we participate in the creation of the speaker just as the speaker must create her own experience if she is to free herself from subservience to external forms. As a result, this poem yields a speaker in search of answers who exploits conventional knowledge only to fall into poetic language through frustration. By listening to the shifts in voice that occur as the language changes, readers can detect the emergence of a community of voices within the speaker. At the end of the poem she is in a position to close her own doors ("Valves") and enjoy the power of "divine Majority." The royal "We" is hers should she choose to assume it.

Listening to the voices that surround the Queen and define her presence reveals the central role assigned time in the Queen's pluralistic dominion. "Some – Work for Immortality ⌣ " (*P* 406, *MBED* 654) proposes a link between time and omniscience that brings to mind the pure potential assumed by the child. The difference is that in this instance the speaker is an experienced adult who knows the world but who still insists that it is possible to attain imaginative inclusivity. Not until the third stanza does the speaker move beyond an intensely ironic use of puns to the extent that her punning begins to magnify rather than undercut the meaning of the line. In the first stanza, we see how the speaker struggles to account for diverse perceptions of time, work, and reward:

> Some – Work for Immortality ＿
> The Chiefer part, for Time -
> He – Compensates – immediately –
> The former – Checks – on Fame –

After opening with a phenomenally vague "Some," the stanza presents the appearance of increasing clarification without actually achieving concrete precision. Each line begins with an indirect reference to some previously identified subject: "Some," "The Chiefer part," "He," "The former." The third and fourth lines surround words with dashes, suggesting uncertainty in the speaker and instability in language. What is meant by "Compensates" and "Checks"? Does the "He" compensate as in reparation for damages, or does "He" compensate as in payment for services rendered? Is there a difference? If "He" is "Time" and "The former" is "Immortality," then the equation could be simple: the minority of people who live for heavenly fame receive assurances in this life while full payment is withheld; on the other hand, the majority who seek immediate gratification receive payment now.

This interpretation of the stanza reduces the words to a simple relativistic truism that makes no effort to account for the dashes or the struggle of the speaker; whereas, if the use of indirect reference is taken seriously, the poem sustains a deep sense of uncertainty, as if the speaker is responding to a prior conversation, saying with all the hesitation of profound disbelief, "Let me get this straight now. . . . This is the way people really live: Some – Work. . . ." Once an inflection of doubt creeps into the presentation, the language gains in richness, complexity, and humor. In such a reading, the low, downward-slanting dash at the end of line 1 might mark the speaker's dubious view of the procedure others follow in their quest for immortality. The dash before "Work" initially ruptures the logic linking "Work" to "Immortality." This rupture is then repeated, commented on and extended by the downward-pointing dash after "Immortality." Readers emerge from the first stanza chuckling at the futility of life constituted according to such bleak alternatives. One objective of the poem, then, becomes that of positioning us with the speaker who stands outside these alternatives. We see that in some sense payment is always insufficient because it presupposes an external and fixed value for life and requires an external authority who either provides compensation or issues checks.[10] From this point of view, the implications of lost time are added to the humiliation of an infantile consciousness forever subject to an adult authority who eternally critiques or checks behavior.

Read in this context, stanza two sounds like a comedy routine where social convention is treated as the straight man. Clichéd metaphors combine with the language of capitalism to show how Christian life has been fashioned as a type of sound investment:

> Slow Gold – but Everlasting –   5
> The Bullion of Today -
> Contrasted with the Currency
> Of Immortality ⹁

The concluding stanza then provides the punch line that makes the entire poem a colossal joke at the expense of a silent Christian everyman:

> A Beggar – Here and There ⹁
> Is gifted to discern   10
> Beyond the Broker's insight –
> One's – Money — One's – the Mine –

Any sense of the possibilities for laughter provoked by the disjunctions dashes create depends on sensitivity to the speaker's deft use of irony as she logically pursues to conclusion an absurd line of thought. The humor surfaces as readers acknowledge both their distance from the conventional reasoning so harshly exposed and their admission that they are intimate with it. Finally, the true subject of the poem emerges as the speaker's and the reader's inability to assert personal authority—as readers we discern the humor because we so desperately want to escape the grasp of conventional Christian thought. The final pun on "Mine" links the notion of physical gold mine and material wealth to the gift of eternal life bestowed on fallen humanity that comes quite independent of human efforts or strategies. We see that the only authoritative "Mine" is the "mine" of personal assertion, the "Mine" of "Mine – by the Right of / the White Election!" The poem leaves us wanting to proclaim our prerogatives and to deny any external authority that would diminish our sovereignty.

Having identified the voices falling under the general headings of child, bride, and Queen, I want briefly to discuss the way these voices interconnect in a grouping of poems from the first fascicle. I argue here that Dickinson's arrangement of poems nineteen through twenty-two reflects the progression from child to bride to Queen. This argument supports the recent assertion of Sharon Cameron in *Choosing Not Choosing* that "different poems in the same fascicle can, through their verbal echoes, be construed as variants of each other, making such poems seem comments on—even incompletely understood, if attenuated, continuations of—each other" (77) and that "one way of explaining the virtual absence of variants in the first ten fascicles is to say that initially Dickinson was understanding her poems *only* in terms of chronological collections" (86).[11]

In "A sepal · petal · and a thorn" (*P* 19, *MBED* 4), the voice of the child communicates the unlimited power that allows her to merge with any sub-ject her imagination touches upon. We see that her identity is not yet rooted in time:

A sepal · petal · and a thorn
Upon a common summer's morn –
A flask of Dew – A Bee or two –
A Breeze - a'caper in the trees ˍ
And I'm a Rose!

Even though the speaker is sufficiently aware of history to admit that she inhabits "a common summer's morn," this knowledge is in no sense restricting. As readers we observe a spectacle within which the ordinary is almost instantaneously transformed. All the features that to a more inhibited consciousness would limit expectation are here revealed as tokens of wonder. The scientific classification of the flower does not strip the flower of mystery, nor does "A Bee or two" or "A Breeze" fail to ignite an imagination thoroughly grounded in the present.

The situation alters drastically in "Distrustful of the Gentian ˍ" (*P* 20, *MBED* 5). We immediately encounter a speaker who has lost faith, who is intensely self-conscious. Nature is an antagonist pointing to the speaker's "perfidy," provoking wishes for a future when sleet will not bring discomfort; nor snow, fear. The voice we hear is alienated from imagination and trapped in time. She senses her distance from pleasure and power, just as the child who first awakens to the limitations of individuation longs to return to the certainty she has left forever:

Distrustful of the Gentian ˍ
And just to turn away,
The fluttering of her fringes
Chid my perfidy –

Weary for my ——   5
I will singing go –
I shall not feel the sleet – then –
I shall not fear the snow.

Flees so the phantom meadow
Before the breathless Bee –   10
So bubble brooks in deserts
On ears that dying lie –
Burn so the Evening Spires
To Eyes that closing go –
Hangs so distant Heaven –   15
To a hand below.

A far cry from the pure potential enjoyed by the child, here we encounter a profound sense of incompleteness. The extended dash or lacuna of line 5 underscores the speaker's inability to contemplate the great loss that pervades the entire poem. Beginning with alienation from nature that first communicates in the perception of a specific flower, the speaker expands her sense of exclusion until all of nature, all of time, and all of eternity reflect her isolation and dependency. We detect in her the voice of the bride.

As the poem progresses, the voices of social and religious convention acquire dominance. The final line affirms the speaker's conformity within the very theological argument that Dickinson so assiduously undermines with her inclusive poetics. And the period that terminates the last line is difficult to accept. Readers want to discover what it was that once filled the gap now signified by a yawning dash. As long as we think we must look outside ourselves to discover an answer, we are in sympathy with the bride who looks to external authority for fulfillment.

"We lose – because we win –" (*P* 21, *MBED* 5) provides the enigmatic key that unlocks the bride's dilemma. The speaker states that victory and loss are both experiences determined by rules we can either accept or reject. As long as we are gamblers, we are in the game, playing because we fully expect to win. Should we at any time lose sight of the fact that the game exists only because we recognize the rules, at that moment we begin surrendering power to external authority.

We lose – because we win –
Gamblers – recollecting which .
Toss their dice again!

The voice we hear in this poem expresses the pure exhilaration that comes with a sudden acquisition of power. Speaking as "we" rather than "me" or "I," the speaker assumes the rights of a majority, dispelling the alienation expressed by the speaker in "Distrustful of the Gentian ‿." Even the movement from lines 1 to 2 shows the way the speaker reasserts the imaginative capacity so pronounced in the child of "A sepal - petal - and a thorn." She links her own experience to that of others, "Gamblers," identifying with, rather than excluding herself from, the world she inhabits.

The power and confidence that begin to emerge in "We lose – because we win –" are given full, mature expression in "All these my banners be" (*P 22, MBED* 6). This is a prime example of the Queen's rejoicing in her dominion. As readers listening to the voice rise and fall, gaining and ebbing in strength, we hear a confidence that toys with the patterns of time:

> All these my banners be.
> I sow my pageantry
> In May –
> It rises train by train –
> Then sleeps in state again –   5
> My chancel – all the plain
> Today.
>
> To lose – if one can find again –
> To miss – if one shall meet –
> The Burglar cannot rob – then –
> The Broker cannot cheat.   10
> So build the hillocks gaily
> Thou little spade of mine
> Leaving nooks for Daisy
> And for Columbine –
> You and I the secret   15
> Of the Crocus know –
> Let us chant it softly -
> "*There* is no more snow!"
>
> To him who keeps an Orchis' heart ‿
> The swamps are pink with June.   20

The voice that speaks initially as a first-person singular "I," becomes a third-person "one," shifts back to "I," adopts the first-person plural "us," and concludes with a third-person singular "him." All this shifting of gears demonstrates the Queen's freedom of movement in and out of majority. Her absolute control of the rules that govern position allow her to deploy voices at will without fear of losing perspective and falling prey to external authority. As a demonstration of her confidence, she lays out the linear progressions of events bound by time, always mindful of her ability to shape the rules that govern play. In this sense, the poem behaves a little bit like a jazz innovation on the gambling theme identified in "We lose – because we win –."[12]

Whether or not Dickinson meant her poems to be read as part of a carefully arranged sequence of interlocking spectacles is less important than the discovery that the poems actually do build on one another. From the first emergence of self-consciousness that introduces the child to history and limitation, to the deliberate polyvocality of the Queen who founds her dominion on invitation, speakers are united in the same growth process. The child's pure potential precipitates the bride's instability that in turn provokes the emergence of the Queen. While such movement does suggest a dialectic, the absence of progress makes the parallel untenable. As we have seen, the Queen in a sense sets herself up for a fall into history. Her very sovereignty depends on her asserting dominion over the rules that govern experience. To do so requires that she take the greatest risks she can imagine in order to embrace all voices and possibilities available to her mind. The height of her achievement is the critique of lesser monarchs, a category within which the Christian God is cast. But to wield such power is precarious at best precisely because "no" is always perceived as a stimulus for the imagination. The Queen who presides over all rules is inevitably a player in many games; as a result, her immersion in the intricacies of time is unavoidable. Thus the speaker that follows the Queen in the first fascicle communicates the child's awakening to diminished power: "I had a guinea golden – / I lost it in the sand –" (*P* 23, *MBED* 7).

In *Emily Dickinson and Her Culture: The Soul's Society,* Barton Levi St. Armand acknowledges the importance of death in the movement from "compensation" to "consummation" so central to that definition of self we have come to think of as constituting a community: "Since both compensation and consummation could be attained only through death, dying was a way of being 'born to the purple,' a coronation as much as a crucifixion" (52). Taking St. Armand's words seriously means accepting the death of speakers as a necessary feature of their participation in the growth that all Dickinson's poems work to articulate. The Queen will necessarily die, expressing her sovereignty to the fullest extent of her imagination. But recollection of her presence will vitalize new voices, new speakers who seek to attain once more the power they sense was once theirs. "We perish – tho' We reign –," Dickinson writes in *P* 458 (*MBED* 775).[13] The movement we observe in these poems is not one that advances by a process of accumulation; it is instead a constant passage from limitation to omnipotence, from mortality to immortality and back again.

Homelessness and the
Forms of Selfhood

 IN A NOVEMBER 1881 LETTER to her parents, Mabel Loomis Todd states that the mythic status accorded Emily Dickinson in her own lifetime came not from any inkling of the almost eighteen hundred poems that have since secured her literary reputation but from the near total reclusivity of the last two decades she lived: "I must tell you about the *character* of Amherst. It is a lady whom the people call the *Myth*. She is a sister of Mr. Dickinson, & seems to be the climax of all the family oddity. She has not been outside her own house in fifteen years. . . . She dresses wholly in white, & her mind is said to be perfectly wonderful. She writes finely, but no one *ever* sees her" (quoted in Sewall 216).

By Dickinson's own account, she had ceased to leave her "Father's ground" by 1869 (*L* 460, #330), seventeen years before her death.[1] Jean Mudge's observation that "Dickinson's image of house or home . . . is perhaps the most penetrating and comprehensive figure she employs" (1) seems the logical extension of such reclusiveness. Yet her letters and poems frequently communicate the view that home is not a comfortable place or, more tellingly, that "homelessness" was a condition she valued. In "To learn the Transport by the Pain ⌣," her speaker declares that homesickness "is the Sovereign Anguish" felt by "'Laureates'" (*P* 167, *MBED* 133). And in "How soft this Prison is" we are told that "Home" is "Incarceration" (*P* 1334; HCL, H ST 22b).

As previous chapters have shown, the poet who both entered and left life in the house her grandfather built aggressively declares the importance of literal and figurative homelessness as a way of interrogating conventional definitions of the self.[2] This chapter focuses more narrowly on the specific challenges such a self poses for Dickinson's readers and for the writer who wishes to express this self in language. Because she lived as a member of one of Amherst's most prominent families while composing poetry that dramatically departed from conventional thought, Dickinson concretely embodied the gathering of contradictory perspectives that characterizes her poetics of inclusion. The poet described in "This was a Poet –," who "Distills amazing sense / From Ordinary Meanings ‿" similarly positions the extraordinary within the ordinary (*P* 448, *MBED* 465). Dickinson's life and the formal choices she made about how to "house" her poetry suggest her determination to simultaneously hold and disperse the predictable patterns of daily life, revealing a universe where "amazing sense" cohabits with "Ordinary Meanings."

For Dickinson, the poet's amazing transformations illuminate the true position of all language users by directing attention to the self's homeless home in heteroglossia. From that unstable locale, the poems tell us, we assent to the limitations implicit in our utterances; we set the balance between the centripetal impetus of history and the centrifugal force of the moment. Learning this truth too suddenly, however, can be dangerous—the heady appeal of personal power can be matched or overmatched by devastating dislocations. As "Tell all the Truth" cautions, the truth must be told, but told indirectly: "but tell it slant –" (*P* 1129, ACL). "Success" in communicating this truth "in Circuit lies," this advocate of slant tells us; too much knowledge of our own power to shape experience can be overwhelming: "The Truth must dazzle gradually / Or every man be blind –." The poet's "Business," therefore, is precisely "to include," forever remaining "touchless" as her words distribute a self never fully localized, never completely at home, ceaselessly expanding its circumference. In her letters Dickinson declares that "My Business is Circumference" (*L* 412, #268) and "to include is to be touchless, for Ourself cannot cease –" (*L* 432, #292).

Dickinson's understanding of "Circumference" connects with important instances of abyss imagery in the letters in ways that can help clarify her presentation of homelessness as a positive, if discomforting, experience. In a letter to Susan, probably written in late 1885, Dickinson describes "Life" in terms that apply directly to the discovery of meaning through language: "Emerging from an Abyss, and reentering it – that is Life, is it not, Dear?" (*L* 893, #1024). With these words, Dickinson briefly alludes to past encounters with deathlike disorientation that for her had become a life-affirming pattern. Crucial to this pattern is both an emergence out of obliteration and the acceptance of a future return. Life is positioned on the verge of the "Abyss," making that edge a figurative locus for experience; the self has one foot in the abyss and one foot on solid ground, so to speak.

In an earlier October 1883 letter, also to Susan, Dickinson expresses this encounter with the abyss in slightly different but equally revealing terms:

"Moving on in the Dark like Loaded Boats at Night, though there is no Course, there is Boundlessness –" (*L* 800, #871). Viewing both of these passages in company with the 1881 letter to Elizabeth Holland where Dickinson claims to sing as firmly in the center of dissolution as in her father's nest (*L* 687-88, #685), we can see the benefits Dickinson attaches to a mapless life that persistently translates darkness into "Boundlessness." The experience detailed in these letters reflects a desire to claim a self obscured by the linear maps of dominant male discourse. Entering the desired dark of the abyss, then, necessitates descent into the darkened expanses through which life circulates in the process of acquiring consciousness. Apprehending that part of the self is impossible except in glimpses or inklings that take one into heteroglossia before the decision to enter specific language reduces the spatiality of pure potential to linear discourse. Dickinson's poetic approach to heteroglossia involves looking into it backward, training her gaze not on the speech that flows out of it but on the richness of the potential self that precedes and surrounds speech.

The "Circumference" that she tells Higginson is her "Business" is rooted in this effort to reclaim the home that can never be fully known even though it is always inhabited. Dickinson's spatial metaphor—"Circumference"—applies to the efforts of consciousness to illuminate the magnitude within which the self dwells. Because perception moves back and away from linguistic containment, it spreads its light in a circle or sphere formed by the borders of discourse, that ever-shifting demarcation where energy is translated into language systems. As such, her poetic project falls outside the aims of self-completion and individual consummation that characterize traditional understandings of the sublime.[3] The illuminated circumference of her poems is produced through disorienting dislocations of self that bring sensations of discomfort that the poems make no effort to soft-pedal. "She staked her Feathers ⌐] Wings" (*P* 798) describes a woman who attempted flight, "Debated – Rose again –" and succeeds "This time" but does so "beyond the / Estimate] inference / Of Envy, or of Men –" (*MBED* 932). Even though she is "now, among / Circumference" and "At home] ease," her "Boat . . . among the / Billows" is unreachable by others.

Given this context, to feel comfortably "at home" in the poems is to deceive oneself. Margaret Dickie hints at this when she argues that in Dickinson the self is never fully realized in any specific instant and "cannot be made uniform, narrated, and organized into a single individual" (19). By opposing the monologic grip of historic unity with the dialogic possibilities of heteroglossia, Dickinson demands that readers consider selves capable of radically inverting perspective. In Mudge's words, "by equating home with consciousness, Emily did not solve a problem; she set herself one. She well knew that the . . . focus of her mind fluctuated, that her interior world turned, shifted, rose or sunk, that, in brief, it was in constant motion or change" (8).[4]

One of the most famous examples of inverted perspective is "My Life had stood – a / Loaded Gun –" (*P* 754, *MBED* 825-26), in which the speaker appears to describe a surge in potency, only to conclude that she lacks the power to die and for that reason feels an overwhelming sense of impotence. The speaker is first "identified" by an "Owner"; then she discovers that she has the power to destroy his foes ("I speak / for Him"; "None stir] harm the second time –"), and at last she admits that she possesses "the power] art / to kill –/ Without – the power to die –." Whether this consciousness of impotence is itself the product of strength or a demonstration of the speaker's subjugation is left for the reader to decide. Was she in a sense stronger before she was alerted to her power? Does her desire for power draw her into a hierarchy that subordinates her, or does she discover a broader understanding that carries with it a recognition of personal limitation? However the reader decides this matter, the speaker's position remains ambiguous so long as the full range of options conveyed through the poem is considered. Our sense that the speaker inhabits a zone that defies final resolution evokes an awareness of how unsettled our own perspective is. As a result, we experience that expansion of alternatives that characterizes homelessness.

The situation is similar in "Shall I take thee, the / Poet said" (*P* 1126, *ACL*), where the speaker describes a process within which decisions made by a specific subject—in this case a poet—provoke responses that seem to come from some mysterious external source. Is the poet therefore contained within a predetermined grid of culturally defined possibilities, or is the poet generating potential through her choices? How we as readers make sense of both poems depends on the importance we ourselves invest in clarity of thought and conscious control of experience. If we view rational understanding as a requisite for personal fulfillment, we will most likely feel dismay at the speaker's inability either to command death in the first poem or to control her own creativity in the latter. The inverse would amount to accepting uncertainty as a component of experience that both speakers acknowledge. What strikes readers as enigmatic, then, is the quick shift of focus that occurs when attention is redirected from a speaker's account of experience to our own assumptions about what constitute the proper aims of speech, poetry, and language.

In simplified terms, dissatisfaction with a speaker's ability to master her situation may reflect reader demands that experience be understood according to stable and predictable systems of logic. Such demands imply desire for stability and a foundation for judging the poem's success or failure. What the poems tell us, however, is that stability of this kind is not part of the speaker's experience, whether she wishes it or not. On the other hand, a complacent acceptance of impenetrability is equally unsatisfactory if for no other reason than that readers and speakers must feel some curiosity before either are motivated to read or utter the words that constitute the poem. Thus, even if we desire poetry that reaffirms our conviction that the world is knowable, we are drawn into language through awareness of our own uncertainty about what we can and cannot know. Regardless of where we stand in relation to the possibility of certainty, we are attracted to possibilities that challenge our desires and slant our perspectives.

Poems like these, so characteristic of Dickinson's work, force readers to acknowledge the complex dialogic nature of their own thought by establishing the appeal of both logical certainty and its absence. One purpose of such poems is to provoke reevaluations of shared assumptions regarding primary distinctions, like those we assume exist between life and death, public and private, creativity and submission. Dickinson's point is that our own desire for stability arises from a pervasive uncertainty that blurs conventional demarcations. For this reason the structure of Dickinson's poems liberates the imagination by interrogating the social conventions that channel perception.

To facilitate this interrogation, Dickinson makes the complexity of perception a special concern through her use of chirographic devices that focus reader attention on the broadest as well as the most minute details of her writing. Doing so enables her to simultaneously acknowledge the appeal of multiple discourses while proclaiming the incomplete character of each, thus directing attention to heteroglossia. To this end, she takes advantage of widely shared assumptions about generic modes of writing by mixing and fragmenting stylistic features that force readers to confront self-limiting expectations. Higginson's observation that Dickinson writes in the tradition of the portfolio is one example of an identifiable genre that Dickinson uses for her own purposes. Yet, as St. Armand has shown, while the portfolio model may have influenced Dickinson, her many innovations significantly alter the genre of portfolio writing.

In her poems we can also see that Dickinson's use of conventions associated with diary and confessional writing contributes to a poetics that absorbs forms, structuring language along the lines Bakhtin attributes to the novel: "Authorial speech, the speeches of narrators, inserted genres are . . . those fundamental compositional unities with whose help heteroglossia . . . can enter the novel; each of them permits a multiplicity of social voices and a wide variety of their links and their relationships (always more or less dialogized). These distinctive links and interrelationships between utterances and languages, this movement of the theme through the different languages and speech types, its dispersion into the rivulets and droplets of social heteroglossia, its dialogization—this is the basic distinguishing feature of the stylistics of the novel" (*Dialogic* 263). By combining the public and private dimensions of the portfolio and the diary, Dickinson formulates a poetic language that functions like the Bakhtinian novel, sustaining dialogue between private and public modes of expression and eluding domination by a single discourse.

"Homelessness" comes, for these reasons, to represent a category of sensations that accompany participation in multiple discourses, none of which dominates and therefore asserts a predictable and fixed logic. House imagery in Dickinson poems is almost always associated with the expectation of warmth, nurturing, and comfort that remain elusive so long as she is successful as an artist. The words of an 1876 letter to Higginson speak to this point: "Nature is a Haunted House – but Art – a House that tries to be haunted" (*L* 554, #459a). Artistic success requires building into artistic creation a hauntedness like that perceived in nature, making "Art" an unsettling, mysterious habitation. Just as nature's vastness eludes comprehension and thus haunts the imagination, so poetry can point to a self exceeding any linguistic domicile.

Contrary to romantic notions of a transcendent self that acquires power through artistic endeavor, Dickinson describes selves that cannot be contained in the vocabularies of specific identity and forever enter existence for the first time. For such selves, there can be no primary voice that acquires greater unity over time, only the reassertion of polyphony. This self constituted by multiple voices coincides with the self Kristeva situates within the signifying practice of modern literature: "The *subject* is only the *signifying process* and [she] appears only as a *signifying practice*, that is, only when [she] is absent *within the position* out of which social, historical, and signifying activity unfolds. . . . It is incumbent upon 'art' to demonstrate that the subject is the absent element of and in [her] practice" (*Revolution* 215).

Here Kristeva directs reader attention away from reification in social identity and toward a prevocal self. Dickinson's artistic project aims to communicate this absence of the subject by positioning the self in heteroglossia, making the speaker an absent presence that most obviously "haunts" the home the artist creates but never fully inhabits.

By approaching Dickinson's poems as the illumination of personal perceptions within larger cultural discussions, we can more fully appreciate the way her poetics presents a culturally determined linguistic house that the speaking subject haunts. Her attentiveness to the boundaries where private and public meet prompts readers to extend the signifying chain themselves and take pleasure in the discovery of dialogic linkages that expand expressive potential. Again, Kristeva is useful in thinking through the role of subjectivity within such a heterogeneous signifying process: "This heterogeneous process . . . is a structuring and de-structuring *practice*, a passage to the outer *boundaries* of the subject and society" (*Revolution* 17). In this passage to "the *outer* boundaries," the discontinuous self that Dickie identifies is much more than merely an authorial attempt to free the self from social and ideological constraints readers in the late twentieth century find unbearably restricting. By enacting speakers' struggles to discover words best suited to the conditions out of which they are writing or speaking, many of Dickinson's poems convey the liminality of subjects whose positions are at all times contingent. Often located within linguistic matrices that both appeal to desire for authority and threaten subjugation, speakers do not fully yield to any of the language systems they encounter. Progress through these matrices can indeed be joyful— so long as the speakers sustain awareness of the possibilities implicit in the discourses they contemplate. From this perspective, each discourse can offer positive opportunities for self-expression that temporarily overshadow the negativity of immersion in specific identity. The implicit promise of linguistic stability and personal security acts as a magnet that draws the speaking subject, while the speaker's refusal to relinquish independence and succumb to the domination of a single system of logic is the source of resistance that sustains poetic tension. Pleasure is the product of the speaker's and the reader's subjective experience of the promises offered by potential identities that are perceived but not realized.

Our appreciation of the poem's development, therefore, depends on the accuracy with which we can detect the spreading circumference of the speaker's personal potential. We must read the poems as challenges to the centripetal force of language that strives to contain the speaker. "As a living, socio-ideological concrete thing, as heteroglot opinion, language," Bakhtin writes, "for the individual lies on the borderline between oneself and the other" (*Dialogic* 293). And because "language is not a neutral medium" (294), speakers who resist being appropriated by the logic of any specific discourse must be aware of the forces that threaten containment. Identifying the ways in which specific poems push against such limits begins with the reader's recognition of a dialogized language that constantly urges thought into unexplored channels, opening centrifugal possibilities as alternatives to monologic containment. Situating the speaker in the boundary between and among many discourses allows for the perception of limitation without total immersion in any single discourse. The tension the reader senses in the speaker is due to the palpable attraction exerted by monologic discourse. In this way, dialogized language drives Dickinson's poems by locating speakers at the boundaries, where it is possible to speak with voices that reflect convention while suggesting the means to resist conformity.[5] Dickinson's poetics of inclusion thus emerges as a delight in limitlessness that is directly proportionate to a speaker's or reader's knowledge of cultural forces that aim at containment.

Too often, critical interpretation fails to acknowledge Dickinson's delight in simultaneity because of the tendency among critics to break from one totalizing interpretation only to assert another in its place. Dickinson's poems work against this tendency by positioning speakers' voices in spatial rather than linear contexts. Because her heterogeneous, dialogized language promotes readings that resist dualistic simplification, readers must combat the logic of their own predispositions if they hope to avoid imposing monologic conclusions. Feminists and New Historians—to take but two of the more appealing critical schools now in vogue—do not fully enter into the sort of reading Dickinson's dialogic-spatial play demands, so long as they insist that social and ideological practices are rooted in either a resurgent patriarchism or synchronic praxis. As Wai-Chee Dimock writes, the problem with such approaches is that they too often reassert static, binary, and hence hierarchic assumptions under the guise of subversive or even revolutionary readings (615-16). Totalizing impulses dominate the reader's experience so that gender and history, for instance, are presented as monolithic rather than multifarious. Diane Price Herndl has suggested that a similar problem exists within dialogic analyses when critics give lip service to polyvocality without doing texts the justice of fully representing a plurality of readings.[6] This question—how to describe the multitudinality expressed in a finite, brief text, like that of a typical Dickinson poem—is one that must be asked if we wish to comprehend Dickinson in a manner not dictated solely by currents that shape our own subjective thought processes. To appreciate Dickinson's presentation of homelessness, we must resist our own desire to feel at home in reading her.

Reading Dickinson, then, demands that we accept the appeal exerted by totalizing language while remaining attentive to the profusion of contrary private perceptions that permeates the public sphere of language. As Juhasz has argued in *The Undiscovered Continent,* Dickinson's decision to withdraw from the larger world "gave her control over her own experience: she could select, apportion, focus, examine, explore, satiate herself exactly as she wished and needed to do" (10). Dickinson selectively addresses public and private spheres without slipping into the hierarchic exclusivity that would deny the importance of one or more features of her life—her sex, her emotions, or her socially determined role—in order to maximize identity as unitary authority. Instead, she behaves in a manner more fully consistent with Irigaray's injunction that "woman" voice a pluralistic, multifaceted body that has been repressed by a phallic logos:

> But if, by exploits of her hand, woman were to reopen paths into (once again) a/one logos that connotes her as castrated, especially as castrated of words . . . then a certain sense, which still constitutes the sense of history also, will undergo unparalleled interrogation, revolution. But how is this to be done? Given that, once again, the "reasonable" words—are powerless to translate all that pulses, clamors, and hangs hazily in cryptic passages. . . . Then. . . . Turn everything upside down, inside out, back to front. *Rack it with radical convulsions,* carry back, reimport, those crises that her "body" suffers in her impotence to say what disturbs her. Insist also and deliberately upon those *blanks* in discourse which recall the places of her exclusion and which, by their *silent plasticity,* ensure the cohesion, the articulation, the coherent expansion of established forms. . . . . *Overthrow syntax* by suspending its eternally teleological order.
>
> [*Speculum* 142]

Whether or not such a project is necessarily feminist—in either essentialist or socially constructed senses—thinking in terms of pluralism rather than unity allows us to accept conventional discourse as one component of Dickinson's inclusive poetics. In simple terms, she fragments constructed discourses that conventionally distinguish internal and external experience so that the unconstructed and infinite might shine through. In words Dimock chooses to describe one admixture of feminism and historicism, readings must respect the "endless mutations and permutations . . . between cause and effect and the structural nonidentity between system and subject" to "open a space for alternatives, however visionary and unsustained," to reveal, in short, "a realm of unexhausted and inexhaustible possibility" (622).

The way Dickinson's inclusive poetics generates possibility can be seen in one of her many poems that describe the speaker's experience of language. These poems, which often discuss the artist's creative engagement with language, can also provide useful information about Dickinson's most distinctive punctuation—her dashes—and the relationship this punctuation has with the generation of voices. As "Shall I take thee" (*P* 1126) demonstrates, speakers can be intensely conscious of their participation in the linguistic process:

```
Shall I take thee, the
Poet said
To the propounded word?
Be stationed with the
Candidates     vainer                          5
Till I have     finer
Tried –         further

The Poet     searched
Philology     probed
And was about to ring                           10
      just     when
for the     suspended
Candidate

There came unsummoned
in  – Advanced
That portion of the Vision                      15
The Word applied to
fill
Not unto nomination
The Cherubim reveal  –
```

Because this poem takes the form of a narrative in the past tense, we are given the commentary of a speaker who may not be the poet whose experience is recounted. Initially, the design suggests a conventional mode of third-person representation stressing distance. This conventional reading takes place on at least three levels: that of the subject (the poet) whose experience is related, that of the narrator (who may be a poet), and that of the relationship of the poet and the narrator (which involves both poetic convention and a poet).

Given the chiasmic structuring that embeds the words of the poet first within a narrative and then within a dialogue of narrative form and narrated experience, we can see how on each of the three levels agency is obstructed by violations of the subject's expectation. For the poet who is searching for the best word, something "unsummoned" supplies the "Word's" "portion of the Vision"; for the narrator, formal narrative ceases when the "Word" fails, transforming the last five lines from narrative resolution into enigmatic aphorism ("Not unto nomination . . ."); for the poet writing of the initial poet's

341

Shall I take thee, the
Poet said
To the propounded word?
Be stationed with the
Candidates   rainer
& Till I have finer
tried -   further

the Poet searched
Philolog,   probed
And / was about To ring
for the just- suspended   when
Candidate
there came unsummoned
in- Advanced
that portion of the Vision
the Word applied to
fill
not until nomination
the Cherubim reveal -

Figure 5. Poem 1126, Amherst College Library. By permission of Harvard University Press and the Trustees of Amherst College Library.

experience *and* the narrator's inability to capture that experience, the narrative disintegrates when one discourse displaces another. This process of considering alternative narratives traces the way each new perspective dissolves the boundary defined by the previous narrative. Within such a reading, boundaries founded on expectation do not limit the subject to a single voice or discourse. Even though we can identify narrative shifts and voice changes, we need not assume that more than one subject exists. Neither need we assume that a single speaker performs multiple roles, speaking with different voices. As readers we must determine if the disjunctions marked by dashes are incompatible with one speaking self.[7]

By recording the poet's frustration at not locating the perfect word, the poem links frustration with homelessness and knowledge of self. In this way, the poem disconnects frustration from a failure to achieve formal unity and connects it to poetic access to new possibilities. And here Dickinson comes very close to her Romantic counterparts in outlining what appears to be an experience of the sublime.[8] But reading the poem as an encounter with the sublime would require that the three stages identified earlier are either transcended by formal unity or that the reader extends the poem's incomplete gestures toward the sublime, achieving individual transcendence.[9] That, at least, would be the aim of a poetics that reifies the self of the egotistical sublime. Dickinson's approach, however, stratifies stages within the creative process in order to undermine the sense that each discrete part discovers a "home" within a coherent whole. Her poems reflect a project quite different from the romanticist concern with the outcomes of poetic language. She is interested in illuminating a plural self that cannot be contained.

Given this context, the dashes at the end of each stanza after "Tried –," "in –,"[10] and "reveal –" raise questions about the linking of one stanza with another. The dash that appears after "reveal" in the final stanza suggests that stanzas need not be linked to other stanzas or even to other words. This pointing away from words betokens the unresolved character of the writer's experience while suggesting a bond uniting all three phases the poem articulates. According to such a reading, poetic creation is at least in part a clarification of conventions that the writer delights in violating. And here Dickinson's 1870 comment to Higginson that poetry makes her "feel physically as if the top of [her] head were taken off" (*L* 474, #342a) affirms the sensation of homelessness available to poet and reader: for both, poetry dislocates the self, releasing sensations of mind and body disorientation. The speaker of "If ever the lid gets off my head" (*P* 1727) uses this imagery of dislocation to expand the world's awareness of the self's flexibility: "If ever the lid gets off my head / And lets the brain away," and "if the world be looking on," it "Will see how far from home / It is possible for sense to live" (no ms.).

This lifting off of the "lid" clearly designates an experience more moving than a casual encounter with a piece of writing. What Dickinson describes is the most desirable kind of reading, the reading that she desires for herself and her readers. Taking the tops of heads off is what Dickinson is all about. She wants her readers physically to encounter limitations and not feel at home within univocal utterances.[11] Such a procedure ensures dialogic vitality by respecting the multiplicity of discourses and voices introduced in poems. As readers we hear multiple voices and resist the silence threatened by monologizing language while passing through the heteroglossia each poem magnifies.[12] And we are alerted to these voices through Dickinson's careful placement of dashes.

Prior to the first dash, for instance, "Shall I take thee, the / Poet said" focuses on the words the poet utters either internally or publicly, depending on whether or not we think the speaker is a poet recalling what she may have thought or an observer of the poet who would not have known what was said unless it was said out loud: "Shall I take thee . . . Be stationed with the / Candidates / Till I have finer] vainer] further / Tried –." The piling up of variants here visually magnifies the poet's appreciation that positive and negative connotations hinge on word choice and the designation of possible meanings. Is the word to be "finer," connoting superiority; "vainer," as in tasteless self absorption; or "further," suggesting the impersonal examination of a longer, "further" list of words? The simultaneous presentation of all three possibilities increases reader sensitivity to the importance of heteroglossia in poetic creation while also clarifying the poem's concern with the poet's thoughts.

Between the first and second dashes, however, the focus shifts from the poet's words to the narrator's words: "The Poet searched] probed / Philology / And was] just] when / about to ring / for the suspended / Candidate / There came] Advanced unsummoned in –." As in the first stanza, variants magnify the speaker's contemplation of word choices and the weight borne by each word. Here the variants emphasize the dramatic character of what is described, so that the poet's efforts are more clearly viewed as having been interrupted by an unsummoned aggressive presence that may have "Advanced" threateningly "when" she "was" "just" about to decide. This dramatic presentation further accentuates the narrative quality of the central unit of the poem while extending the sense that the poem is exploring tensions between internal and external experience.

Following the second dash, the poem's focus shifts away from the search for words to the "portion of the Vision" that the "Word applied to / fill" and the concluding reflection: "Not unto nomination / The Cherubim reveal –." These shifts tell us that we have moved out of dramatic narration into a more reflective meditation on the function of words (nomination) by means of a metalanguage spoken by a philosophic observer. And here the poem presents no variants, as the distance of reflection sufficiently detaches the speaker from the precariousness of immediacy, suggesting that the anxiety of weighing discourse possibilities has passed.

All of these speakers contribute to the poem; each conveys an experience that is both linked to and independent of the others. Should we as readers choose to collapse these speakers and merge their voices, we must do so in the face of visual markers—the dashes—that militate against such an act. In this way the poem makes the reader's desire to achieve resolution itself a subject of investigation by contesting the expectation that resolution is possible. One aim of the poem, then, is to awaken readers to their own monologizing impulses.

If we consider "Shall I take thee, the / Poet said" to be about the way multiple meanings impinge on the thought processes of poets and readers, we can begin to imagine poetic creation as the use of language to free all subjects from monologic subjugation. Read with this possibility in mind, we can reduce some of the mystery that adheres to the "portion of the Vision" that enters the poem "unsummoned." What is the "portion" that can both be crucial to the creative experience of a poet and not involve words? A simple answer to this question is punctuation, the one feature of the poem that contributes to rhythm and meaning while sustaining an authority equal to or even greater than that of words. If we accept this answer to the riddle posed by the poem, we have to look seriously at dashes, as there is no other punctuation. As we have already seen, dashes delineate shifts in speaker, for in three successive stanzas the focus shifts from poet's words to narrator's words to the words of a metacommentator. This movement alone indicates that the poetic experience is polyvocal. The final dash then raises questions about what is next, about what additional voice or voices might enter the poetic process. I suggest that this dash tells us what the prior dashes have also told us: that there are always other voices and that any decision to limit voice is the product of personal choice. The poem then ends after having established that (1) poets use words to think about composing with words; (2) poets engage in a process whereby language becomes more than words; (3) poets reflect on the otherness out of which language comes.

The point is that through this poem and others like it, Dickinson casts doubt on the accuracy with which any specific discourse conveys information about the self. In a poem like "Shall I take thee, the / Poet said," we see how speakers "suspend" words and thus engage language spatially. As a result, we as readers begin using language that becomes opaque in proportion to our awareness of multiple meaning possibilities. Transparency, on the other hand, is a function of immersion in a specific discourse. When we are told that "Not unto nomination / The Cherubim reveal –," for instance, "nomination" conflates democratic and monarchical notions of naming (as for office or for familial identity), and we can imagine that the speaker is exhorting us not to trust in hierarchies. At the same time, however, we hear the speaker saying that "Cherubim reveal," prompting the conclusion that even in the act of rejecting hierarchy, hierarchic language ("Cherubim") enters speech. This sense—that language always grows out of other language and hence contains within itself the seeds of objectionable discourse—becomes the basis for spatial readings that acknowledge the heterogeneous, unstable processes of language. Dickinson's arrangements of variants and her lineation visually enhance such spatial readings through their direct manipulation of the poem's material habitation.

The primary difference between what I am calling linear and spatial readings is that the former stress beginnings and endings, conclusions and climaxes; whereas spatial readings have no initiating moment and therefore cannot reach climax and resolution. Poems like Dickinson's that constantly oppose linear readings with spatial ones succeed as works of art when readers identify the attraction of monologic specificity but pass beyond it, breaking out of linear constructs into spatial possibilities. They feel the tops of their heads lifted off.

Such readings imply that knowledge of self relates to the spatialization of identity. By emphasizing the opacity of language, Dickinson counters narcissistic impulses based on the belief that transparent language conveys a true image of the self. This tension between transparency and opacity is crucial to any full appreciation of Dickinson's stature as an artist; her practice of opposing readings grounded in conventional notions of transparency with readings that demonstrate opacity sustains the dialogism crucial to her grounding of self-knowledge in the experience of homelessness.

Reading "Like Eyes that looked on Wastes –" (*P* 458, *MBED* 775) as the thoughts of a speaker looking at her reflection clarifies the way Dickinson manupulates transparency and opacity to communicate homelessness:

Like Eyes that looked on Wastes –
Incredulous of Ought
But Blank – and steady Wilderness –
Diversified by Night –

Just Infinites of Nought –   5
As far as it could see –
So looked the face I looked upon –
So looked itself – on Me –

I offered it no Help –
Because the Cause was Mine –   10
The Misery a Compact
As hopeless – as divine –

Neither – would be absolved –
Neither would be a Queen
Without the Other – Therefore –   15
We perish – tho' We reign –

The poem is split between the first two and the last two stanzas as the speaker shifts from passively commenting on her reflection to actively taking possession of it: first she asserts distance: "So looked itself – on Me –"; then she takes possession of it: "Because the Cause was Mine –." This division provides an unusually accessible critique of self based on what the speaker finds both encouraging and troubling in her reflection. On the surface, she comes to terms with a disturbing expression in her eyes by placing what disconcerts her in the context of a positive goal: to "be a Queen." This reading ignores Dickinson's syntax and her use of dashes. As in "Shall I take thee, the / Poet said," there is a riddle buried in the lines that emerges once the poem is read as a self-conscious discussion of the subject's relationship to language.

If the speaker is looking at herself, the "Wastes" she observes in the first line represent not the external otherness the language at first suggests, but an otherness the speaker acknowledges in herself. Immediately, internal and external opposition is complicated so that one is not easily separated from the other. Even though the poem asserts the presence of such a distinction, the play of presence and nonpresence that is a main concern of the poem appears here in the speaker's efforts to affirm a self that exceeds the validating discourses of culture. In addition to punning on "Eyes" and "I's," the poem focuses attention on what can be perceived as either the absences Porter identifies as having existed "where authority should have stood" (170) or the infinity alluded to in "Infinites of Nought" mentioned in line 5. An inclusive reading must consider the way potential is denied by terms like "Ought," "Nought," and "Blank" that denote absence but do so with such force that the reader imagines what the language negates.

Because Dickinson tropes on the notion that language can achieve transparency, the repeated assertion of absence triggers the consideration of its opposite: the "Queen" the speaker refers to in the last stanza. Again, the "Eyes/I's" pun sets up an inclusive sense of otherness that confers positive complements for the terms denoting negativity in the first two stanzas. As Roland Hagenbüchle has noted, "The experience of total loss, of total poverty, of total ignorance, of total nothingness always turns into the experience of its very opposite" (146). Thus the exaggerated use of negative terms draws attention to itself as a metaphor that inverts denotative meaning, stimulating expansive visions of the literal fields of reference attached to specific words. The entire poem becomes an elaborate play on reflection or the reversal of perception characteristic of mirrors, so that infinite negativity surfaces as a domain fit for a queen.

Opening as it does with the simile, "Like Eyes that looked on Wastes –," the poem's language incorporates a self-conscious awareness of its own artifice that immediately undermines the finality and accuracy of what follows. Partially because the poem makes us wait so long before learning the subject of the simile, we are aware of the speaker's difficulty locating language to describe what she sees. Through her effort to define the self that she seeks in the mirror, the speaker discovers a multitude of intervening phenomena that she must interpret. The uncertainty of this process implies that she stands both within and without the interpretive possibilities she contemplates—she is the infinite potential "Incredulous of Ought." Such a compounding of uncertainty directs attention to the meaning potential of words magnified by dashes and shifts in speaker.

As we confront this kaleidoscope of possibilities, we begin to focus increasingly on the labyrinthine character of a verbal landscape that is ostensibly composed to clarify our understanding of what the subject sees. The initial simile, "Like Eyes that looked on Wastes –," describes what we finally learn in line 7 is "the face I looked upon." But before we arrive at the face, we are given a figure of speech with an unspecified referent that is first "Incredulous of Ought / But Blank –" and may be contained within or added to "steady Wilderness –," which in turn may or may not be "Diversified by Night," depending on the degree of disjunction attributed to the dashes. The buried riddle has to do with the way all references to absence are simultaneously assertions of plenitude. As with other Dickinson poems, opposing fields of reference position the speaker at neither extreme but rather in the border region from which she can embrace the widest range of options.

Naturally, such play holds enormous implications for Dickinson's notion of what constitutes useful knowledge of the self. Cameron's observation that "for all its self-reflective terms, the poem seems strangely without a subject" (142) points to the futility of searching for a unified self. For Cameron, the poem describes the speaker's failure to "reify absence" through her reflection. She tries unsuccessfully to "hold on to it as personified identity" in an effort to deny Derridean "differance" and escape the pain of loss. Because the speaker insists on "contingent identities that will not accept boundaries," the ultimate outcome is "disintegration" and pain.

Contrary to this reading, I propose that the speaker, fully aware of her liminal position, speaks to us from the boundary—that is, out of heteroglossia—that enables her to touch all the discourse possibilities her imagination encounters. Instead of feeling defeated by her inability to reify a lost self, she revels in the growth of perspectives figured by reflection; she realizes that the past can no longer accommodate her because her horizon has expanded. The sense of loss she registers thus performs the double duty of both distancing her from what she was *and* affirming the attraction the past still exerts. The outcome is her awareness that she feels pain because the past retains meaning within an expanded present self. Far from expressing a fear of disintegration, the poem suggests that pain can signify that the circumference of experience has grown.

By concentrating on Derrida's proposition that speech is "an aspect, a species of writing" (8), we can see how Dickinson's speaker translates her perception of what might be described as "differance" into the basis for self-knowledge. As Derrida states in *Of Grammatology,* once language is freed from ultimate grounding in truth and is instead perceived as deriving from primary ideological assumptions, the meaning attributable to signifiers is never fully exploited in any linguistic construction (62-63). Rather, the potential field of reference is limitless, and any grammatical construction reveals a speaker's ideological predisposition, not external truth. Language is never fully centered in any statement but "differed" by or "different" from whatever the syntax imputes.[13] As Cameron suggests, poetry can provide a means of sustaining contact with the past, but it does so by vitalizing all experiences of "differance" in proportion to our memory of that which is gone.

To facilitate a reading that focuses on the dialogic richness of this specific Dickinson poem, I want to consider a monologic reading of the sort encouraged by its earliest editors. The poem's first appearance in *Bolts of Melody* in 1945 differs markedly from the manuscript version, primarily through the regularization of punctuation and capitalization designed to promote unitary closure. The result is a poem that progresses in linear fashion, placing great weight on the final lines. This strategy makes the "Therefore" in line 15 a pivotal word culminating the logic of the previous lines and situating the poem in the context of didactic verse of the sort Poe disdainfully regarded as having committed "the heresy of *The Didactic*" (416).

> Like eyes that looked on wastes,
> Incredulous of aught
> But blank—and stead [*sic*], wilderness
> Diversified by night—
>
> Just infinite of naught   5
> As far as it could see,
> So looked the face I looked upon.
> So looked itself on me.
>
> I offered it no help
> Because the cause was mine,   10
> The misery a compact
> As hopeless as divine.
>
> Neither would be absolved,
> Neither would be a queen
> Without the other—therefore   15
> We perish, though we reign.

According to this arrangement of the poem, a speaker perceives "wastes" reflected in her own eyes and decides that she will not reach out to herself ("I offered it no help"). She tells us that her refusal to help is based on her perception that "the cause was mine," implying that she chooses not to violate the integrity of a self, albeit her own self, because that self has a purpose (a "cause") that must be honored. This choice, then, reflects deep respect for a unified self, a self she perceives as at present "hopeless" but ultimately "divine." Lastly, we are given a formula that unites the two opposing sides of the self, stating that each is dependent on the other: "Neither would be a queen / Without the other." The resulting poem reveres the unity of self to such an extent that the speaker is willing to accept absence or "wilderness" as a necessary sacrifice to a larger "regal" unity. Knowledge, according to this reading of the poem, is the recognition that dedication to a larger purpose requires sacrifice. The self must be contained and made obedient to a hierarchic system of values.

Less conventional interpretations become possible once the chirography of the manuscript is accepted as a serious guide to reading; linear and hierarchic assumptions encouraged by the 1945 version seem like reinscriptions of conventions the poem explicitly interrogates. Immediately upon considering the possibilities opened by dashes and capitalization, we recognize that words subordinated within the syntax of a unitary reading stand out like unruly children fleeing from a teacher. Once the dashes are acknowledged, however, the syntactic narrowing of meaning coincident with conventional grammar is challenged, thereby illuminating the seams of unified interpretations. Words like "Wastes," "Blank," and "Nought" acquire meaning in terms of alternative discourses like those associated with mirroring, metaphorical play, and linguistic opacity, discussed earlier. As a result, the poem can be read as a dialogic activation of discourses effaced by convention. A fairly blatant objective of a poem like this one would therefore be to question the possibility of a unified self. More precisely, this poem calls attention to the sacrifice required when readers erase dashes and eliminate from consideration alternatives to convention.

As Kristeva writes in *Revolution in Poetic Language,* sacrifice is the "other side of symbolism," reproducing "the process of its production" (77). Along with sacrifice comes an "expenditure of semiotic violence" that "tends to dissolve the logical order" and "generally precedes sacrifice" (79). Such is the progression in the Dickinson poem where the logic of absence is dissolved before the sacrifice designed to institute a new order is proposed. The poem tells us that the "Therefore" is not a natural resolution of apparent oppositions but a forced containment of self demanded by assumptions the speaker finds less than compelling. Bakhtin observes of terms such as "therefore" that they are "used to maintain a logical sequence" that loses authority when complicated by more than one voice or discourse (*Dialogic* 305), as is the case here. The result is a questioning of the benefits of sacrifice that the speaker sees as requisite to her becoming a queen. Built into the poem, therefore, is the ironic recognition that the speaker contemplates a sacrifice in order to acquire power she already possesses—she already wields an omnipotence that makes her more powerful than any ordinary queen.

As a means of situating this poem in its historical context and exploring its engagement with conventional literary practices, I want to examine the poem's adaptation of the conventional literary form that Thomas H. Johnson, Barton Levi St. Armand, and others refer to as "Poetry of the Portfolio." As St. Armand describes it, this "largely female art form" (5) first achieved public notice through Washington Irving's 1819 *Sketch Book* and was later described as a separate genre by Ralph Waldo Emerson in an 1840 *Dial* essay entitled "New Poetry" (4). In Emerson's words, "*Verses of the Portfolio*" made up a uniquely American genre that democratically drew on other established forms, like the confession. He writes that the manuscript verses of the portfolio possessed a special charm: "'they were confessions; and the faults, the imperfect parts, the fragmentary verses, the halting rhymes had a worth beyond that of a high finish'" (4). Notable for their intimacy and unpolished presentation, portfolio verses provided what St. Armand identifies as "Dickinson's art . . . of assemblage, a 'quilting' of elite and popular ideas onto a sturdy underlying folk form, frame, or fabric" (9).

This "quilting" reflects the private and eclectic nature of the "portfolio genre" that St. Armand defines as "a loose repository of musings, views, portraits, copies, caricatures, and 'studies from nature' . . . an idiosyncratic 'Book of the Heart'" (5). As a model for what he imagines to have been Dickinson's mode of composition, St. Armand devotes considerable time to the fully intact portfolio of Mary Warner, a close friend of Dickinson's. His purpose is to treat the portfolio as "a guiding anthology of ideas, models and patterns" of the sort that would have influenced Dickinson's writing (31). My intention is to extend St. Armand's interest in the highly personal character of portfolio entries without accepting his conclusion that Dickinson "weaves folk, popular, and elite strands of culture together so effortlessly as to make the result appear seamless" (37). I see Dickinson drawing on the form in order to expose seams in all writing, including her own. Any effort to duplicate an external form would require the sort of self-sacrifice Dickinson avidly resists.

Without exploring all the intricacies of each strand, I want to stress Dickinson's determination to expose at least a few of the seams all too easily effaced by her culture. In this way, she uses the poems that may or may not have derived from her portfolio in a manner consistent with the typical use of a diary as described by contemporary authors and diarists. Jane H. Hunter's research in diary writing led her to the conclusion that "Girls' diaries offered them a compromise—a way to release and contain rebellious impulses, however circumscribed, without breaking with families" (58). Diary writing allowed girls to experiment with forms of expression not countenanced in the home, so that keeping "secret diaries facilitated the development of a multifaceted self" (Hunter 61). In this sense, diaries would have been natural repositories for the young girl's experiences of homelessness at home.

Not surprisingly, diaries could take on confessional attributes, as in this entry written by Harriet Burton in the late 1880s:

> I am in a very hilarious frame of mind today, and can hardly curb my prancing spirits enough to "wright" as this scrawl bears witness. My silvery voice has been heard at all hours of the day rolling forth in diabolical waves of laughter, and striking terror into the souls of the inhabitants of the house. My mind is so filled with plans which wont come true that

I'm nearly crazy. My emotions for other people . . . become so conflicting that they brake from the narrow bounds of my inner man and find
vent in a mad race around the house.
      [Hunter 68]

Hunter associates the use of diaries to vent unacceptable facets of the self
with the view of women's writing expressed in Charlotte Perkins Gilman's
1892 "The Yellow Wallpaper." In that work, the physician-husband forbids
his wife to write, thinking that doing so would only "'lead to all manner of
excited fancies'" (69). Hunter's point is that access to diaries afforded young
women the opportunity to develop a sense of self that extended beyond the
role dictated by male-dominated culture. That this unorthodox self was so
closely affiliated with women's writing in general and the diary in particular
has special implications for Dickinson's writing, where the work ultimately
destined for public consumption was initially a private and highly restricted
form of publication carried on between a reclusive author and a few carefully
selected friends.

      Read as a response to the tradition of women's diaries and personal con-
fessions, "Like Eyes that looked on Wastes −" clearly trades on a number of
prominent conventions. The initial use of the mirror as a figure for writing
of an intimate and reflective nature establishes the speaker's sense that her
primary audience is herself, as would be the case in a diary. However, Dickinson's having written her poems primarily for private consumption during her
lifetime does not preclude her having had future readers in mind for whom
she was drawing on the diary/portfolio format because it offered an identi-
fiably female context that she sought to elevate to the level of art. Doing so
would allow her to combine the popular and elite strands that St. Armand
speaks of; it would also account for her idiosyncratic use of dashes, line breaks,
capitalization, and other visual effects more common in less polished forms
such as diaries and portfolios. In addition, the poem's concern with what
the speaker sees in her own eyes is consistent with the sort of personal confession a writer might try to work through in the privacy of her diary.

      Given the concern with private and public spheres so prominent in Dick-
inson's life and so much a part of the function of women's writing in general,
it is not surprising that writers like Gilman and Dickinson should exploit the
power of language to release multifaceted selves that conventional and patriarchal practice strives to contain. As Stonum has convincingly demonstrated
in the portion of *The Dickinson Sublime* that he titles "The Influence of Elizabeth Barrett Browning," Dickinson recognized a similar impulse at work in
Barrett Browning's poetry. Describing Barrett Browning as a writer second

only to Shakespeare in Dickinson's esteem, Stonum goes on to state that Browning's primary influence was that of steering Dickinson away from didactic verse and encouraging the sort of poetry that empowers readers to think and write for themselves: "Browning's influence inspires or legitimizes what I have called an ethic of productivity" (46) according to which an author's creation "initiates at best a richly productive process of response" (47) wherein "the poet becomes the more modestly honored initiator of a process that continues long after." Such an approach directs readers away from the search for unified meaning and rather incites them to look through the language of the author to realize meanings possible only through their personal encounter with the text. In this way language would be treated as a matrix offering an array of interpretive possibilities instead of constellating all reading around a single dominant discourse. As such, language would not present readers with a discrete image they were expected to reflect accurately in their own readings.

Dickinson may well have been familiar with Barrett Browning's 1850 poem "Confessions," in which a woman debates with her mirrored image the merits of the physical love that her culture condemns. In that poem, the speaker concludes that she will accept God's judgment and remain rebellious despite the exhortations to conform uttered by her moralistic self. Separating herself from her reflected image, the speaker demonstrates that the social values metaphorically embodied in the mirror cease to compel her conformity even though she acknowledges the power of dominant Christian belief. In taking this stand, the speaker agrees to meet God as an equal, much as Aurora does in *Aurora Leigh,* when she asserts that she will live according to her own authority and deal with God "As He and I were equals" (340). This assertion of personal freedom so great that it allows the speaking subject to face omnipotence as an equal epitomizes Dickinson's inclusiveness: Dickinson's speakers can also refuse to sacrifice their own power at the same time that they acknowledge an infinite power that apparently opposes them.

Precisely such an assertion of personal authority occurs in Dickinson's poem when her speaker hesitates at the point of accepting "Misery" as a "Compact." The speaker's reluctance to relinquish her hold on either the "divine" or the "hopeless" presents a difficulty the final formula in that poem attempts to resolve by emphasizing the "Queen" side of the equation when "perish" is subordinated to "reign" in the last line: "We perish – tho' We reign." The highly ambiguous character of this last line leaves the reader poised either to admit that perishing is necessary for any queenly "reign," by ending the reading with emphasis on the "reign" part of the equation, or to insist that the benefit of any queenly "reign" is severely compromised by a perishing that undermines the possibility of queenly authority. Because the poem draws attention to the difficulties of deciding on one reading over another, the reader pauses between possible readings, conscious of the appeal of both positions.

This hesitation, one that makes difficult the customary acceptance of sacrifice as a means to authority, reveals the speaker's discomfort with any discourse that denies the validity of her own experience. Here the speaker departs from that mode of diary entry that commends sacrifice, moving instead in the direction of possibilities that lie outside the woman's sphere. In her discussion of diary conventions, Hunter argues that the diary similarly contributed to the emergence of a new woman less dependent on traditional definitions of womanhood: "The diary could soften behavioral commands issued by internalized authority" (70), allowing girls access to a form of writing that "affirmed their rights to a degree of autonomy" (75). Like the diarists who repeatedly dedicate themselves to more disciplined lives but realize at the moment of resolution that they will fail, Dickinson's speaker recognizes the impotence of her words even as she struggles to utter them.

Our understanding of the poem now draws on monologic readings that link linguistic transparency to conventional values, plus readings that see words and punctuation combining to urge the contemplation of unconventional discourse. At this point, then, we become concerned with the artistic implications of language that becomes opaque as heteroglossia gains prominence. Our own interests in the poem take us away from the social and historical dimensions of the work while nevertheless remaining dependent on those dimensions; without them we would not perceive the text as a dialogic expression of a pluralistic self. Such an inclusive reading, for these reasons, adds a horizontal dimension to the vertical semantics of hierarchic discourse while adding vertical syntax to the linear punctuation of monologic thought. This move toward opacity and spatiality is evidence of Dickinson's participation in a literary avant-garde concerned with breaking from formal conventions of writing and raising questions about knowledge and truth as these concepts apply to the concrete experience of daily life.[14] And here, links with other works that explicitly identify the difficulties faced by artists who are not granted cultural authority become particularly relevant.[15] The struggles of the lower-class male artist in Rebecca Harding Davis's 1861 short story, "Life in the Iron Mills," and Charlotte Perkins Gilman's 1892 depiction of a disenfranchised professional woman, "The Yellow Wallpaper," typify the sort of struggle increasingly prominent in literature in the second half of the nineteenth century.

Both of these stories explore the ways that creativity is translated into pain and suffering when not directed though channels condoned by social, political, and economic institutions. Harding Davis concentrates on the class structure implicit in the distribution of cultural power, while Gilman focuses more narrowly on the destructive influence of social conventions that thwart female ambition. In "Feminism, New Historicism, and the Reader," Dimock stresses the importance of considering both historical context and gender when reading "The Yellow Wallpaper," arguing that the isolation of either discourse would provoke a reification of power relations and gender. To avoid falling back on binary interpretations, Dimock recommends an approach to reading that corresponds closely to the dialogic and spatial readings of Dickinson that I have presented and that can be applied to her poems as well as to the fiction of Harding Davis and Gilman. Acknowledging the historical presence of an emerging social order like that Hunter associates with the "new woman" in girls' diaries, Dimock goes on to emphasize the need to focus on spatial elements in literature: "Gender . . . is to be understood not as an incidental addition to a stable historical field but as a principle productive of uneven textures, productive of the discrepancy between the dominant and the emergent, inflecting and disturbing the very shape of historical time, challenging not only normative temporality but also its spatial disposition of margins and limits" (621). Though Dimock is primarily concerned with demonstrating the interrelatedness of feminism and historicism, her interest in multiplying discourses corresponds to the efforts of avant-garde writers who emphasize the function of art as a means of evaluating not just social practice but the institutionalization of artistic conventions. The point is that these writers also position readers at the boundaries out of which new conventions develop.

As a way of uniting her interest in the artistic ambitions of a newly self-conscious American literati and her concern with the exclusion from public institutions felt keenly by women, Dickinson created a poetics that instructs readers in the experience of living inclusively, on the boundaries that illuminate the choices undergirding conventional life. She transmits knowledge essential to the acceptance of such a liminal existence through poems that take readers into these boundaries and allow them to experience for themselves the limitlessness their own lives can possess when binary thought is included as an option rather than a necessity. Dickinson's frequent mention of the experience of "homelessness" acquires special significance in this context in which stability and monologic certitude are equated with the sacrifice of personal freedom.

Conclusion

 AS A FINAL COMMENT, I want to speculate briefly on implications for readings of Dickinson's life and work suggested by Constance Fenimore Woolson's 1880 short story "Miss Grief." Of particular interest are the multiple correspondences with Dickinson's life, her complicated relationship with readers, and her reluctance to publish. In Woolson's story, Aarona Moncrief, a forty-three-year-old spinster (260), asks an established male writer to read her work. After grudgingly agreeing, he discovers to his surprise that she is a writer of genius: "I . . . sat up half the night," he tells us, and "felt thrilled through and through" (256). He believes, however, that there are "faults . . . many and prominent" that Miss Moncrief should eliminate before going to a publisher. When he generously offers to edit her work, she demurs: "'No,' she answered softly, still smiling. 'There shall not be so much as a comma altered'" (260).

The parallels between this scenario and Dickinson's relationship with Thomas Wentworth Higginson are clear. Miss Moncrief stands as her own tribunal, appreciative of her editor's acknowledgment but unflinchingly refusing editorial advice. "You think my gait / 'spasmodic'" is the famous Dickinson counterpart, "You think me 'un- / controlled' – I have / no Tribunal" (BPL Higg 52, *L* 408-09, #265). Higginson, of course, plays tribunal after Dickinson dies and together with Mabel Loomis Todd initiates a tradition of posthumous editorial intervention.

With Miss Moncrief the situation is different: her editor, wishing to serve her interests and not embarrass himself, decides to overrule her objections and amend her text in private, while she is still living. In the process he is astonished to discover that all his best efforts are frustrated: "I amended, altered, left out, put in, pieced, condensed, lengthened; I did my best, and all to no avail. I could not succeed in completing anything that satisfied me, or that approached, in truth, [her] work just as it stood" (Woolson 264). At last he reaches the end of his patience, admitting what Dickinson's editors have only recently begun to acknowledge: "I was forced at last to make up my mind that either my own powers were not equal to the task, or else that her perversities were as essential a part of her work as her inspirations, and not to be separated from it" (265). In the end, he abandons his efforts to "improve" her manuscript, tells her that the work will be published as she wrote it—though he knows that this will never happen—and consigns the unyielding manuscript to the oblivion of a "locked case" (268).

Both the short story by Woolson and the life of Dickinson present us with women writers searching for an able readership. Both connect with editors who recognize their genius, but who believe the "perversities" of their work will preclude widespread or commercial acceptance. I want to argue that this state of affairs was not *only* the result of a male literary establishment's insensitivity to female genius, though that explanation certainly contributes to the problem. Rather, as the episodes I have touched on suggest, the writing of these women itself produced, even demanded, a problematic relationship with the reader. Recent work on Dickinson has argued in various ways that "discomfort," "unfixity," and "wickedness" (to use some of Betsy Erkkila's words[1]) are all characteristics of women's writing during this period. I want to extend these ideas into the realm of the reader's aesthetic, exploring the way Dickinson's life and Woolson's fiction show that able readers were necessarily implicated in these disturbing aspects of women's writing.

The narrator/editor of "Miss Grief" (who remains nameless) has an extremely uncomfortable relationship with her writing, as the summary I have given suggests. Although he is "thrilled through and through" at first reading, he has a simultaneous and contradictory impulse to try and change the text, as if he had not immediately appreciated its unruliness. The work seems to have alerted him to the narrowness of his preconceptions, forcing him to consider new aesthetic possibilities. Yet his response is to try and conventionalize the text. The fact that he cannot bring himself to do this, despite all attempts, proves that he was indeed that rarest of beings: the reader capable of perceiving brilliance in unconventional writing. But his immediate attempt to control and domesticate the text suggests that he is also deeply challenged and disturbed by it. In a related incident, the narrator attempts to control the text by showing Miss Moncrief's poems to a woman he knows will be shocked by them. By purposefully exposing them to someone who will not see beyond their departure from orthodoxy, the narrator seems to, in a slightly different way, attempt to reduce their power.

The narrator's main experience with the work, then, is one of discomfort. This discomfort extends to his personal relationship with Miss Moncrief herself. Though the two have very little in common personally, they are strangely bonded because of their shared abilities as readers and writers. Upon meeting Miss Moncrief, the narrator is amazed by the extent of her familiarity with his writing. She surprises him not only by quoting his work from memory but by affirming his own secret evaluation. In her recitation he discovers a "full, almost overfull, recognition which," he says, "startled me. For she had understood me—understood me almost better than I had understood myself" (Woolson 252). Most uncannily of all, she singles out for praise the one scene in his work that he admired most but that the public ignored.

The sureness of her emotional and intellectual grasp, founded solely on her abilities as a reader, establishes the basis for their relationship, as Miss Moncrief suggests when she tells the narrator, "If you had not written that scene I should not have sought you" (Woolson 253). For his part, the narrator is not overly enthusiastic about helping her because she has made it clear that what she admires in his writing is the exception and not the rule. The appeal each has for the other rests on a recognition of ability that in no way diminishes their ideological differences. If anything, they are only too aware of the inconvenience provoked by a reading aesthetic they grudgingly share. From the beginning, then, while they are united as members of a small fellowship of able readers, their communication suggests that this relationship is one of unease and discomfort.

Just as the narrator attempts to distance the power of her text, so he seems to work hard to keep Miss Moncrief herself at arm's length. He never refers to her by her true name, but rather by the name "Miss Grief." This made-up name distances him from the person, turning her into a symbolic victim rather than acknowledging her individuality. He distances her in a slightly different way when he steers what could become a highly personal discussion about her work into cooler, more professional avenues. By responding to her manuscript instead of to her personally, he is able to offer Miss Moncrief the perspective of a potential publisher, thereby placing the conversation on a professional footing. He does this even though, from the beginning, Miss Moncrief had made it clear that publication was not her goal; when she first asked him to read her manuscript, she told him that she understood his opinion would be of little service "'in a business way'"; rather, she would value his "'assistance personally'" (Woolson 253). After his positive response, the writer tearfully exclaimed that his personal judgment was all that mattered to her: "My life was at a low ebb: if your sentence had been against me, it would have been my end" (258). When he confronts her with the query, "Was it not your idea that I might help you in obtaining a publisher?" (259), she answers, "Yes, yes," but her manner lacks enthusiasm, and she looks at him "apprehensively," her behavior at odds with her words. Instead of sympathizing with Miss Moncrief's confusion, the narrator sees her ambivalence as an opportunity to steer the conversation away from the unwanted intimacy: "I followed up my advantage, opened up the little paper volume and began to read." As in his treatment of the manuscript, the narrator's distancing of Miss Moncrief is an index of his discomfort with her and her work.

Dickinson's relationship with Higginson contains some of the same characteristics of uneasy partnership, discomfort, and distancing. When, during his summer 1870 visit, she tells Higginson of the powerfully unsettling effect poetry has on her, she could be describing, though in very different terms, the core aesthetic experience conveyed in "Miss Grief." Higginson records her having said that she knows when she is reading poetry because "it makes my whole body so cold no fire can ever warm me" and "feel physically as if the top of my head were taken off" (*L* 473-74, #342a). Like Miss Moncrief and the narrator, Dickinson models what it means to be a true and able reader. Also like Miss Moncrief, she appears to have found a reader for her poetry in her would-be editor.

In yet another parallel with Miss Moncrief's editor, Higginson had a problematic personal relationship with Dickinson. His ambivalence is perhaps best expressed in the letter he wrote to his wife describing his 1870 visit: "I never was with any one who drained my nerve power so much. Without touching her, she drew from me. I am glad not to live near her" (*L* 476, #342b).[2] Dickinson personally presented a challenge to Higginson that was matched by the challenge contained in her work. And, as was the case with Miss Moncrief's editor, his response seems designed to distance the poet. She was, again like Miss Moncrief, not primarily concerned with publishing but with finding an able reader for her work. But Higginson, like the narrator in "Miss Grief," pressed the publishing issue in a way that may have seemed to Dickinson like a diversionary tactic. "I smile when you suggest that I delay 'to publish'_that being foreign to my thought, as Firmament to Fin–," she writes in the June 1862 "Tribunal" letter (BPL Higg 52, *L* 408, #265). Dickinson's smile presents the possibility that Higginson's withdrawal into the rhetoric of publication is a familiar evasion on the part of readers who seek to control intimacy. Her smile is both sardonic and grateful, because the evasive tactic demonstrates that she has touched her reader, albeit too close for his comfort.

Both the real and fictional relationships between reader and writer I have been examining suggest that uneasiness dominates the reader's experience of powerful writing. The common ground between Woolson and Dickinson is not necessarily shared politics or ideology.[3] Rather, their most profound commonality lies in the fact that both encounter the difficulties inherent in developing a new aesthetic, one dependent on shaking up the reader instead of making him or her comfortable. This new aesthetic could be understood as the reader's experience of what Betsy Erkkila terms "'wickedness'" (15), that feature of women's writing that presents "unfixity, struggle, and ongoing transformation among and within women writers . . . as the underlying dynamics" (16). Both Dickinson and Woolson suggest that the reader's rightful habitation is on slippery ground. As a result, reading their work cannot be comforting, and may even be unpleasant; able readers may find themselves endorsing work they find deeply troubling. And we can see through Higginson and Miss Moncrief's editor that good readers may mistakenly believe they are on solid ground until they try to bring the work into line with conventional practice. In this sense, both Dickinson and Miss Moncrief use familiar means to coax their readers into uncharted territory. The poet who "Distills amazing sense / From ordinary Meanings" (*P* 448, *MBED* 465) may be wicked indeed.[4]

Like cartoon characters who unknowingly run beyond the edges of cliffs, readers attracted to the next word suddenly discover that the solid earth of print convention lies behind them. In Dickinson's poems and letters, this experience communicates variously as the "homelessness" readers and writers discover when they recognize that what most attracts them draws them away from domesticated verbal habitations. This is the point Mudge makes when she observes that "by equating home with consciousness, Emily did not solve a problem; she set herself one. She well knew that the . . . focus of her mind fluctuated, that her interior world turned, shifted, rose or sunk, that, in brief, it was in constant motion or change" (8). Thus, poets who seek to extend the limits of what is expressible learn "the Sovereign Anguish" that poem 167 ascribes to "'Laureates'" who stay their "homesick feet / Upon a foreign shore" (*MBED* 133). And readers, about whom we are told in "This was a Poet –," learn that the "Poet" who "Distills amazing sense / From ordinary Meanings . . . Entitles Us [readers] . . . To ceaseless Poverty" (*P* 448, *MBED* 465).

As these examples suggest, "homelessness" can be equated with an aesthetic coincident with thwarted expectations, a collapse of unity, and a wicked rejection of allegiances to identity, schools of thought, and historical tradition. Moreover, the prominence of house and home imagery in Dickinson's poems affirms that, for her, thwarting the desire for security is crucial to a reader's aesthetic. As an artist, she measures her success according to the degree that she can challenge the stability of discourse the reader trusts most. In this sense, her poems serve to vacate linguistic domains the reader believed the proven habitations of truth. Her spring 1876 letter to Higginson speaks to this point: "Nature is a Haunted House – but Art – a House that tries to be haunted" (*L* 553-54, #459a). As Mudge has noted, Dickinson here embeds "her aesthetic theory in the language of architecture" (147); that is, the artistic aim of capturing in language a sense of incompletely departed spirits. To make this house haunted, the artist must undermine assumptions of truth that readers invest in discourse, so that readers experience both the presence and the departure of that truth. The writer who succeeds will necessarily evoke feelings of resentment or anger as well as admiration.

It comes as no surprise, then, that Thomas Wentworth Higginson and Susan Huntington Gilbert Dickinson, certainly two of Dickinson's most important readers, had turbulent relationships with her. That Sue and Emily periodically expressed anger at one another should not be the basis for questioning their mutual respect when it comes to literary art; in fact, had their relationship been untroubled, we might have a stronger basis for doubting Sue's role as a primary reader. Martha Nell Smith suggests as much when she concludes that Dickinson's "singular relationship" with Sue "makes . . . a good standard of comparison for all of Dickinson's other relationships" (*Rowing* 33).

That stormy relationships often are based on sensitive readings is a point that Woolson makes with great force in her 1886 short story "At the Chateau of Corinne." Here Woolson points to the danger of assuming that an able reader could make a compatible life partner. Mrs. Katharine Winthrop, the protagonist, is a poet who chooses to marry a man who is one of the few among her readers who dislikes her poetry (Woolson 231). She marries him, we learn, because his antagonism for her writing passionately registers a force other readers have missed. As offended as she is by his accusations of "a certain sort of daring" that he considers "its essential, unpardonable sin" (233), his evaluation strikes her as not governed by convention; despite his outward conformity, she considers him "'the only man [she has] met in years who seems to feel no desire to flatter [her]'" (231).

When he finally proclaims his love for her, he does so in terms suggesting that his feelings have exceeded his control: "'Do with me as you please,' he beseeches her, 'I must bear it. But believe that I love you with all my heart. It has been against my will; I have not been willing to admit it to myself; but of late the certainty has forced itself upon me so overwhelmingly that I had no resource left save to come to you'" (Woolson 241). Katherine recognizes the timeliness of his proposal—it comes when she has lost her fortune—and assents to marriage, knowing that doing so means she will cease to write (246). This last astonishing concession comes after John admits that he is jealous of her strength as a writer. In this context, her acceding to silence places the power of her voice at the center of their marriage. By mutual agreement, then, her strength as an author is perpetually affirmed. A wicked solution, indeed!

The problems such a conclusion poses are, of course, plain, and my feeling is that Woolson wrote "At the Chateau of Corinne" as part of her larger project of outlining the options available to women artists in search of able readers. If, unlike Dickinson, women writers required economic security and sought to gain it without compromising their artistic achievement, marriage to a man humbled by their brilliance might have been appealing. Woolson, however, does not recommend this option. Rather, she seems to be saying that the attraction of such marriages may explain why more women are not publicly engaged in literary experimentation. At the other extreme, writers like Aarona Moncrief, who have sacrificed health and material well-being to create works of impeccable integrity, have likewise fallen outside of literary history.

And here is where Woolson's and Dickinson's interest in a readers' aesthetic touches on the issue of women writers and publication. In light of Woolson's concerns with the twin obscurities women found in marriage and spinsterhood, Dickinson emerges as a shrewd observer of the literary climate of her day. She might even have figured as the exemplary artist in a Woolson story who possessed family wealth sufficient to write without peril to her health, as well as the savvy to appreciate the liabilities attached to any single reader, no matter how able he or she may have been. As a result she did what Aarona Moncrief and Katherine Winthrop were incapable of doing: she did not seek publication and she never stopped writing. "How dreary –," she wrote in "I'm Nobody! Who are you?" (*P* 288), "to be _ Somebody! / How public — like a Frog –/ To tell your] one's name – the livelong / June –/ To an admiring Bog!" (*MBED* 209). She would bide her time.

Notes

INTRODUCTION

1. PF #19, *L*914, ACL. All references to Dickinson's letters and prose fragments come from Thomas H. Johnson and Theodora Ward's *The Letters of Emily Dickinson*. In all citations I precede the page number(s) with an italicized capital L (*L*) and give the prose fragment (PF) or letter number preceded by the symbol #. (ACL) indicates that the manuscript is located under the PF number at Amherst College Library.

2. See the variorum for a more complete analysis of poems written each year, as well as an account of rough and fair copy (Dickinson, *The Poems of Emily Dickinson*, ed. Johnson, 1201).

3. In all references to Dickinson's poems, I cite the Johnson variorum numbers prefixed with an italicized capital P (*P*), and I provide page numbers for Franklin's *The Manuscript Books of Emily Dickinson* (*MBED*). When no manuscript exists, or when a manuscript is not contained in the Franklin edition, I make a special note: (no ms.) indicates that no holograph manuscript exists; (ACL) indicates that the holograph manuscript is not in Franklin and but can be located according to the Johnson number at the Amherst College Library. This procedure provides the information necessary to locate holograph manuscripts for all the poems considered in this study. When manuscripts exist in addition to Franklin's fascicles and sheets, the variorum states where. In most instances, I indicate either in the text or in a note when more than one manuscript version of a poem exists.

All discussions of the poems are based on manuscript readings. One of my motives is practical: print versions of the poems are based on editorial translations of Dickinson's chirography, whereas the manuscripts present the poems as Dickinson left them. My other motive is to base readings on the totality of Dickinson's visual arrangements; punctuation and lineation, for example, acquire meaning within interconnected visual, syntactic, and semantic systems, not in isolation. Even when my conclusions do not differ markedly from those based on print versions, my procedure ensures that all Dickinson built into the poem has at least been available for my consideration. Photographic facsimiles of the poems and letters contained in this work may not be as revealing as the actual manuscripts, but they capture more of what she wrote than any print format. Nevertheless, I attempt to match print to Dickinson's chirography as closely as possible.

I owe much to recent Dickinson scholarship for clarifying the importance of Dickinson's manuscripts. Susan Howe's work with calligraphy has opened many eyes to Dickinson's visual intentions and her resistance to print conventions. At the end of *The Birth-mark* Howe summarizes her rationale for including holographs and attempting to capture manuscript peculiarities in print (152-53). Martha Nell Smith shares Howe's perception that Dickinson's poems and letters are a form of manuscript art that eludes containment in print: "By her handwritten productions, she deprived a primarily male corps of its copyright on what constitutes serious poetic technique" (*Rowing in Eden* 61). Smith argues further that Dickinson "published" herself through her correspondence and manuscript books (15-16). In *Choosing Not Choosing*, Sharon Cameron focuses on the fascicles, recommending that they be viewed as Dickinson "might herself have regarded them: as definitive, if privately published, texts" (8). Like Howe and Smith, Cameron sees variants as integral to poetic structure.

4. See the opening of *Comic Power in Emily Dickinson* (1-6) where Juhasz, Miller, and Smith provide a good overview of recent efforts to connect the person and the poetry. See also Juhasz, *The Undiscovered Continent* (2-14).

5. The many voices that I argue are central to her poems frequently depart from this stereotypic image. For this reason, I believe that Dickinson's status as stereotypic spinster may have been instrumental in elevating her sensitivity to the way language enforces cultural values that unacceptably restrict thought and behavior. Though discussion of the spinster is not a central concern of this study, it is useful to think of Dickinson as exposing strands in the web of conformity that she struggled with personally. In Mary Daly's words, spinsters like Dickinson turn their marginalized identities to positive ends by illuminating and thereby reducing the power of patriarchy to impose false consciousness: "Absorbed in Spinning, in the ludic cerebration which is both work and play, Spinsters span the dichotomies of false consciousness and break its mindbinding combinations" (386).

6. See Erika Scheurer in "'Near, but remote': Emily Dickinson's Epistolary Voice" for further discussion of the way language "must *also* periodically, temporarily *stop:* become whole, tangible, embodied" (89).

7. Porter offers a wonderful description of his discovery of the importance of Dickinson's manuscripts:

> Finding Dickinson requires an intricate going-back-through. A reader must penetrate the print that she did not authorize, with its straight lines and capitals, its even margins and spacing, the stanzaic regularity, the *visual deftness*; go through the contorted syntax and beyond the unanchored tropes; back despite the absent tissue of her work and through her reclusion and her silence to the immediacy of the scraps and pencil. Formalist criticism, my own earlier studies included, worked from the book and the Dickinson who emerged was a formalist creation. Printing of necessity had done to her what camera and editing do to the live performance of an actor, and so formalism has missed the deepest and fullest identity. The critical convenience of seeing her poems as one long poem is a further distortion of the fact of the text. [3]

8. Two manuscripts for this poem exist. Johnson uses a variant located at the Amherst College Library that is probably based on the fascicle version I have employed. That version eliminates word variants, alters lineation, and eliminates stanza breaks, but otherwise retains much of the fascicle's open-endedness. Even though discussions of manuscript variations would be illuminating, my focus here is on the way the fascicle poem resists print conventions visible in the 1891 published version.

9. As Gilbert and Gubar argue in *The Madwoman in the Attic,* dashes are extremely important in exposing the seams erased by monologic discourse: "Tiny and clear, they are elegant as 'Tucks—of dainty interspersion,' fine stitches joining split thoughts seam to seam" (641). In the next chapter I explore the way dashes make a special contribution to the centrifugal force of Dickinson's poems; here I am more interested in establishing the general sense that many manuscript features dialogize language.

10. My discussion of performance here and elsewhere takes into account the ways Dickinson's poems notify readers of their role in the creation of meaning. For this to happen, the poems must cease to function transparently and instead call attention to their status as symbolic structures. Only then can readers act with awareness of their own power to authorize meaning. Juhasz, Miller, and Smith make an important observation about this dimension of performance: "Theories of reading and performance question whether or not a literary text can exist outside its reading performances. . . . Outside interpretation, it might be said, literature devolves to meaningless marks on the page" (*Comic* 13). My point is that Dickinson presents readers with such a plenitude of possible meanings that language actually becomes the marks on the page. Readers then act with the understanding that they make the marks meaningful.

11. Keeping the voices straight is not always easy. Malini Johar Schueller explains this general difficulty in dialogic readings:

> This notion of the speaking voice is far more complex than (although it includes) related concepts used by narratologists and reader response critics. . . . Shifts in syntax and tone may indicate different voices even within passages demarcated as direct speech. On the other hand, because a word is 'born in a dialogue as a living rejoinder within it,' there are different interacting voices within each word. Each word participates in a network of social interactions. *Voice* thus refers to an ideological speaking presence in the text, whether broadly thematic (though these are not synonymous) or minutely lexical. At no point, however, is it possible to identify all the voices in a text or an utterance so that it has a definite social or ideological referent.
> [*The Politics of Voice*, 9-10]

12. See Cameron's *Choosing Not Choosing,* Howe's *The Birth-mark,* and Smith's *Rowing in Eden.* Each of these authors incorporates holographs into her text and works out a different strategy for representing manuscripts in print.

13. The Dickinson Editorial Collective was organized in 1992 following the first international Emily Dickinson conference. For more information about this organization see Martha Nell Smith's "The Importance of a Hypermedia Archive of Dickinson's Creative Work" in *Emily Dickinson Journal* (4.1:75-85).

CHAPTER 1. DASHES AND THE LIMITS OF DISCOURSE

1. Wylder proposed that Dickinson used the dashes as elocutionary marks based on Ebenezer Porter's *The Rhetorical Reader,* a textbook Dickinson studied. With Porter's influence on Dickinson as her guide, Wylder argues that the poet's "punctuation system is an integral part of her attempt to create in written form the precision of meaning inherent in the tone of the human voice" (4). Her understanding of the dash, then, appears to rest on viewing it as a device Dickinson uses to narrow the

range of meanings otherwise available to written language. But despite her apparent belief that the dash restricts meanings, Wylder writes of the monotone notation (flat dash): "surely the monotone is a guarded tone (and therefore often ambiguous)" (44).

2. The text for this poem comes from *Poems 1890-1896 by Emily Dickinson,* a facsimile reproduction of the Todd-Higginson editions, edited by George Monteiro (1967).

3. See Margaret Dickie's analysis of the ambiguity of "simple News" (*Lyric Contingencies,* 33).

4. Evidence of established discourse presenting Nature as sympathetic, even motherly, are abundant. I will draw from two widely known sources to briefly anchor this point.

The opening lines to Lydia Sigourney's famous poem "The Mother of Washington" present Nature as honoring George Washington's mother though her grave has been neglected by the living:

> Long hast thou slept unnoted. Nature stole
> In her soft ministry around thy bed,
> Spreading her vernal tissue, violet-gemmed,
> And pearled with dews.
> [Walker, *American Women Poets of the Nineteenth Century,* 5-6]

The audience of the poem receives instruction from Nature's example and reverently acknowledges the achievements of motherhood: "But now we come / To do thee homage—mother of our chief!" In this way motherhood acquires special virtue as a reflection of Nature's mothering.

Nature is even more directly linked to motherhood in Longfellow's poem "Nature":

> As a fond mother, when the day is o'er,
>   Leads by the hand her little child to bed,
> . . . .
> So Nature deals with us, . . .
> [McQuade, *The Harper American Literature* 2128]

5. Sharon Cameron dedicates much of her argument in *Choosing Not Choosing* to exploring Dickinson's rejection of the notion of exteriority. In a portion of her argument that relates directly to the dash, she takes up Geoffrey Hartman's assertion that Dickinson's dash functions like a hymen "'because it both joins and divides'" (quoted in *Choosing* 3). Cameron argues that "what the dash emphasizes is not in fact singularity, 'stasis,' or 'impasse,' as Hartman claims, but rather that unboundedness which admits of making radical connections" (179n).

My understanding is that the dash awakens readers to the way they consciously or unconsciously consent to the closure required by the exclusive logic of discourse. Dickinson's poems demonstrate that external authority depends on the consent readers grant whenever they speak and therefore enter history. One part of her poetry, then, illustrates the contingent nature of exteriority while affirming its reality. At the same time, she presents individual decisions as occurring in socially and politically charged environments where language must work against itself in order to loosen the hold of preexisting discourse. In this sense, thought is always related to language and can never originate in an Edenic wilderness uninformed by processes of socialization.

6. Even though Bakhtin is well known for having stated in "Discourse in the Novel" that "in the majority of poetic genres (poetic in the narrow sense) . . . the internal dialogization of discourse is not put to artistic use . . . and is artificially extinguished" (*Dialogic Imagination* 284), I am using his thought as a means of clarifying Emily Dickinson's poetics. I do so precisely because she does not write with a unified voice but rather employs a multitude of speakers whose utterances are the primary subject of the poems. As Tzvetan Todorov observes in *Mikhail Bakhtin: The Dialogical Principle*, "It isn't that the representation of discourse, and therefore of its utterer, is impossible in poetry, but it just isn't aesthetically valorized there as it is in prose" (64). In "The Problem of the Text," written near the end of his life, Bakhtin himself questions the possibility that any creative use of language could be as devoid of dialogism as he had previously thought was the case with poetry:

"Is not any writer (even the pure lyricist) always a 'dramaturge' in the sense that he directs all words to others' voices, including to the image of the author (and to other authorial masks)? Perhaps any literal, single-voiced word is naive and unsuitable for authentic creativity" (*Speech Genres and Other Late Essays*, 110).

My reading of Dickinson suggests that her poetry displays many of the traits the young Bakhtin considered the exclusive domain of the novel. A precise determination of genre is less important than is finding ways to discuss the functions of speakers and voices in the poems. Perhaps the best solution is to think of Dickinson not as poetic in the "narrow sense" the young Bakhtin had in mind but as perfectly poetic in the broader sense the elder Bakhtin perceives even in "the purist lyricist."

7. Porter offers these conclusions in *Dickinson: The Modern Idiom*: "Dickinson's poems do not invoke a full world. Instead, they are the vast hoard of a traveler's snapshots without an itinerary of the trip or a map showing the destination" (293). Greg Johnson responds to Porter's comments by admitting that the poems "may appear to be 'utter miscellaneousness'" but actually represent "the vast range of a mind . . . compelled to record every stage of its quest" (8). In *Emily Dickinson: Perception and the Poet's Quest*, Johnson sets out to show that Dickinson does in fact provide a map: "Although many of her poems typically describe lyric 'moments' of insight, these moments may be safely placed at various points along a critically conceived map of the poet's movement toward knowledge and a final, idealized illumination" (6).

My position is much closer to Stonum's. He points out that Dickinson's departure from established "authorial practice" exposes the way "other writers exert considerably more control over how their works are to be read and over what aims and standards they are to be judged against" (*The Dickinson Sublime*, 8). In a conclusion that could apply equally to Johnson, Stonum states that "Porter's assumptions about normal and desirable literary practice indicate an overwhelmingly author-centered esthetics" that has "long been central to our understanding of literature and which has especially dominated romantic and postromantic values" (8-9) Accordingly, "our expectations about the author's directive role lend themselves to specifically heroic conceptions of literary vocation" (9).

8. A single closing bracket ( ]) immediately following a word, as with "Vol-canic]" here, indicates that a manuscript variant follows. In this instance, "Volcano" is the variant for "Volcanic."

9. Roseanne Hoefel similarly points to Dickinson's movement away from exclusivity. In "Emily Dickinson Fleshing Out a New World," she observes that Dickinson "is dreaming of a new discourse . . . one *not* based on binary opposites and thus exclusivity" (64).

10. The sense of "romanticism" used here comes directly from a standard handbook definition that defines the term in the following manner: "Although *romanticism* tends at times to regard nature as alien, it more often sees in nature a revelation of Truth, the 'living garment of God,' and a more suitable subject for art than those aspects of the world sullied by artifice" (Holman and Harmon, *A Handbook to Literature*, 416). My point is that Dickinson does not subscribe to either the view that nature is alien or that "Truth" exists independent of human perception.

11. Cynthia Griffin Wolff argues convincingly for the influence of William Paley's *Natural Theology* and his "'Argument from Design'" in her biography, *Emily Dickinson* (80-83).

12. See Wendy Barker's *Lunacy of Light: Emily Dickinson and the Experience of Metaphor* (especially 55-73) for more on the way Dickinson's use of sun imagery moves beyond traditional associations with male power; see also Martha Nell Smith's comments on Susan as the subject of sun imagery (*Rowing*, especially 114). In later chapters, I look more closely at some of the ways Dickinson departs from this traditional figure for male power. At this point, however, the approach suggested by Pollak establishes the appropriate context for reading "A Wife – at Daybreak –" (*P* 461, *MBED* 781).

13. Three manuscript versions of this poem exist. Johnson bases his text on the third version, not the second (fascicle) version that I have drawn from here. In constructing his text, Johnson follows closely the lineation of the Mabel Loomis Todd transcription housed in the Amherst College Library. All three Dickinson versions present line breaks that Johnson regularizes in the variorum. My contention is that Dickinson's lineation violates common ballad and common measure meter in order to isolate or quote accepted discourse for the purpose of interrogating it. By following Loomis Todd's lead, I believe Johnson has significantly effaced an important feature of Dickinson's poem.

Here are transcriptions of the initial penciled version and the third version Johnson uses. Readers can readily see that Dickinson consistently rejected regularized lineation. This is the penciled version:

> A Wife – at Daybreak
> I shall be –
> Sunrise – hast thou a flag for me?
> At midnight – I am yet a
> maid –   5
>
> How short it takes to make
> it Bride!
> Then – Midnight – I have passed
> from thee
>   *over*
> Unto the East – and Victory –   10
> Midnight – Good night – I hear
> them call –
> The Angels bustle in the hall ⌐
> Softly – my Future climbs the
> stair ⌐
> I fumble at my Childhood's
> prayer –

So soon to be a Child – no more –
~~The Vision flutters in the door~~ -
Master – I've seen the face   20
before ⌐
     Eternity! I'm coming, Sir –

The third version:

A Wife ⌐ at Daybreak
I shall be –
Sunrise – Hast thou
a Flag for me?
At Midnight, I am   5
but a Maid,
How short it takes to
make it Bride –
Then ⌐ Midnight, I have
passed from thee   10
Unto the East, and
Victory –
Midnight – Good Night!
I hear them call ⌐
The Angels bustle in   15
the Hall –
Softly my Future climbs
the Stair,
I fumble at my Childhood's
prayer   20
So soon to be a Child
no more –
Eternity, I'm coming ⌐
Sir,
Savior – I've seen   25
the face – before!

All three versions are located at the Amherst College Library.

    14. Harriet Beecher Stowe provides an excellent example of the way the expectation of dramatic personal change was commonly associated with marriage. In a 6 January 1836 letter to Georgiana May, the as-yet-single Miss Beecher informs her friend of an absence of transformation similar to that expressed by the bride in Dickinson's poem: "Well, my dear G., about half an hour more and your old friend, and companion, school mate, sister, etc. will cease to be Hattie Beecher, and change to nobody knows who. My dear, you are engaged, and pledged in a year or 2 to encounter a similar fate, and do you wish to know how you shall feel? Well, my dear, I have been dreading and dreading the time, and lying awake all last week wondering how I should live through this overwhelming crisis, and lo! it has come, and I feel *nothing at all*" (Lerner 59). I provide a more detailed commentary on this letter and Dickinson's in chapter 5.

    15. Bakhtin comments on the relationship of consummation or wholeness to the life of the subject in "Author and Hero in Aesthetic Activity." As I explain in chap-

ter 5, his choice of terms is particularly appropriate and even playful when applied to the bride who speaks in this poem: "If I am consummated and my life is consummated, I am no longer capable of living and acting. For in order to live and act, I need to be unconsummated, I need to be open for myself—at least in all the essential moments constituting my life; I have to be, for myself, someone who is axiologically yet-to-be, someone who does not coincide with his already existing makeup" (*Art and Answerability*, 13).

Chapter 2. Playing with Elite and Popular Traditions

1. Dale M. Bauer and S. Janet McKinstry provide a helpful overview of feminist dialogics in their introduction to *Feminism, Bakhtin, and the Dialogic*. They take the position that "a feminist dialogics is not agonistic or oppositional; it also suggests an identity in dialectical response, always open and ongoing" (3).

2. Jerome J. McGann describes what I am referring to as the reader's awareness of the poem's physicality in *Social Values and Poetic Acts*. There he analyzes the way certain poems draw attention to the ideological horizons within which they are situated in order to loosen the hold of these same ideologies. In the process, a certain kind of "poetic performativity" challenges the dominance of "ideological performativity": "Although the work defines itself, ideologically, in relation to a particular point of view within a specific horizon of human interests, the representational structure of poetic discourse multiplies and complicates the communicative act. Poetic performativity overtakes and finally overcomes ideological performativity as the poetic strives to thicken and realize the entirety of the communicative field" (91). I am calling this thickening of the communicative field the emergence of physicality that occurs as communicative possibilities displace the communication of discrete meanings. The poem performs on this physical level when linguistic transparency disperses sufficiently to make opacity a part of the reader's experience.

3. Bakhtin and Kristeva attend to the relation of historical change to artistic innovation in ways that both extend and complement Buell's argument. Bakhtin asserts that periods of intensified historical change reduce monologic claims on artistic discourse (*Marxism and the Philosophy of Language*, 23-24; see also Todorov, *Bakhtin*, 58), and Kristeva observes that poetic language "accompanies crises within social structures and institutions—the moments of their mutation, evolution, revolution, or disarray" (*Desire in Language*, 125).

4. Elizabeth Phillips describes the demands on Dickinson's time in *Emily Dickinson: Personae and Performance*, 23ff. Jay Leyda also records numerous events related to the war that affected Amherst life, especially the death of Frazar Stearns (*The Years and Hours of Emily Dickinson*, 49-50). More directly, Leyda includes a letter Dickinson sent to Louise and Frances Norcross late in 1862. The document is worth noting because it describes the growing influence of the war on her daily experience. "Sorrow seems more general then it did, and not the estate of a few persons, since the war began; and if the anguish of others helped one with one's own, now would be many medicines. 'Tis dangerous to value, for only the precious can alarm. I noticed that Robert Browning had made another poem, and was astonished—till I remembered that I, myself, in my smaller way, sang off charnel steps" (*Letters*, 1931; quoted in Leyda, *Years*, 2:72).

5. In *The Politics of Domesticity*, Barbara Leslie Epstein defines the sphere appropriate for female aspiration: "Girls were told to limit their aspirations to marriage

and motherhood and to cultivate modesty and malleability appropriate to a dependent role. They were advised to quell whatever ambitions they might have" (74). Carroll Smith-Rosenberg defines the "Cult of True Womanhood" created by "the new bourgeois men of the 1820s, 1830s, and the 1840s" as similarly confining women to "a female role bounded by the kitchen and nursery, overlaid with piety and purity, and crowned with subservience" (*Disorderly Conduct*, 13).

6. Opening a correspondence with Higginson is evidence of Dickinson's affinity for revolutionary change. His participation in the effort to grant blacks full standing as citizens plays into well established alliances between female reform movements and abolitionism. Though Dickinson did not openly agitate for political change, much of my discussion argues that she quietly waged war on the field of language—a symbol system that always extends far beyond the purely private. Her highly ironic 1862 poem "I cannot dance upon my Toes – / No Man instructed me ‿ " (*P* 326, *MBED*, 411-12) is but one example of the many poems that undermine power imbalances central to patriarchal politics.

7. Because I advocate an inclusive approach to Dickinson's poems, my aim is to add to the body of existing readings, not to impose limits. My purpose is to affirm the contributions of all perceptive readings, like the one Maryanne M. Garbowsky provides in her book *The House without the Door*. There she argues that "the mental, emotional, and physical states described here are identical with panic attack" (95). The one disagreement I might have with critics like Garbowsky is that their interpretations often are presented as definitive explanations of Dickinson's poems. I am convinced that no matter how profound Dickinson's psychological trauma, or her romantic disappointment, she was also an artist who crafted her poems in a manner sensitive to the work of other writers. A full picture of the poet's work must therefore examine her poems in terms of their commentary on prevailing cultural practice.

8. In his discussion of this poem, Johnson presents both "Bosom" and "Buckle" as variants for "Boddice." This seems right. Seeing all three words as potentially functioning in that line further underscores the speaker's growing confusion at the tide's invasion of her private self. The reader's consideration of variants on the bottom of the second page interrupts reading, requires considerable eye movement, and the turning of the page necessary to shift vision between "Boddice" and the variants. Dickinson's introduction of these demands establishes a physical link between the speaker's agitation and the reader's experience. Doing so also draws attention to the physical and constructed nature of the poem by requiring that readers participate in the authorial role of considering word choices.

9. This element of romanticism is clearly identified by M.H. Abrams in *The Mirror and the Lamp:* "(1) Poetry is true in that it corresponds to a Reality transcending the world of sense" (313). "(2) Poetry is true in that poems exist, are very valuable, and are the product and cause of actual emotional and imaginative experiences" (314).

10. Gerardine Meaney provides an incisive historical overview of the sublime from Longinus to Kristeva in *(Un)Like Subjects* (192-214). Central to the experience of the sublime, she argues, is "the identification of subject with object, the loss of self in other, which is the sublime state" (208). In this state, "the space which western philosophy has constructed as the space in which 'I' exist" collapses into "the internal space which is 'I'." Part of my argument is that in Dickinson's writing this "I" has been so consistently exposed as the product of social construction that there is no binary distinction between self and other to collapse. In my view, the sublime is an ideal born out of ontological dualism that loses meaning as it is absorbed in Dickinson's inclusive poetics. Kristeva's description of the sublime in *Powers of Horror* further asserts the

dependence of the sublime on the existence of an "I": "Not at all short of but always with and through perception and words, the sublime is a *something added* that expands us, overstrains us, and causes us to be both *here*, as dejects, and *there*, as others and sparkling" (12). I am arguing that this split between here and there is a characteristic of the self in language, a self Dickinson acknowledges; but her purpose is to claim the prevocal self not yet subject to the binary logic that presupposes such separations. Therefore, according to my reading the sublime provides a solution to the alienation or abjection of a self that has forgotten its infinite potential. Dickinson's aim is to awaken readers to that self.

11. Ronald J. Zboray argues in "Antebellum Reading and the Ironies of Technological Innovation" that "the capitalization of printing—seen most readily in stereotyping and electrotyping—altered the relationship of publishers to authors and, through advertising, to readers" (182). More to the point, Buell writes of the deliberate rejection of the ideal of "genteel amateurism" by younger writers: "The continual breakdown of the ideal is seen in the younger writers who found support in Emerson (often to his discomfort) for anticonventional, risk-taking commitment to their expressive gift at the cost of forfeiting any chance of integration into the ranks of the socially proper. Among them were Thoreau, Ellery Channing, and Emily Dickinson, all of whom cultivated the sense of their differentness and, in their more confident moments, positively rejoiced in the thought that their writings were caviar to the general. 'Give me a sentence,' demands Thoreau, 'which no intelligence can understand'" (*New England Literary Culture*, 62).

12. Dickinson's parodic treatment of Emerson is not in itself a novel literary gesture, though her decision to mock him would certainly have necessitated a degree of daring. Perhaps the most famous of all parodies of the eyeball passage is that by Thoreau in *Walden*. At the beginning of the "Solitude" chapter, he describes himself walking "along the stony shore of the pond" imbibing "delight through every pore" (174). Having shifted his organ of perception from Emerson's eye and its intellectual connotations to the far more earthy pore, Thoreau completes his inversion of Emerson by concluding that there is nothing of particular interest in the scene he has described: "I see nothing special to attract me."

13. Susan M. Anderson's essay "'Regard[ing] a Mouse' in Dickinson's Poems and Letters" argues that Dickinson's use of the mouse figure "does not mean that she invokes triviality or smallness" (85). Writing specifically of "I started Early," Anderson makes the case that the speaker's mouselike appearance enables her to dupe men into mistaken confidence in the power they have over her. She then uses their unfounded confidence to enhance the considerable power she unleashes when she "started – too." My reading of the poem differs from Anderson's, but her sensitivity to the deceptive character of imagery like the mouse is an important feature of Dickinson's style that I also see in much of Dickinson's writing.

14. Roland Hagenbüchle's essay "Sign and Process" is particularly useful in pinning down differences between the two writers' understandings of language. The following conclusion bears directly on the function of transparency in Emerson and Dickinson: "All this evidence points to the conclusion that the dependence of language on nature as found in Emerson contrasts sharply with Dickinson's emphasis that words are part of an autonomous symbolic system" (141). He makes the point even more forcefully later in the essay: "The organic unity between nature and the poetic artifact, however, which for Emerson and the other Transcendentalists is a basic assumption, runs counter to [Dickinson's] whole poetic credo" (151).

Margaret Homans also stresses Dickinson's rejection of the transparency so central to Emerson. "To achieve his proof of the transparency between natural facts and spiritual facts," she writes, he uses analogies "between the seasons and the sequence of human life," for instance, that "figure largely in Dickinson's poems, but their validity is constantly questioned" (*Women Writers and Poetic Identity,* 183).

CHAPTER 3. DASH AND VOICE IN THE LETTERS

1. The manuscript for this document is located at the Houghton Library of Harvard University, in box nine of the Dickinson Papers.
2. Judith Farr's analysis of Sue's obituary usefully clarifies the significance of Sue's describing Dickinson as a poet. Farr argues that Sue wrote the obituary "at a time when she was somewhat alienated from Emily and Lavinia" (*The Passion of Emily Dickinson,* 11) as a result of Austin's involvement with Mabel Loomis Todd. That she should have written the obituary testifies to the family's "reluctant respect for her long friendship" with the poet. Farr notes particularly Sue's "remarkable linkage of Dickinson's 'worth' with her 'work'": presenting Dickinson as a poet meant positioning her outside the sphere appropriate to "a proper lady in the nineteenth century." The tensions Farr identifies as part of the obituary's composition and content further heighten concerns with audience that I see as central to Sue's comments.
   Martha Nell Smith writes extensively of Sue's intimate participation in Dickinson's life as a poet. See especially "To Be Susan Is Imagination: Dickinson's Poetry Workshop" and "Fame Is a Fickle Food: 'Sister Sue' as Producer of Poems" in *Rowing.* Smith concentrates on Sue's obituary notice at the beginning of the latter chapter (207-12).
3. HCL refers to Harvard College Library, where this letter is listed in the letters to the Hollands (H).
4. Marta L. Werner offers an exceptionally clear overview of what might be considered primary stages in the development of Dickinson's style. Her *Emily Dickinson's Open Folios: Scenes of Reading, Surfaces of Writing* concentrates on writing after 1870, when Dickinson abandons the fascicles to more completely "inscribe herself outside institutional accounts of order" (4). Drawing largely on the work of Susan Howe, Sharon Cameron, Martha Nell Smith, Jeanne Holland, and R.W. Franklin, Werner implies three distinct phases: the period up to 1858 or 1859, when Dickinson begins to assemble the fascicles; the period from 1858 or 1859 to 1870, when Dickinson abandons the fascicle project; and the period of radical experimentation that extends from 1870 until Dickinson's death. My concern in this chapter is primarily with the earliest phase and roughly the first third of the second.
   I see Dickinson beginning to make the stylistic decisions that will characterize her poetry as early as 1849. According to my way of thinking, the fascicles conclude a decade of experimentation during which time Dickinson defines her poetic identity and rejects editorial conventions as unacceptably restrictive. My treatment of letters written following Dickinson's initial correspondence with Higginson in 1862 aims at demonstrating stylistic and thematic consistency after that time. The consistency I see grows out of illocality and might be described as the embracing of open-endedness that Werner and many others identify as source for further experimentation.
5. HCL L54 indicates Harvard College Library, number 54 in the collection preserved by Lavinia Norcross Dickinson or Susan Gilbert Dickinson or their heirs.

6. Richard Rorty is useful in thinking about the way Dickinson's use of voices relates to assumptions about knowledge that validate conventional discourse. When Dickinson rejects the monologic language evident in the letters of the mid-forties, she does so by reintroducing the dash and establishing multiple voices for each speaker. This move suggests that thought is not unified but discontinuous, that decisions are founded on specific circumstances and not certainty. In *Philosophy and the Mirror of Nature*, Rorty argues that all knowledge is propositional and that we have much to gain by dropping the search for certainty and instead proceeding with the understanding that all discourse is provisional. Such an approach treats discourse as conversation rather than the presentation of unified givens founded on a reality that determines and hence limits human perception: "If we see knowledge as a matter of conversation and of social practice, rather than as an attempt to mirror nature, we will not be likely to envision a metapractice which will be the critique of all possible forms of social practice" (171).

In stating this position, Rorty advocates the liberation of individual thought from conformity to external standards not grounded in individual belief. By shifting the focus of the search for knowledge from "the relation between human beings and the objects of their inquiry to the relation between alternative standards of justification" (390), Rorty establishes a basis for the sort of dialogic conversation that Dickinson presents in her poems. Rorty helps clarify Dickinson's wish to remain open to alternative discourses and not mistake "home" for the limitations of any single point of view, no matter how comforting such a home might prove.

7. At this stage in her writing, Dickinson is experimenting with forms of punctuation; the mark that resembles a circumflex occurs with some frequency in this letter and other letters of this period. In my view, this circumflex and other variations reflect a stage of experimentation that culminates in the construction of the fascicles that begins in 1858 or 1859. Once fascicle construction begins, Dickinson's placement of marks becomes an integral feature of her visual art that she monitors closely. After she ceases constructing fascicles around 1870, she expands the visual effects that became increasingly prominent in later fascicles and that Martha Nell Smith, Jeanne Holland, and Marta Werner have remarked on in their studies. I see the circumflex as part of a less structured period of experimentation, in which Dickinson is exploring options for punctuation that disrupts the prose line. I leave to later studies the precise determination of what the circumflex signals to the reader; for my purposes, it can be read as part of the category of marks designated dashes that introduce varying degrees of disjunction.

8. Referring to critical comments in a recent letter from her brother, Austin, Dickinson responds with the following narrative in her 29 June 1851 letter to him:

> I feel quite like retiring, in presence of one so grand, and casting my small lot among small birds, and fishes – you say you dont comprehend me, you want a simpler style. *Gratitude* indeed for all my fine philosophy! I strove to be exalted thinking I might reach *you* and while I pant and struggle and climb the nearest cloud, you walk out very leisurely in your slippers from Empyrean, and without the *slightest* notice request me to get down! As *simple* as you please, the *simplest* sort of simple – I'll be a little ninny – a little pussy cat, a little Red Riding Hood.
> [*L* 117, #45]

Eleven years later, Dickinson expresses a similarly disdainful response to criticism of her style. This time her remarks are directed to an established critic she has never met, a man who will play an increasingly important role in her life as she contemplates the possibility of publishing. The following passage from a 7 June 1862 letter to Thomas Wentworth Higginson will be explored at greater length later in this chapter:

> You think my gait
> "spasmodic" – I am
> in danger – Sir –
> You think me "un-
> controlled" – I have
> no Tribunal.
> [BPL Higg 52; *L* 409, #265]

9. The manuscript is located at the Boston Public Library, listed in the Higginson papers as Higg 112. Johnson and Ward judge the metrics and use of capitals that begin with "And then" and conclude with "by it / yet –" sufficient basis for setting these lines apart from the text as a distinct quatrain. I respect Dickinson's decision to leave the lines embedded in the letter. Her arrangement asks more from her reader and by doing so both honors the eye and ear of her friend—by assuming that she can spot the lines on her own—and invites her to share in Dickinson's unorthodox fusion of poetry and letter genres. Part of the compliment to Helen Hunt Jackson, then, is the inserting of conventional poetic features within a letter. Dickinson's decision to do this is important as a formal innovation that significantly influences the way the words are read. For that reason, I believe that placing the lines in a conventional quatrain setting unacceptably alters the meanings available through Dickinson's arrangement. I do not impose quatrain form on any of the letters.

10. Dickinson's August 1860 letter to Bowles demonstrates how playful she could be, even when asking for forgiveness: "I am much ashamed. I misbehaved tonight. I would like to sit in the dust. I fear I am your little friend no more, but Mrs Jim Crow. I am sorry I smiled at women" (*L* 366, #223). An October 1861 letter to Bowles demonstrates how Dickinson could combine intimacy with humor and a declaration of imaginative power: "Cant I bring you something? My little Balm might be *o'erlooked* by wiser eyes – you know – Have you tried the Breeze that swings the Sign – or the Hoof of the Dandelion? *I* own 'em – wait for *mine*!" "This is all I have to say – Kinsmen need say nothing – but 'Swiveller' may be sure of the 'Marchioness'" (*L* 382, #241).

11. The "continuum" referred to here is a natural outgrowth of Dickinson's close focus on the experience of speaking subjects seeking to express themselves in language. Because her poems concentrate on the subject's relation to discourses within culture, her language is necessarily dialogic and resistant to any single version of truth. Julia Kristeva refers to this logic as the "*power of the continuum*" that "transgresses rules of linguistic code and social morality" by never privileging a monologic narrative ("Word" 41). As Kristeva states in *Revolution in Poetic Language,* "poetic language puts the subject in process/on trial through a network of marks and semiotic facilitations" (58). Once "on trial," the subject transgresses the restrictive boundaries of social identity emerging as a potentially new identity in an altered context. This process informs the range of speakers in Dickinson poems whose voices span the intellectual and emotional spectrum from initial self-consciousness to deliberate self-creation. For the sake of brevity, I encapsulate this spectrum under the general headings of child, bride, and Queen.

12. Letters in brackets indicate the order of holograph pages.

13. Susan M. Anderson's analysis of mouse imagery in this letter presents similar conclusions about Dickinson's skill at manipulating readers. She argues that Dickinson is actually displaying her poetic ability while professing need for a mentor: "In a statement that claims to admit her inadequacy as a poet, then, Dickinson attests to the sophistication of her poetic skills" ("'Regard[ing] a Mouse,'" 87).

14. Robert McClure Smith analyzes Dickinson's frequent reversal of male and female roles in traditional seduction scenes where she invests the seemingly dependent and weak female with startling rhetorical power. In the first of two essays treating this subject, his conclusion applies directly to the use of irony I have identified in Dickinson's fifth letter to Higginson: "in creating that subversively ironic space, Dickinson . . . uses the mechanism of rhetorical seduction to wrench authority away from her correspondent in order personally to assume it" ("'Inferential Knowledge—The Distinctest One,'" 238). Smith's second essay more specifically addresses the way Dickinson's poems make use of similar rhetorical poses: "When the female speaker of a Dickinson poem appears to set up and validate a traditional male/female hierarchy within the scene of seduction, she is simultaneously engaged in a subtle questioning and sometimes an inversion of the very same power coordinates that support that hierarchy" ("'He' Asked If I Was His," 60).

15. Thomas H. Johnson identifies 1862, 1863, and 1864 as Dickinson's most prolific years. In the variorum he attributes 366 poems to 1862; 141 to 1863; and 174 to 1864 (1201).

Chapter 4. Listening to the Child

1. Two manuscript versions of this poem exist; in the variorum Johnson uses the version Dickinson sent to Sue.

2. As the speaker of *P* 870 observes, "Finding is the first / Act / The second, loss" (*MBED* 1043). The first act in life is childhood, a constant "Finding" that ceases only with the "loss" that initiates early adulthood. The perception of the first is contingent upon the second. Consequently, the voice of the child emerges retrospectively, after or during the discovery of loss coincident with the end of childhood, for only then does childhood enter history and acquire status as an object of discourse.

3. Julia Kristeva describes this pure potential as the "chora" in *Revolution in Poetic Language*. Her perceptions help explain the way Dickinson's construction of the child can reflect the language of a subject that has not yet entered history: "Discrete quantities of energy move through the body of the subject who is not yet constituted as such and, in the course of his development, they are arranged according to the various constraints imposed on this body—always already involved in a semiotic process—by family and social structures. In this way the drives, which are 'energy' charges as well as 'psychical' marks, articulate what we call a *chora*: a nonexpressive totality formed by the drives and their stases in a motility that is as full of movement as it is regulated" [25]. By giving voice to the child, Dickinson acknowledges the "nonexpressive totality" Kristeva designates as the chora. Hearing the voice of the child becomes a matter of listening for words uttered at the moment linguistic expression is first attempted.

4. The recognition that childhood is a more exalted state than adulthood was by no means unique to Dickinson. She does differ from her contemporaries, however, in her equating of childhood with an infinity that is excluded from adult experience. The following passage from Barbara Leslie Epstein's *The Politics of Domesticity* outlines changes in the perception of childhood in New England that provide the foun-

dation for Dickinson's elevation of the child: "The authors of nineteenth-century women's books told mothers that their babies were innocent and pure and must be shielded from the corrupting influences of the outside world. . . . Such sentiments stand in stark contrast to the Puritan belief that children are born in sin and that it is the responsibility of parents to discipline and educate them out of their innate depravity" (81).

5. Although I disagree with Mossberg's argument that Dickinson desires a unified identity, her description of the crisis Dickinson and her speakers face when they contemplate the identities society offers corresponds closely to my reading: "She is caught in the gap between girlhood and womanhood as a Daughter in a perpetual identity crisis" (*Emily Dickinson*, 52).

Diehl's comments on "I'm ceded ⁀" apply even more directly to the sort of bind I see expressed by Dickinson's speaker: "Though all the choice is hers, the speaker understands the demand or call as emanating from outside, as external. She wears the crown, and the religious emblem acquires, through its identification with royalty, not only the choice of independent authority but also a distinctly orthodox cast that modifies the radicalism of her self-bestowal" (*Women Poets and the American Sublime*, 36-37).

6. This is the same "too" that appeared in line 16 of "I started Early" (Poem 520). Dickinson habitually writes "too" in this manner. Though I do not draw attention to every instance, I believe Dickinson's treatment of the word demonstrates the extent to which she made visual play a consistent feature of her writing.

7. In her "Reading Dickinson Reading" chapter in *Rowing in Eden*, Martha Nell Smith discusses Dickinson's awareness that she joins readers in the process of reading her texts. The following passage outlines the relationships Smith explores at length: "Imagining readers who interact with works to produce texts, this consciousness does not put anxiety over or battles for meaning center stage, but spotlights the meaning-producing processes of give and take between author and text, text and reader, reader and author, inevitable in reading" (52).

8. Helen McNeil comments on Dickinson's use of "diadem" as a metaphor for her independent signifying practice that distributes meaning evenly without granting "primacy of meaning" to "the signified" (*Emily Dickinson*, 136). Such a practice is consistent with the child's effort to discover speech and meaning in the same act.

9. In a reading of "I'm ceded –" (*P* 508) that focuses closely on the religious implications of Dickinson's speaker, Diane Gabrielson Scholl argues that the speaker discovers a "new resplendent self, radiant in transfiguration" ("From Aaron 'Drest' to Dickinson's 'Queen,'" 8). Scholl sees the speaker as acquiring the stature of a "female Christ" (9) and therefore reinscribing a symbolic pattern that maximizes her power through unified identity. I agree with this reading and see it as a clear example of the way Dickinson viewed all forms of reification as limiting.

10. Certainty is attributed to the codes of adulthood only after the child becomes conscious of external limitations that restrict her freedom. The certainty of earliest childhood derives from a sense of unlimited power, while the certainty of adulthood is predicated on authority achieved through mastering the rules of society.

11. Johnson uses the version of this poem that Dickinson sent Higginson in her first letter to him (15 April 1862, *L* 403, #260). That version presents only one stanza break—at the line "Homesick for steadfast Honey –"; it also eliminates word variants, alters lineation, and replaces two dashes with commas. The poem sent to Higginson may well be a scaled-back version of the fascicle poem that Dickinson judiciously normalized to make it less difficult for Higginson to swallow.

12. As Dickinson indicated in her August 1862 letter to Higginson (*L* 414-15, #271), fraud is an adult experience because it depends on the subject's conformity within socially determined values: one cannot be defrauded without sharing the defrauder's assumptions about experience. See my comments on this letter in chapter 3.

13. A similar voice says, "I taste a liquor never brewed –" in *P* 214 (*MBED* 227). Only in this poem, the positioning of the child has a considerably more pronounced ironic dimension. The third and fourth stanzas situate the events described within conventional time but do so in a manner that urges acceptance of the less transient power of the child. When the last judgment arrives and "Seraphs swing their snowy hats _ / And saints - to windows run –," they will see "the little Tippler / From Manzanilla Come!]Leaning against the – Sun." The apparent comic diminishment of the child is here countered by the employment of what Henry Louis Gates describes as a self-conscious parody designed to undermine the status of those who control the terms of discourse. Gates employs Bakhtin's notion of the "hidden, or internal, polemic" that is part of parody in *The Signifying Monkey* (110-11).

14. Here, degree is not the adult degree of hierarchy, but the absolute denial of subserviency—it is the power of dominion.

15. Martha Nell Smith provides the most complete examination of Dickinson's resistance to print conventions in *Rowing in Eden*. She writes specifically of "A narrow Fellow" at the beginning of her first chapter (11-12).

Chapter 5. The Community of Self

1. See discussion of the three manuscript versions of this poem in chapter 1.

2. Mossberg refers to this voice as emerging from a "sexual limbo," where the speaker prizes the benefits of social acceptance but also resists out of recognition that this construction of "womanhood" brings confinement in identity:

> The period just before a girl enters puberty is the time in her life when she is most free from the identity of girl or woman. There is an absence of pressure to conform to a sexually determined role; girls at this time, unrestrained by social expectations/restrictions for women are lively, aggressive, and independent.... Significantly, it is this sexual limbo in which we often find Emily Dickinson's "supposed person" in the poems and letters. In these writings, she retains the sensibility of an eleven- or twelve-year-old, on the brink of maturity, precocious, defiant, and rambunctious. But because she does not go beyond this stage to become a "woman" or "wife," she experiences the pain, discomfort, and insecurity we see in "I'm 'wife.'"
> [*Emily Dickinson*, 47]

In my discussion of "I'm 'wife' – I've finished that –" (*P* 199, *MBED* 781) later in this chapter, I argue that the speaker expresses regret over having surrendered the freedom that was hers as long as she remained in social limbo.

3. Kristeva outlines such an assessment of writing in her description of "literature" and "text." In *Revolution in Poetic Language*, she writes of the "sum" of conflicting relations that together constitute a form of struggle: "If there exists a 'discourse' which is not a mere depository of thin linguistic layers, an archive of structures, or the testimony of a withdrawn body, and is, instead, the essential element of a practice involving the sum of unconscious, subjective, and social relations in gestures of

confrontation and appropriation, destruction and construction—productive violence, in short—it is 'literature,' or, more precisely, the *text*" (16).

4. Johnson's variorum commentary identifies a variant of the first stanza, probably sent to Sue about two years after composing the fascicle poem, or about 1864.

5. Martha Nell Smith provides an important caution about reading this most quoted of all Dickinson letters as a simple expression of heterosexual female sexual anxiety. Smith recommends approaching the letter in light of Dickinson's growing intimacy with Sue; in this context it presents a form of "comic exaggeration" through which "Dickinson both warns and seeks to delight her friend, hopefully making herself more appealing" (*Rowing* 170). This view of Dickinson as competing with and even belittling, rather than cowering before, patriarchal power is consistent with my own reading of her comic posturing in letters and her determination to transform the stultifying "No's" society imposes on women into sources of creative affirmation.

6. I readily acknowledge that my brief reference to Wittig does not do justice to the complexity and force of her argument in *The Straight Mind*. My decision to include some mention of Wittig is based on my belief that I would be remiss were I not at least to hint at the richness her line of argumentation offers to future Dickinson criticism. Wittig's interest in exploring the ontological foundations of sexuality is especially appropriate to what I understand as Dickinson's effort to position poetry at the point where limitless possibility intersects with the limitations of discourse.

7. Mossberg identifies a "humorous ambiguity" at the heart of this poem's social critique. Though Mossberg doesn't specifically address the multiple discourses examined in the poem, her presentation clarifies both the speaker's dilemma and the poem's commentary on that dilemma:

> [Dickinson] sets off the words "Wife" and "Woman" in quotation marks to show that while she is equating herself with those titles as roles or concepts, they are essentially foreign to her—"quotes," as it were, from society's voice, states of being that society prescribes. We see her in a dilemma, then, because she is trapped in an alien identity as a "woman," and having "finished" her girlhood, has burned her bridges behind her. . . . The metaphor of death (going to heaven) is superimposed onto marriage so that a woman's supposed "happy ending" in marriage is her literal demise as well.
>
> Whether the persona is dead or merely married is not made clear, but the poem's humorous ambiguity on this point signifies that marriage or maturity is a kind of death for a woman.
> [*Emily Dickinson*, 46]

8. R.W. Franklin makes a strong case for treating the last stanza of "I tie my Hat" as a different poem (*MBED* 534). But I find even more compelling Sharon Cameron's argument that the lines are "metrically, imagistically, and thematically consonant with, as well as a direct continuation of the sense of, [*P*]443" (*Choosing* 33, n 19).

9. Johnson's variorum notes that Dickinson sent a variant of the first stanza to Sue about two years after she wrote the fascicle poem, or around 1864.

10. The "checks" alluded to in the poem could be the sort that train conductors issued by announcing the train's location to passengers. This sort of "check" would add to the poem's interest in the ways people seek to certify their progress toward immortality.

11. My comments on this first fascicle should not be viewed as equally applicable to other fascicles. My remarks are intended to describe a meaningful sequence of voices identifiable in the earliest of Dickinson's private publications; therefore, this sequence may be the basis for later thematic and stylistic innovations while not taking the form I describe here. Other poems examined in this chapter indicate that the relationships I see linking the poems in this fascicle are reiterated in single poems Dickinson wrote later in life.

12. This poem does represent a certain gamble inasmuch as setting up events rooted in time, like the sequence of seasons and the building of "hillocks," requires that the speaker risk being swept up in linear progressions. Perhaps that is why the last six lines focus so closely on "the secret" mentioned in line fifteen. If the speaker were conscious of ebbing control, that would also account for the final two lines that act as a sort of paraphrase of the previous four lines. Such an interpretation might also explain Dickinson's decision to concentrate on loss in *P* 23: "I had a guinea golden–/ I lost it in the sand–."

13. In her discussion of *P* 458, Mossberg argues that the poem details an unfortunate identity conflict the poet must enter as daughter and woman seeking to assert power in a world that defines her as powerless: "At the end of the poem, 'Me' and 'it' are fused into 'We.' There has been a progression from a schism between the objectified self (the mask) and the creating poet self to an affirmation that they are one, and when so combined, formulate an identity of a 'Queen–,' a poet defined in specifically feminine terms. In other words, a Queen is a daughter and poet in conflict, a woman at odds with her femininity. The pained woman in the self is no longer banished, but becomes the integral dominant ingredient in the poet's identity" (180-81).

My reading is fundamentally different from Mossberg's, though I agree with her conclusion that the Queen inclusively embraces other voices. Where Mossberg describes Dickinson as a writer shattered by the discourse of culture, I see Dickinson repeatedly asserting both that language is never an adequate home for the self and that the desire for an identity within a specific discourse is the product of unacceptable self-limitation. In my view, Mossberg too quickly attributes to Dickinson the wish for a unified identity that would allow her status and prestige as defined by patriarchal conventions.

CHAPTER 6. HOMELESSNESS AND THE FORMS OF SELFHOOD

1. My designating the last seventeen years of Dickinson's life as the period of her reclusivity is somewhat conservative in light of general critical practice. In their introduction to *The Letters of Emily Dickinson,* for instance, Thomas H. Johnson and Theodora Ward observe: "There came a time in Emily Dickinson's life, very near her thirtieth year, when she deliberately chose never willingly to leave her home" (xix). This would mean that Dickinson was a recluse for at least twenty-five years, or more than half of her adult life. However, Johnson and Ward qualify their position by writing that Dickinson never "willingly" left her home, tacitly acknowledging the trips she made to Boston in 1864 and 1865 as a result of eye problems. Such qualifications suggest that the inclination for reclusivity preceded the actual adoption of a strictly reclusive practice. To avoid quibbles over intent and practice, I have accepted Dickinson's own words in her 1869 letter as establishing a date by which she had definitely become a recluse.

2. In *Emily Dickinson*, Helen McNeil dedicates her "The House without the Door" chapter to an examination of house imagery as "a kind of test case for the presence the house of the father can have in the writing of the daughter" (112). Her analysis of "home" usefully points out associations with permanence and timelessness that set home apart from the transience of "house," particularly house-as-body and site of temporal identity.

My reading differs from hers over the issue of the subject's relation to the house of language. McNeil argues that as a woman writer Dickinson never sees "resemblance" in language and therefore "*should not* claim immediate knowledge when, as we know, the house from which she would look is not hers" (128). In my view, Dickinson recommends the illocality that comes from knowing that the self does not find its semblance in language. For her, illocality is a positive accomplishment, not a diminished form of experience. The self that *mistakenly believes* that accurate resemblances are available in language risks surrendering personal authority to social convention.

3. Joanne Feit Diehl presents Dickinson as creating "an uncanny, death-haunted American Sublime" (*Women* 40) in which "poem after poem strives to release death's hold by imagining his death as her freedom" (42). This description accurately accounts for the repetition central to the poems, but Diehl unnecessarily regards repetition as a binary conflict through which Dickinson "first must resolve through aggression her need for supremacy in imaginatively murderous acts that recur because murder of the tradition is a most illusory triumph." My position is that Dickinson is fully appreciative of the illusory character of triumph in general—at least as aware as any of us are—and that she avoids the binary trap by refusing to participate in the monologic discourse of a unified self. As a result, she does not fulfill the basic requirement of the sublime: return to unified selfhood. Rather, I would agree with Diehl that Dickinson's subject "achieves no resolution" and that "conflict over death becomes, indeed, a form of poetic life" (43). The difference is that I do not read the speaker's failure to triumph as a mark of deferred completion, but as a flat declaration that any achievement of harmony within the self is an illusion. Therefore, no further completion is sought.

In *The Dickinson Sublime*, Gary Lee Stonum cogently describes the sublime both as a part of Romantic tradition and as it pertains to Dickinson. His discussion of the sublime in "the Sublime as Design" (67-80) portion of his "Cherishing Power" chapter is particularly helpful. Even though I do not concur with his assertions about the role of the sublime in her poetry, I fully accept his conclusion that "the sublime object is structured as an absolute, self-contained harmony" (145). It is precisely because of the accuracy of this conclusion, however, that I see no role for the sublime as an aim in Dickinson's poetry. This is a matter I explore at greater depth later in this chapter.

4. Mudge's *Emily Dickinson and the Image of Home* is a storehouse of information related to homelessness. Her analysis of "home" in *Webster's* is especially useful in identifying the cluster of concepts and discourses Dickinson attaches to the term (11-12). However, even though I share her conviction that "house" and "home" figure prominently in Dickinson's poetry, my conclusions differ from hers. Mudge wants to show that Dickinson desired the unity a home would provide: "the central struggle of her life finally became, in effect, an endless pursuit of this ever-elusive locus" (8). For Mudge, home functions as "a psychic spatial formula or unifying form" (11). I see Dickinson as acknowledging the attraction of home but resisting the containment posed by any "unifying form."

5. In *Emily Dickinson's Poetry*, Robert Weisbuch deftly articulates Dickinson's simultaneous recognition and denial of the power of logic:

It is Dickinson's desire to madden logic, to inject it with an individual sense of crisis. Yet it is equally her desire to create this sense of crisis without making the word or the world a mere extension of the self's emotional problems. At another level, the conflict is analogous: one aim is to dramatize the act of language-making, with all its difficulties, as emblematic of the struggle with human limits in general; another aim is not to allow the dramatization of this struggle to interfere with a produced effect, a deepening and expansion of the meanings of language. [71]

6. Commenting on the difficulty of writing criticism that acknowledges polyvocality, Herndl makes the following observations in "The Dilemmas of a Feminine Dialogic": "This kind of criticism would resist offering 'a reading' and offer, instead, 'readings.' It would therefore resist the masculine-monologic place of asserting any one meaning, because the meaning would always be 'not one.' This dialogic feminine criticism would not just pay lip-service to two readings while clearly privileging one (which is what many post-structuralist writings tend to do); it would, instead, emphasize the plural meanings—even contradictory meanings—in the text" (18).

7. Many Dickinson scholars have detected multiple personae in the poems and have distinguished them differently. Though there is general agreement that a child, a bride, and a Queen all speak in the poems, there is no clear agreement as to which poems or which parts of poems represent the voices of which speakers. My point is that the design of the poems is such that readers are bound to differ in these matters, just as no two people are likely to agree at precisely which point or at what degree of disjunction voices no longer belong to a single speaker.

8. In "Sign and Process," Roland Hagenbüchle introduces this poem to illustrate the way "the organic unity between nature and the poetic artifact . . . which for Emerson and the other Transcendentalists is a basic assumption, runs counter to [Dickinson's] whole poetic credo" (151). He argues that, for her, "the creative process and the struggle with language become virtually the same." Though he chooses ultimately to collapse "the search for the word, the meaning, and the vision" into a single "epiphany," he asserts the power of simultaneity that sustains tripartite distinctions of the sort that I identify.

9. Stonum does an excellent job of presenting the traditional stages of the sublime and opposing his version of a reader's sublime to a more traditional authorial sublime in the "Cherishing Power" chapter of *The Dickinson Sublime*. There he states: "Dickinson's poetry takes the established patterns of the romantic sublime and gives them an additional twist, one which works to circumvent the otherwise deep complicity between sublimity and mastery" (68). From my point of view, Stonum is correct only insofar as he accounts for the authority Dickinson insists on according the reader; I disagree with his efforts to impose an experience of the sublime on Dickinson's texts. In his chapter titled "The Dickinson Sublime," he concludes that "without abandoning the structure of the romantic sublime and indeed by making specific use of its forces and phases, Dickinson defers to the reader the moment of final commitment. . . . The Quintessential Dickinson sublime is a hesitant sublime" (141). He democratizes access to the sublime by placing readers and authors on the same level, but he persists in asserting traditional Romantic aims. My argument is concerned with the way specific discourses, like that on the sublime, are unraveled in Dickinson's poetry. Unlike Stonum, I am more concerned with the way her resistance to convention directs attention to the logic upon which discourse is founded.

10. The position of "Advanced" in the manuscript conveys a kind of spatial

uncertainty here: is it the conclusion of the second stanza that Johnson ends after the word "in" or is it, as Johnson suggests, a variant for "there came"? In my reading, the arrangement of variants visually expresses the poet/speaker's spatial engagement with language that simultaneously offers possibilities for expression and imposes limits. In this case, the presence or nonpresence of "Advanced" further complicates and hence magnifies the potential disjunction suggested by dashes. As a result, I choose both to affirm the Johnson decision to conclude the line with a dash and to assert the visual disjunction of Dickinson's manuscript that resists the metrically appropriate stanza break by simultaneously asserting the presence and absence of "Advanced."

11. As Dickie has noted in her comments on "A nearness to Tremendousness" (*P* 963, *MBED* 980), the release of imagination Dickinson urges can be accompanied by physical discomfort: "In Dickinson's poem, there is an odd conflation of the two states of pain and imagining in which the speaker appears to be feeling the 'Agony' as a process of self-transformation" (*Lyric*, 49).

12. Mary Loeffelholz refers to the ways romanticism in general and the egotistical sublime in particular silence the voices of women by treating language as natural rather than as fabricated. Her point is that, according to such a conception, women are positioned within nature as the objects of greatest value and therefore subject to the laws men have designed to govern the exchange of natural objects. "For the female speaker," she writes, "the language of absolute natural value verges all too nearly upon the law in which woman is the highest—and most silent—value in nature; the transparent 'envelope' of value around her, in Irigaray's metaphor, prevents her voice from being heard" (*Dickinson and the Boundaries of Feminist Theory*, 35). Loeffelholz's reference to Irigaray is particularly instructive here because of Irigaray's insistence that women's experience is at all times plural and at odds with the monologizing impulses that fuel patriarchal hierarchies. See especially pages 84-85 in Irigaray's *This Sex Which Is Not One*.

13. Christopher Norris provides a helpful overview of Derrida's use of "differance" in *Deconstruction: Theory and Practice* (32). For a useful application of Derridean "differance" to Dickinson, see Helen McNeil's "Dickinson and Difference" chapter in *Emily Dickinson* and her discussion on pages sixteen and seventeen.

14. Dickinson is commonly regarded as part of an avant-garde and my purpose is not simply to reassert a widely held perception; rather, I propose that choices she made about formal artistic innovations—especially punctuation and other visual features—play a more central role in future discussions. My understanding of what constitutes an "avant-garde" is consistent with the definition Charles Russell provides at the beginning of his book *Poets, Prophets, and Revolutionaries:* "I believe the term avant-garde can be profitably used to distinguish writers and artists who believe not only that the world they inhabit is essentially modern and that they need to find an aesthetic language to express this newness, but also that they are in some manner in advance of a future state of art and society which their innovative works help to bring into existence" (viii).

15. Situating Dickinson in the company of other nineteenth-century American women poets is difficult. As Cheryl Walker states in her introduction to *American Women Poets of the Nineteenth Century*, "The more one reads Emily Dickinson, the less like her contemporaries she seems" (xxviii). This, together with evidence that Dickinson "paid little attention to American women poets popular in her lifetime" (xxxvi), has prompted my looking to Elizabeth Barrett Browning and American women prose writers for examples of women who shared her interests. However, I do not agree with Walker's conclusion that meaningful connections with contemporary women do not

exist; whether or not Dickinson paid attention to other American women poets, she shared many of their concerns. Scholars will surely discover numerous links to other writers of the kind so clearly suggested by Helen Hunt Jackson's grim assertion of homelessness in "Found Frozen":

> And yet
> 'Twas in the place she called her home, she died;
> And they who loved her with the all of love
> Their wintry natures had to give, stood by
> and wept some tears, and wrote above her grave
> Some common record which they thought was true;
> But I, who loved her first, and last, and best,—*I* knew.
> [Walker, *American*, 287]

CONCLUSION

1. Erkkila introduces these terms on page 15 of *The Wicked Sisters*.

2. For additional discussion of this letter and letter #265 mentioned below, see chapter 3, pp. 78, 80-81.

3. This is not to say that Dickinson and Woolson do not express similar political and ideological positions. In her chapter "A Woman Born Midcentury" in *Constance Fenimore Woolson*, Cheryl B. Torsney makes a strong argument for the ideological and political rootlessness of women writers like Woolson and Dickinson who were born too late to be a part of the Cult of True Womanhood and too early for the New Woman.

4. Much recent Dickinson scholarship points to the way her writing defies containment within conventional boundaries. Such a view may be explained as the reader's encounter with the boundaries that Mary Loeffelholz argues "exist to be breached" so that metaphorical borders that separate self from other "might be seen deconstructively, not as irreducibly 'primary,' but as the effect of [their] own undoing" (*Dickinson*, 111). In Erkkila's words, Dickinson articulated "a kind of creative work and a kind of writing that would enable her to exist simultaneously inside and on the margins of the system" (23). In *The Birth-mark*, Susan Howe has described Dickinson's participation in a wicked antinomian strain in American writing that traces its roots to Anne Hutchinson's direct assault on established authority.

Works Cited

Abrams, M.H. *The Mirror and the Lamp: Romantic Theory and the Critical Tradition.* New York: Oxford U P, 1953.

Anderson, Susan M. "'Regard[ing] a Mouse' in Emily Dickinson's Poems." *Emily Dickinson Journal* 2.1 (1993): 84-101.

Bakhtin, Mikhail. *Art and Answerability: Early Philosophical Essays.* Trans. Vadim Liapunov. Ed. Michael Holquist and Vadim Liapunov. Austin: U of Texas P, 1990.

———. *The Dialogic Imagination: Four Essays.* Ed. Michael Holquist. Trans. Caryl Emerson and Michael Holquist. Austin: U of Texas P, 1981.

———. *Marxism and the Philosophy of Language.* Published under V.N. Volosinov. Trans. Ladislav Matejka and I.R. Titunik. Cambridge: Harvard U P, 1973.

———. *Problems of Dostoevsky's Poetics.* Ed. and trans. Caryl Emerson. Minneapolis: U of Minnesota P, 1984.

———. *Rabelais and His World.* Trans. Helene Iswolsky. Bloomington: Indiana U P, 1984.

———. *Speech Genres and Other Late Essays.* Trans. Vern W. McGee. Ed. Caryl Emerson and Michael Holquist. Austin: U of Texas P, 1986.

Barker, Wendy. *Lunacy of Light: Emily Dickinson and the Experience of Metaphor.* Carbondale: Southern Illinois U P, 1987.

Bauer, Dale M., and Susan Janet McKinstry, eds. *Feminism, Bakhtin, and the Dialogic.* Albany: State U of New York P, 1991.

Bennett, Paula. *Emily Dickinson: Woman Poet.* Iowa City: U of Iowa P, 1990.

Browning, Elizabeth Barrett. *Aurora Leigh.* Chicago: Academy Chicago Ltd., 1979.

———. *The Poetical Works of Elizabeth Barrett Browning.* London: Oxford U P, 1932.

Buckingham, Willis J., ed. *Emily Dickinson's Reception in the 1890s: A Documentary History.* Pittsburgh: U of Pittsburgh P, 1989.

Budick, E. Miller. *Emily Dickinson and the Life of Language: A Study in Symbolic Poetics.* Baton Rouge: Louisiana State U P, 1985.

Buell, Lawrence. *New England Literary Culture: From Revolution through Renaissance.* New York: Cambridge U P, 1986.

Cameron, Sharon. *Choosing Not Choosing: Dickinson's Fascicles.* Chicago: U of Chicago P, 1992.

———. *Lyric Time: Dickinson and the Limits of Genre.* Baltimore: Johns Hopkins U P, 1979.

Capps, Jack L. *Emily Dickinson's Reading, 1836-1886.* Cambridge: Harvard U P, 1966.

Cody, John. *After Great Pain: The Inner Life of Emily Dickinson*. Cambridge: Belknap Press of Harvard U P, 1971.

Daly, Mary. *Gyn/Ecology: The Metaesthics of Radical Feminism*. Boston: Beacon P, 1978.

Derrida, Jacques. *Of Grammatology*. Trans. Gayatri Chakravorty Spivak. Baltimore: Johns Hopkins U P, 1974.

Dickie, Margaret. *Lyric Contingencies: Emily Dickinson and Wallace Stevens*. Philadelphia: U of Pennsylvania P, 1991.

Dickinson, Emily. *Bolts of Melody*. New York: Harper & Brothers, 1945.

———. *Collected Poems*. Ed. Peter Siegenthaler. Philadelphia: Courage Books, 1991.

———. *The Letters of Emily Dickinson*. 3 vols. Ed. Thomas H. Johnson and Theodora Ward. Cambridge: Belknap Press of Harvard U P, 1958.

———. *The Manuscript Books of Emily Dickinson*. 2 vols. Ed. R.W. Franklin. Cambridge: Belknap Press of Harvard U P, 1981.

———. *Poems 1890-1896 by Emily Dickinson: A Facsimile Reproduction of the Original Volumes Issued in 1890, 1891, and 1896, with an Introduction by George Monteiro*. Ed. Mabel Loomis Todd and T.W. Higginson. Gainesville, Fla.: Scholars' Facsimiles & Reprints, 1967.

———. *The Poems of Emily Dickinson: Including Variant Readings Critically Compared with All Known Manuscripts*. 3 vols. Ed. Thomas H. Johnson. Cambridge: Belknap Press of Harvard U P, 1955.

Dickinson, Susan Huntington Gilbert. Box 9. Dickinson Papers. Houghton Library, Harvard University, Cambridge, Mass.

Diehl, Joanne Feit. *Dickinson and the Romantic Imagination*. Princeton: Princeton U P, 1981.

———. *Women Poets and the American Sublime*. Bloomington: Indiana U P, 1990.

Dimock, Wai-Chee. "Feminism, New Historicism, and the Reader." *American Literature* 63.4 (1991): 601-22.

Dobson, Joanne. *Dickinson and the Strategies of Reticence: The Woman Writer in Nineteenth-Century America*. Bloomington: Indiana U P, 1989.

———. "'The Invisible Lady': Emily Dickinson and Conventions of the Female Self." *Legacy* 3.1 (1986): 41-55.

Donoghue, Denis. "Reading Bakhtin." *Raritan: A Quarterly Review* 5.2 (Fall 1985): 107-19.

Douglass, Ann. *The Feminization of American Culture*. New York: Doubleday, 1977.

Eberwein, Jane Donahue. *Dickinson: Strategies of Limitation*. Amherst: U of Massachusetts P, 1985.

Emerson, Ralph Waldo. *Nature*. In *Selections from Ralph Waldo Emerson*. Ed. Stephen E. Whicher. Boston: Houghton Mifflin, 1957.

———. "The Poet." In *Selections from Ralph Waldo Emerson*. Ed. Stephen E. Whicher. Boston: Houghton Mifflin, 1957.

Epstein, Barbara Leslie. *The Politics of Domesticity: Women, Evangelism, and Temperance in Nineteenth-Century America*. Middletown, Conn.: Wesleyan U P, 1981.

Erkkila, Betsy. *The Wicked Sisters: Women Poets, Literary History and Discord*. New York: Oxford U P, 1992.

Farr, Judith. *The Passion of Emily Dickinson*. Cambridge: Harvard U P, 1992.

Franklin R.W. *The Editing of Emily Dickinson: A Reconsideration*. Madison: U of Wisconsin P, 1967.

Garbowsky, Maryanne M. *The House without the Door: A Study of Emily Dickinson and the Illness of Agoraphobia*. Rutherford, N.J.: Fairleigh Dickinson U P, 1989.

Gates, Henry Louis, Jr. *The Signifying Monkey: A Theory of African-American Literary Criticism.* New York: Oxford U P, 1988.

Gelpi, Albert J. *The Mind of the Poet.* Cambridge: Harvard U P, 1965.

Gilbert, Sandra M., and Susan Gubar. *The Madwoman in the Attic: The Woman Writer and the Nineteenth-Century Literary Imagination.* New Haven: Yale U P, 1984.

Griffith, Clark. *The Long Shadow: Emily Dickinson's Tragic Poetry.* Princeton: Princeton U P, 1964.

Hagenbüchle, Roland. "Sign and Process: The Concept of Language in Emerson and Dickinson." *ESQ* 25.3 (1979): 137-55.

Hart, Ellen Louise. "The Elizabeth Putnam Whitney Manuscripts and New Strategies for Editing Emily Dickinson's Letters." *Emily Dickinson Journal* 4.1 (1995): 44-74.

Herndl, Diane Price. "The Dilemmas of a Feminine Dialogic." *Feminism, Bakhtin, and the Dialogic.* Ed. Dale M. Bauer and S. Margaret McKinstry. Albany: State U of New York P, 1991.

Higginson, Thomas Wentworth. "Letter to a Young Contributor." *Atlantic Monthly* 9 (April 1862): 403-5.

Hoefel, Roseanne. "Emily Dickinson Fleshing out a New Word." *Emily Dickinson Journal* 1.1 (1992): 54-75.

Holman, Hugh C., and William Harmon. *A Handbook to Literature.* 6th ed. New York: Macmillan, 1992.

Holquist, Michael. *Dialogism: Bakhtin and His World.* New York: Routledge, 1990.

Homans, Margaret. *Women Writers and Poetic Identity: Dorothy Wordsworth, Emily Brontë, and Emily Dickinson.* Princeton: Princeton U P, 1980.

Horowitz, Howard. *By the Law of Nature: Form and Value in Nineteenth-Century America.* New York: Oxford U P, 1991.

Howe, Susan. *The Birth-mark: Unsettling the Wilderness in American Literary History.* Hanover: U P of New England, 1993.

———. *My Emily Dickinson.* Berkeley: North Atlantic Books, 1985.

Hunter, Jane H. "Inscribing the Self in the Heart of the Family: Diaries and Girlhood in Late-Victorian America." *American Quarterly* 44.1 (1992): 51-81.

Irigary, Luce. *Speculum of the Other Woman.* Trans. Lillian C. Gill. Ithaca: Cornell U P, 1985.

———. *This Sex Which Is Not One.* Trans. Catherine Porter and Carolyn Burke. Ithaca: Cornell U P, 1985.

Johnson, Greg. *Emily Dickinson and the Poet's Quest.* Tuscaloosa: U of Alabama P, 1985.

Johnson, Thomas H., ed. *The Poems of Emily Dickinson: Including Variant Readings Critically Compared with All Known Manuscripts.* 3 vols. Cambridge: Belknap Press of Harvard U P, 1955.

Juhasz, Suzanne. *The Undiscovered Continent: Emily Dickinson and the Space of the Mind.* Bloomington: Indiana U P, 1983.

———, ed. *Feminist Critics Read Emily Dickinson.* Bloomington: Indiana U P, 1983.

Juhasz, Suzanne, Cristanne Miller, and Martha Nell Smith. *Comic Power in Emily Dickinson.* Austin: U of Texas P, 1993.

Kristeva, Julia. *Desire in Language: A Semiotic Approach to Literature and Art.* Trans. Thomas Gora and Alice Jardine. Ed. Leon S. Roudiez. New York: Columbia U P, 1980.

———. *Powers of Horror: An Essay on Abjection.* New York: Columbia U P, 1982.

———. *Revolution in Poetic Language*. Trans. Margaret Walker. New York: Columbia U P, 1984.

———. "Woman's Time." *The Kristeva Reader*. Ed. Toril Moi. New York: Columbia U P, 1986.

———. "Word, Dialogue and Novel." *The Kristeva Reader*. Ed. Toril Moi. New York: Columbia U P, 1986.

Lechte, John. *Julia Kristeva*. New York: Routledge, 1990.

Lerner, Gerda, ed. *The Female Experience: An American Documentary*. New York: Oxford U P, 1977.

Leyda, Jay. *The Years and Hours of Emily Dickinson*. 2 vols. New Haven: Yale U P, 1960.

Lindberg-Seyersted, Brita. *The Voice of the Poet: Aspects of Style in the Poetry of Emily Dickinson*. Cambridge: Harvard U P, 1968.

———. *Emily Dickinson's Punctuation*. Oslo: U of Oslo, 1976.

Loeffelholz, Mary. *Dickinson and the Boundaries of Feminist Theory*. Chicago: U of Illinois P, 1991.

McGann, Jerome J. *Social Values and Poetic Acts: The Historical Judgment of Literary Work*. Cambridge: Harvard U P, 1988.

McNeil, Helen. *Emily Dickinson*. New York: Pantheon Books, 1986.

McQuade, Donald, et al. *The Harper American Literature*. Vol. 1. New York: Harper & Row, 1987.

Meaney, Gerardine. *(Un)Like Subjects: Women, Theory, Fiction*. New York: Routledge, 1993.

Melville, Herman. *Moby-Dick*. New York: Norton, 1967.

Miller, Cristanne. *Emily Dickinson: A Poet's Grammar*. Cambridge: Harvard U P, 1987.

Miller, Ruth. *The Poetry of Emily Dickinson*. Middletown, Conn.: Wesleyan U P, 1968.

Mossberg, Barbara Antonina Clarke. *Emily Dickinson: When a Writer Is a Daughter*. Bloomington: Indiana U P, 1982.

Mudge, Jean McClure. *Emily Dickinson and the Image of Home*. Amherst: U of Massachusetts P, 1975.

Norris, Christopher. *Deconstruction: Theory and Practice*. New York: Routledge, 1982.

Patterson, Rebecca. *The Riddle of Emily Dickinson*. Boston: Houghton Mifflin, 1951.

Phillips, Elizabeth. *Emily Dickinson: Personae and Performance*. University Park: Pennsylvania U P, 1988.

Pitts, Mary Ellen. "The Holographic Paradigm: A New Model for the Study of Literature and Science." *Modern Language Studies* 20.4 (1990): 80-89.

Poe, Edgar Allan. "MS. Found in a Bottle." In *Great Short Works of Edgar Allan Poe*. New York: Harper & Row, 1970.

Pollak, Vivian R. *Dickinson: The Anxiety of Gender*. Ithaca: Cornell U P, 1984.

Porter, David. *Dickinson: The Modern Idiom*. Cambridge: Harvard U P, 1981.

Porter, Ebenezer. *The Rhetorical Reader; Consisting of Instructions for Regulating the Voice, with a Rhetorical Notation . . .* New York: Dayton & Newman, 1842.

Reynolds, David S. *Beneath the American Renaissance: The Subversive Imagination in the Age of Emerson and Melville*. New York: Knopf, 1988.

Rich, Adrienne. "Vesuvius at Home: The Power of Emily Dickinson." *Parnassus: Poetry in Review* 5.1 (Fall-Winter 1976): 49-74.

Rorty, Richard. *Philosophy and the Mirror of Nature*. Princeton: Princeton U P, 1979.

Rubin, Joan Shelley. *The Making of Middlebrow Culture.* Chapel Hill: U of North Carolina P, 1992.

Russell, Charles. *Poets, Prophets and Revolutionaries: The Literary Avant-garde from Rimbaud through Postmodernism.* New York: Oxford U P, 1985.

St. Armand, Barton Levi. *Emily Dickinson and Her Culture: The Soul's Society.* New York: Cambridge U P, 1984.

Salska, Agnieszka. *Walt Whitman and Emily Dickinson: Poetry of the Central Consciousness.* Philadelphia: U of Pennsylvania P, 1985.

Scheurer, Erika. "'Near, but remote': Emily Dickinson's Epistolary Voice." *Emily Dickinson Journal* 4.1 (1995): 86-107.

Scholl, Diane Gabrielson. "From Aaron 'Drest' to Dickinson's 'Queen': Protestant Typology in Herbert and Dickinson." *Emily Dickinson Journal* 3.1 (1994): 1-21.

Schueller, Malini Johar. *The Politics of Voice: Liberalism and Social Criticism from Franklin to Kingston.* Albany: State U of New York P, 1992.

Sewall, Richard B. *The Life of Emily Dickinson.* 2 vols. New York: Farrar, Straus and Giroux, 1974.

Shurr, William H. *The Marriage of Emily Dickinson: A Study of the Fascicles.* Lexington: U P of Kentucky, 1983.

Small, Judy Jo. *Positive as Sound: Emily Dickinson's Rhyme.* Athens: U of Georgia P, 1990.

Smith, Martha Nell. *Rowing in Eden: Rereading Emily Dickinson.* Austin: U of Texas P, 1992.

———. "The Importance of a Hypermedia Archive of Dickinson's Creative Work." *Emily Dickinson Journal* 4.1 (1995): 75-85.

Smith, Robert McClure. "'He Asked If I Was His': The Seductions of Emily Dickinson." *ESQ* 40.1 (1994): 27-65.

———. "Inferential Knowledge—The Distinctest One': Rhetoric, Seduction and the Male Reader of Emily Dickinson's Letters." *Prose Studies* 15.2 (August 1992): 225-41.

Smith-Rosenberg, Carroll. *Disorderly Conduct: Visions of Gender in Victorian America.* New York: Oxford U P, 1985.

Stonum, Gary Lee. *The Dickinson Sublime.* Madison: U of Wisconsin P, 1990.

Stowe, Harriet Beecher. "To Georgiana May." (6 Jan. 1836) In *The Female Experience: An American Documentary.* Ed. Gerda Lerner. Indianapolis: Bobbs-Merrill, 1977.

———. *Uncle Tom's Cabin or, Life Among the Lowly.* New York: Penguin Books, 1981.

Thoreau, Henry David. *Walden and Civil Disobedience.* New York: Penguin Books, 1983.

Todorov, Tzvetan. *Mikhail Bakhtin: The Dialogical Principle.* Trans. Wlad Godzich. Minneapolis: U of Minnesota P, 1984.

Tompkins, Jane. *Sensational Designs: The Cultural Work of American Fiction, 1790-1860.* New York: Oxford U P, 1985.

Torsney, Cheryl B. *Constance Fenimore Woolson: The Grief of Artistry.* Athens: U of Georgia P, 1989.

Walker, Cheryl, ed. *American Women Poets of the Nineteenth Century.* New Brunswick: Rutgers U P, 1992.

———. *The Nightingale's Burden: Women Poets and American Culture before 1900.* Bloomington: Indiana U P, 1982.

Wardrop, Daneen. "'Goblin with a Gauge': Dickinson's Readerly Gothic." *Emily Dickinson Journal* 1.1 (1992): 39-53.

Watters, David H. "'I Spake as a Child': Authority, Metaphor and *The New England Primer*." *Early American Literature* 20.3 (Winter 1985-86): 193-213.

Webster, Noah. *An American Dictionary of the English Language*. 2 vols. New York: S. Converse, 1828.

Weisbuch, Robert. *Emily Dickinson's Poetry*. Chicago: U of Chicago P, 1972.

Werner, Marta L. *Emily Dickinson's Open Folios: Scenes of Reading, Surfaces of Writing*. Ann Arbor: U of Michigan P, 1995.

Wittig, Monique. *The Straight Mind and Other Essays*. Boston: Beacon P, 1992.

Wolff, Cynthia Griffin. *Emily Dickinson*. New York: Knopf, 1986.

Woloska, Shira. *Emily Dickinson: A Voice of War*. New Haven: Yale U P, 1984.

Woolson, Constance Fenimore. "Miss Grief." In *Women Artists, Women Exiles: "Miss Grief" and Other Stories*. Ed. Joan Myers Weimer. New Brunswick: Rutgers U P, 1988.

Wylder, Edith. *The Last Face: Emily Dickinson's Manuscripts*. Albuquerque: U of New Mexico P, 1971.

Zboray, Ronald J. "Antebellum Reading and the Ironies of Technological Innovation." In *Reading in America: Literature and Social History*. Ed. Cathy Davidson. Baltimore: Johns Hopkins U P, 1989.

Index of First Lines of Poems

Note: Poem numbers given are from the variorium edition of Thomas H. Johnson; page numbers are provided from *The Manuscript Books of Emily Dickinson*, edited by R.W. Franklin.

Index of Letter Numbers

Note: Letter numbers given are from the edition of Thomas H. Johnson and Theodora Ward.

General Index